THE ORDINATION OF WOMEN AS RABBIS

Studies and Responsa

Volume XIV in the **Moreshet Series,**
Studies in Jewish History, Literature, and Thought

A CENTURY OF ACHIEVEMENT

1886–1986
תרמ״ו–תשמ״ו

THE ORDINATION OF WOMEN AS RABBIS

Studies and Responsa

Edited by Simon Greenberg

A Centennial Publication
The Jewish Theological Seminary of America
New York 1988

Copyright © 1988
The Jewish Theological Seminary of America

Library of Congress Cataloging-in-Publication Data

The Ordination of women as rabbis.

(Moreshet series ; v. 14)
Includes index.
1. Conservative Judaism—Doctrines. 2. Ordination
of women—Conservative Judaism. 3. Women in Judaism.
I. Greenberg, Simon, 1901–   . II. Jewish Theological
Seminary of America. III. Series.
BM197.5.073   1987   296.6'1   87-2782
ISBN 0-87334-041-8
ISBN 0-87334-042-6 (pbk.)

Manufactured in the United States of America

Contents

Preface

All of the papers included in this volume were written by members of the faculty of The Jewish Theological Seminary of America. Among other things, they record the history of the process that led to their being written. The authors of two papers that were originally presented to the faculty requested that they should not be included in this volume. One gave no reason for his request and the other said that the papers of his colleagues had changed his mind.

No substantive changes of any significance were made in the papers from the time they were first presented to the faculty. A certain amount of repetition in the papers was inevitable, since all of them were dealing with the same subject and had recourse to essentially the same source materials. But each paper sets the same sources within its own distinctive context and structure. No attempt was made to establish uniformity of transliterations of Hebrew or Aramaic quotations throughout the volume. It was task enough to establish uniformity within each one of the essays. There are differences of opinion expressed in this volume on matters far more urgent than the problems of transliteration.

For a variety of reasons I decided that Rabbinic terms and quotes found in this volume would be listed not in a glossary but in the index. These terms are variously defined and used by the contributors. Their meaning therefore, depends ultimately on how they are used. The index will indicate the various places where these terms appear.

It is hoped that this volume will in some adequate measure reflect the depth and the passion of the attachment of the Conservative Movement to the Halakhah, even as it reflects the

conviction that the future of our people's loyalty to the Halakhah will depend upon reactivating the creative potentialities
that inhere in it. It was the courageous use of these "creative
potentialities" that made it possible for the Halakhah to serve
our people so well for at least two millenia within a vast variety
of political, economic, religious and cultural environments.

My sincere thanks are due to Dr. Zevulon Ravid for his
helpful suggestions regarding the text of the Hebrew essay
included in this volume, to Dora Levine for her patient careful
typing and retyping of the English essays and to Bernard
Scharfstein for concernedly seeing the manuscript through the
press and making the volume available to the public.

The discussion only partially recorded in this volume and
the historic decision to which it led could not have taken place
on the high scholarly and spiritual level herein reflected, if it
were not for the courageous and wise leadership of Professor
Gerson D. Cohen, who was then serving as the Chancellor of
the Seminary. It was at his request that I agreed to serve as
editor of this volume. I am grateful that I have this opportunity
publicly to express my gratitude to the Almighty that I had the
privilege of enjoying the personal friendship of Dr. Louis
Finkelstein and Dr. Gerson D. Cohen and of being closely
associated with them during the excitingly creative years when
each of them served as Chancellor of the Seminary. May we
continue to be blessed for many more years by their presence,
and always inspired by their example.

Dr. Simon Greenberg
The Jewish Theological Seminary
of America

March 17, 1987

THE ORDINATION OF WOMEN AS RABBIS

Studies and Responsa

Introduction

GERSON D. COHEN

It is, I believe, particularly appropriate for the Jewish Theological Seminary of America, during its centennial year, to issue this collection of responsa written by members of its faculty six and seven years ago. This hundredth year of one of the major contemporary institutions of Jewish scholarship constitutes a milestone. In its first century, the Seminary has been a significant influence on Jewish communities not only throughout North America, but also in Israel, Latin America, Scandinavia, and elsewhere. It has had a major impact on many aspects of intellectual and spiritual activity.

The issue of women as rabbis, with which this volume is concerned, is but one of several questions on which the Seminary has taken a stand not unanimously applauded by all observers, or even by all the members of its own faculty. Through much of its history, the Seminary faculty has resisted taking a stand as a faculty on halakhic issues, and this reluctance has been widely criticized as an abdication of responsibility.

I disagree with that criticism. In the past I even applauded this posture of aloofness. The issue discussed in this volume, however, could not be sidestepped. Since the central question was criteria for admission to an academic program, a faculty

1

decision was clearly required. In this volume, members of the faculty have articulated the bases for their positions, and presented the arguments on which the faculty decision was ultimately based.

I became an advocate of the acceptance of women as fully matriculated rabbinical students in consequence of the hearings of the Commission which I chaired on the question, as well as in consequence of the responsa published in this volume. At the outset of the Commission hearings, I had leaned slightly toward the *status quo,* i.e., to opposition to the admission of women. In the light of the arguments that I heard and read, I found that position to be neither halakhically mandatory nor morally defensible. I therefore became a fervent advocate of the admission of women.

Now that that issue is a matter of history, and, indeed, a woman has already been ordained as a rabbi by the Seminary, I think it should be made clear that the vote of the Seminary faculty was only on the issue before them. Their decision has no implications for other questions of female egalitarianism in the synagogue. The acceptability of women as rabbis will ultimately be decided by Jewish communities the world over, each congregation making the decision for itself. As of this writing, for example, the ordination of women as rabbis in the Conservative communities of Israel is not even an arguable issue. That the question will someday arise in Israel I am confident, but there are many bridges yet to be crossed there before that happens. In the final analysis, each section of the Jewish world will work out its own dialect within the overall framework of the tradition.

The principles of Conservative Judaism, and the yardsticks it adopts for continuity and for change of Jewish practice, will have to be halakhic as well as in accord with the ethical values of the Jewish spiritual value complex. The question of the halakhic acceptability of women as candidates for the rabbinate arose in the North American communities because it was there that women had been gaining progressive recognition and equality, educationally and professionally as well as religiously. Women were increasingly accepted as members of the minyan, thanks to the 1973 decision of the Joint Committee on Jewish Law and Standards of the Rabbinical Assembly. But the implementation of that decision and others like it has ultimately depended on local acceptance: that is, on the rabbi and congregation of a particular community.

Doubtless the acceptance of women as candidates for the rabbinate will encourage feminists to work for the legitimization and equalization of women in other areas. It will also encourage exponents as well as opponents of change to mobilize their sympathizers in organized fashion, an effort which has already been started. What may well emerge is a delineation of the limits of pluralism within the Conservative Movement. If the debate is conducted on a high level of moral responsibility, with full articulation of the theory underlying each point of view, it can only have the beneficial consequence of increasing religious awareness, knowledge, and commitment. I hope this book will initiate that process of constructive criticism and public debate on the development of *halakhah*. Its significance in this centennial year lies in its indicating a promising path for our Movement to follow as it moves into the twenty-first century.

These responsa, I believe, will be of interest to any student of *halakhah* and not only to a student of the place of women in Jewish law, for underlying the opinions on the admission of women to the Rabbinical School is the fundamental question of the social role of religion, or more particularly of Jewish religion. The Seminary position, as expressed in this case by the majority of the faculty, can only be legitimately effective if a *halakhic* rationale can be found for it. But to others that is only one aspect of the problem. For them religion must bespeak the atmosphere of and the continuity with the past. It is not enough that the admission of women to the Rabbinical School does not contravene Jewish law. The admission must also be in accordance with the regnant spirit of the Jewish community of our time and place. This is a question that cannot be resolved by vote, nor can it be settled by us in our lifetimes. To say that one is in favor of change, provided only that that change does not violate Jewish law, is to betray lack of concern for community. To be governed only by community is to reflect a lack of courage and religious conviction. Those of us who are not committed to Jewish orthodoxy must live in tension with ourselves. That is part of the challenge of such a place as our Seminary.

Final Report of the Commission for the Study of the Ordination of Women as Rabbis

January 30, 1979

I. PREAMBLE

The deliberative body issuing this report was formed at the behest of the Rabbinical Assembly, which, at its annual convention held in May 1977 in Liberty, New York, passed the following resolution:

> Be it resolved that the Rabbinical Assembly respectfully petitions the Chancellor of The Jewish Theological Seminary of America to establish an interdisciplinary commission to study all aspects of the role of women as spiritual leaders in the Conservative Movement.

> Be it further resolved that this study commission, whose membership shall reflect the pluralism and diversity of the Conservative Movement, shall be responsible for a progress report on its findings to be presented to the Executive Council of the Rabbinical Assembly in the spring of 1978, and for a final report and recommendation at the 1979 Convention of the Rabbinical Assembly.

The formation of the Commission was announced in October 1977 by Gerson D. Cohen, Chancellor of the Jewish Theological

Seminary of America, and Chairman of the Commission. Shortly thereafter, the Commission convened a series of meetings which continued throughout 1978, and which will be described below. With the submission of this final report to the 1979 Convention of the Rabbinical Assembly, the Commission terminates its career.

The fourteen men and women who accepted invitations to serve on the Commission represented a wide array of disciplines, backgrounds, and geographical regions. Their names follow:

(1) Gerson D. Cohen (Chairman), Chancellor, The Jewish Theological Seminary of America.

(2) Haim Z. Dimitrovsky, Professor of Talmudic Exegesis, The Jewish Theological Seminary of America.

(3) Victor Goodhill, Professor of Otologic Research, University of California at Los Angeles.

(4) Marion Siner Gordon, Attorney, Royal Palm Beach, Florida, and Lenox, Massachusetts.

(5) Rivkah Harris, Assyriologist, Chicago, Illinois.

(6) Milton Himmelfarb, Editor, *American Jewish Year Book*, and Director of Information, American Jewish Committee, New York, New York.

(7) Francine Klagsbrun, Author, New York, New York.

(8) Fishel A. Pearlmutter, Rabbi, Congregation B'nai Israel, Toledo, Ohio.

(9) Harry M. Plotkin, Attorney, Washington, D.C.

(10) Norman Redlich, Dean, New York University School of Law.

(11) Elijah J. Schochet, Rabbi, Congregation Beth Kodesh, Canoga Park, California.

(12) Wilfred Shuchat, Rabbi, Congregation Shaar Hashomayim, Westmount, Quebec.

(13) Seymour Siegel, Professor of Theology, The Jewish Theological Seminary of America.

(14) Gordon Tucker (Executive Director), Assistant to the

Chancellor, The Jewish Theological Seminary of America.*

The first task which the Commission faced was the definition of the problem it was to consider, and an interpretation of its mandate. Although the resolution of the Rabbinical Assembly was intentionally broad, referring as it did to "all aspects of the role of women as spiritual leaders in the Conservative Movement," it was decided at the outset that this Commission would deal specifically with the question of whether qualified women may and should be ordained as rabbis by the Rabbinical School of The Jewish Theological Seminary of America. Ruled outside of the scope of the Commission's deliberations were such issues as the investiture of women as cantors, and more general forms of ritual participation and leadership. The question of whether women already ordained by a recognized rabbinical seminary ought to be considered for membership in the Rabbinical Assembly, although related to the main question, was considered by the Commission to be subordinate to it. In any event, it was the Commission's understanding that the sense of the 1977 Rabbinical Assembly Convention was that any action by the Rabbinical Assembly on membership procedures for women should and would be deferred until the Commission reported its findings on the question of ordination at the Seminary, and until the Seminary's faculty took action on the basis of the report. Thus, the Commission's inquiry focused on the posture it would recommend to the Seminary with respect to female applicants to its Rabbinical School.

This final report on the Commission's activities will have the following form: first, the procedures which were followed will be described. Then, the specific areas of inquiry will be treated, and a summary of the evidence gathered and the subsequent discussion will be provided. Following that, the recommenda-

---

*As executive director, Rabbi Tucker was also responsible for the writing of this report, which was carefully reviewed and approved by the signatories to both the majority and minority opinions.

tion of the majority of the Commission on the main question will be presented and elaborated, along with some additional recommendations which the Commission felt a responsibility to offer at this time. Finally, a separate section will contain those opinions and recommendations of members of the Commission which diverged from the majority view.

II. PROCEDURES

Several operating principles were established at once at the Commission's initial meeting on December 12, 1977.

(1) Each member of the Commission had been invited to serve by dint of personal experience and expertise, and not as a representative of any organization or institution to which he or she belonged.

(2) The Commission would actively consult as wide a sampling of the constituency of the Conservative Movement as possible: rabbis, organizational leadership, synagogue leadership, and to the extent that it was possible, individuals as well.

(3) The Commission would approach the main question from the perspectives of the many disciplines which impinged upon it. Those included *halakhah*, ethics, economics, sociology, psychology, and education. Pragmatic and symbolic considerations were also deemed to be important objects of deliberation.

(4) Most important, despite the acknowledgment of the many facets considered relevant to the inquiry, the Commission was unanimous in its commitment to the following guideline: *no recommendation would be made which, in the opinion of members of the Commission, after having heard the testimony of experts, would contravene or be incompatible with the requirements of halakhah as the latter had been theretofore observed and developed by the Conservative Movement.* Thus, the Commission not only committed itself to recognizing the primacy of the role played by the *halakhah* in

Conservative Judaism but in effect decided that in matters which profoundly affect the future course of the Movement, *halakhic* considerations and constraints must be of primary significance.

The specifics of procedure for the life of the Commission were as follows:

(a) The meeting of December 12, 1977, in New York determined operating guidelines and was otherwise devoted to a general discussion of the issues to be considered.

(b) A second meeting took place over a three-day period in New York, from March 12 to March 14, 1978. During that time, invited testimony was heard from the leadership of the Rabbinical Assembly, the United Synagogue of America, and the Women's League for Conservative Judaism. Those who presented testimony were thoroughly questioned by Commission members. The first extensive discussion of the *halakhic* dimensions of the issue took place at this meeting, and several members undertook to research that particular aspect thoroughly in the ensuing months, in keeping with the Commission's insistence on conformity with Jewish legal norms. Plans were made for establishing lines of communication with the general constituency of the Movement, the implementation of which will be described in the paragraphs immediately following.

(c) Public meetings were arranged for various locales in North America, at which all persons affiliated with the Conservative Movement were invited to present testimony before several members of the Commission. These meetings were not for the purpose of counting "votes" pro or con, but rather for the purpose of gathering information on the problems which concerned the rank and file of the Movement, and the arguments which were being formulated by the laity. It was felt to be a fundamental principle of Jewish practice that any decision concerning Jewish usage, even an *halakhically* based decision, must take account of what will be reasonably acceptable to the community. Accordingly, meetings were set up as follows:

(a) Vancouver, British Columbia, on July 20, 1978.
(b) Los Angeles, California, on September 5–6, 1978.
(c) Minneapolis, Minnesota, on September 13, 1978.
(d) Chicago, Illinois, on September 14, 1978.
(e) Washington, D.C., on September 17, 1978.
(f) New York, New York, on November 1–2, 1978.
(g) Toronto, Ontario, on November 22, 1978.
(h) New York, New York (for members of the faculty and student body of The Jewish Theological Seminary of America) on December 3, 1978.

All of the above-mentioned public meetings were taped, and the transcripts have been made available to the public upon request. Arguments which were heard in the course of these meetings will be incorporated in the discussion of the substantive issues below: Nevertheless, some general, qualitative observations on these meetings should be made at this point:

(i) Although no tally was made, or indeed ever contemplated, it was manifest that the overwhelming majority of those who chose to testify at these meetings strongly favored the ordination of women.
(ii) It became equally clear that women are very much interested in continuing their drive toward full religious equalization with men; moreover, many young women are seriously interested in the rabbinate as a career.
(iii) By and large, those women who aspire to become Conservative rabbis have a strong commitment to traditional values and law. In fact, many of those women could probably be characterized as having a pattern of religious observance lying near the more traditional end of the spectrum of Conservative Jewish practice.

(iv) The Conservative communities, as they were represented at these public meetings, seem to be prepared to
accept, even if gradually, rabbinic leadership by women.

Needless to say, these observations must be considered in
the light of the uncertainty concerning just how representative
a sampling of the community were those who took the trouble
to testify at the hearings. In spite of the fact that there was
fairly wide and general publicity in advance of each meeting,
there was evidence that, for whatever reason, some persons
who would oppose the ordination of women did not take the
trouble to attend the hearings. On the other hand, those who
did make the effort to testify probably constituted a better
sampling of those Conservative Jews who have strong feelings
on the subject, and that in itself is significant. In that connection, the following should be noted: the Commission took great
satisfaction and pride in the fact that in community after
community across North America, Conservative Jews were
motivated by this issue to seriously contemplate their own
personal stances not only with respect to the issue at hand, but
also with respect to Jewish commitment generally. In many
cases, people took the initiative in reading and studying about
the issue, and in that sense, the Commission's enterprise was
an educative force in the community.*

---

*A survey of the Conservative Jewish community of a more scientific
nature was considered to be desirable as well. As a result, very generous
professional assistance was secured from two quarters. The first was the
market research firm of Yankelovich, Skelly, and White, which designed a
questionnaire and a tabulation plan, and provided advice on methods of
choosing a sample and distributing the questionnaires. Special thanks are
due to Ms. Florence Skelly and Mr. Arthur White, as well as to their
associates, Mr. Sanford Deutsch and Ms. Ann D. Clurman. Second, Dr. Saul
Shapiro lent his assistance in programming and running the tabulation of the
completed questionnaires. In all, fourteen Conservative congregations were
sent some 300 questionnaires each. The Commission only had the benefit of
some preliminary results, due to some unavoidable delays in the processing
of the data. However, fully tabulated and cross-correlated results have now
been obtained, and the Commission hopes that the bodies which will bear
the responsibility for considering, debating, and perhaps implementing the
recommendations made herein will consult those results in the process.

The Commission met again in New York on December 6–7, 1978. During those two days members shared and discussed the results of their own researchers and investigations, considered new evidence from various sources (e.g., the regional hearings, and the unsolicited communications which were addressed to the Commission fairly steadily throughout its lifetime), and eventually arrived at tentative conclusions. Subsequently, Commission members communicated via the mails and the telephone in order to arrive at the final version of this report.

Thus, the Commission was active for slightly less than fourteen months, during which time it met as a complete body for six full days, convened six public hearings plus one hearing for the Seminary community, received considerable testimony, both solicited and unsolicited, and itself commissioned a scientific survey of the Conservative laity on the issue being confronted.

III. THE ISSUE

There are certain aspects to the question at hand regarding which it was at once established that there was unanimity among members of the Commission. These are some of the more obvious considerations which come to mind: the ability and willingness of women to perform rabbinic duties as well as men, the right to equal job opportunities, the right to pursue a career of one's choice. Indeed, it could be said that with respect to the context in which general feminist issues are discussed, there was never any serious dispute among Commission members, nor apparently within the community either. There were and are, for example, many men who fully accept the fact that their wives are pursuing careers, as well as women actually pursuing careers, who nevertheless oppose the ordination of women.

It was therefore determined at the outset that this could not be treated solely as a feminist issue. From that point of view, there was plainly very little to discuss. The complexity of the issue at hand stemmed from the fact that, although there is general agreement concerning the questions which characterize general feminist debates, there is still a wide range of other considerations of which account must be taken. Those considerations include some peculiar to the rabbinate, to Jewish practice in general, and to Conservative Judaism in particular. It was about these special considerations that discussion and debate revolved.

A. Halakhic Considerations

As indicated above, the demands of *halakhah* led the list of matters to be resolved. Even though the Commission was not charged with developing an *halakhic* stance or approach for the Conservative Movement, its commitment to the notion that legitimacy within Conservative Judaism must be measured first and foremost by an *halakhic* standard made theoretical discussions concerning the processes of *halakhah* indispensable.

The Commission eventually adopted the classical position which had been embraced by the religious leadership of the Conservative Movement since its founding. That stance maintains that the body of Jewish law is not uniform in texture, but is rather composed of materials which fall into two main categories, usually referred to as *de-oraita* (biblically ordained) and *de-rabbanan* (rabbinically developed). That which is *de-oraita* can be considered to be the very core of the system, which holds it in place and provides a frame of reference. It therefore must be treated as inviolable. Tampering with what is *de-oraita* is tantamount to destroying the core of the Jewish pattern of life as it has existed for millennia. There is positive precedent for doing so only in the most dire of circumstances, and even then with extreme caution and conservatism.

The much greater (that is, in terms of volume) overlay which is *de-rabbanan*, on the other hand, comes with procedures for change and development. What is *de-rabbanan* can develop, is in fact meant to develop, as the conditions of the Jewish community change. That is what ensures the vibrancy and the continuity of the *halakhah* as the coordinate system which roots all Jewish communities.

It is a commonplace among Conservative Jews that the recognition of the flexibility and fluidity of the *halakhah* is one of the hallmarks of Conservative Judaism, and this is certainly true. It is equally the case that this recognition constitutes in many ways a major distinction between Conservatism and Orthodoxy. Yet it ought not to be forgotten that there are important similarities between Conservatism and Orthodoxy which need reemphasis. In particular, it cannot be stressed too strongly that the strength of Conservative Judaism depends as much on its continuation as a movement devoted to tradition as it does on its continued devotion to *halakhic* development. The two are inseparable in classical terms, and the centrality of tradition expresses itself in the conditions under which development becomes acceptable. Those conditions include:

(1) The core which is *de-oraita* may not be altered or displaced. The general principles of, for example, *kashrut* or *Shabbat* could never be displaced as central pillars of Conservative Judaism.

(2) Development in the domain of *de-rabbanan* must not be abrupt or discontinuous, must be rooted in traditional exegetical methodologies, and above all, must be ratified by the community of the committed and the informed.

(3) The impetus for development in what is *de-rabbanan* must come from *within* the community of the committed and the informed, and not be an external influence originating outside the concerned Jewish community.

When the Commission determined that it would not recommend anything which would contravene the *halakhah*, it was to this view of the *halakhic* process that it was appealing. Faithfulness to this process constitutes, in the opinion of the Commission, a *sine qua non* for legitimacy within the Conservative Movement. Of course, the view outlined above is not univocal or free of ambiguities. Indeed, there is a certain amount of inherent ambiguity attending all three of the conditions lately listed. There is, in fact, no clear-cut demarcation line between *de-oraita* and *de-rabbanan*. Nevertheless, the existence of gray areas does not negate the fact that the areas which are clearly black or white are well distinguished, and it certainly does not preclude the use of criteria which give rise to those gray areas. Given the obvious fact that some ambiguities will be unavoidable, the alternative would be paralysis, which could not possibly serve the cause of *halakhah*.

Once agreement was reached on the philosophical and theoretical level, the specific *halakhic* problems which arise were addressed. As is well known from the recent literature on this issue, there are a variety of *halakhic* criteria which have traditionally distinguished between men and women. Primary among these are the following:

(1) According to some sources, women may be ineligible to be appointed to any office of communal responsibility in the Jewish community.
(2) Women are exempted from the obligation to study Torah (except for the acquisition of knowledge concerning obligations they do have), although there is no problem presented by their voluntarily assuming that obligation.
(3) Women are exempted from positive time-dependent commandments, with a few notable exceptions. The most relevant commandments under this category for purposes of this Commission are those relating to public worship, for exemption from performance raises problems concerning eligibility to discharge the obligation of another person who cannot claim exemption.
(4) Women are traditionally ineligible to serve as witnesses in judicial proceedings, including the execution of documents determining personal and familial status.
(5) Women are, by virtue of (4) above, considered by most traditional authorities to be ineligible to serve as judges.

All of these sex-role distinctions of the *halakhah* were discussed and researched by members of the Commission. The results of those deliberations will now be summarized:

The role of the rabbi as we know it today is not one which is established in classical Jewish texts, but rather is one which has evolved through social need and custom. Consequently, there is no specifiable *halakhic* category which can be identified with the modern rabbinate, nor with the currently accepted mode of ordination. Ordination at the Jewish Theological Seminary of America is done in a way which is nearly indistinguishable from the granting of an academic degree at the successful completion of a course of study. Of course, it still has a profound religious and symbolic significance not shared by any academic degree. In other words, issues relating to ordination are not *halakhic* issues per se, though it is certainly true that there may be serious ramifications of decisions concerning ordination which can lead to a confrontation with certain *halakhic* principles. Strictly speaking, point (1) above is general enough to present an *halakhic* problem concerning ordination. That point has its origin in a passage in the *halakhic* midrash on the Book of Deuteronomy, the *Sifre*. On the verse in Deuteronomy 17:15, "You shall be free to set a king over yourself," the *Sifre* comments, "A king and not a queen." Extrapolating from this comment, Maimonides in *Laws Relating to Kings* 1:5 says, "Only men may be appointed [to positions of authority] in Israel."

Insufficient as Halakhic Barrier.

After considering the opinion of Maimonides on this matter, the Commission decided that it was beset by numerous ambiguities and uncertainties and should not be accounted as an immutable provision of the *halakhah*.

The modern rabbinate cannot be analogized to an appointment on the order of magnitude of the ancient monarchy. The many obvious high-level appointments of women in modern Jewish life indicate the passing of this principle from general Jewish usage. The Commission therefore determined that this *halakhah* as formulated by Maimonides was insufficient to pose an *halakhic* barrier to the ordination of women.

With respect to point (2) above, the Conservative Movement has already taken the strongest possible stand in favor of obligating women to study Torah on a basis equal to that of men. The Movement's introduction of *Bat Mitzvah* half a century ago, its educational programs in Camp Ramah, United Synagogue Youth, Leaders Training Fellowship, and last but not least, the schools of the Jewish Theological Seminary of America, all bear witness to that stand. Indeed, the history of the Conservative Movement on the issue of the religious education of women not only vitiates the force of point (2), but actually constitutes a consideration in favor of ordaining women, as will be noted below.

Points (3), (4), and (5) are a group in several respects. First, they have all been dealt with to some extent by a constituent arm of the Conservative Movement. Second, they are all *halakhic* sex-role distinctions which are secondary to the issue of ordination, as will be explained. Third, although they are secondary to the ordination issue *logically*, they are closely connected to the rabbinic role *practically*. These points accounted for most of the *halakhically* based discussions during the Commission's proceedings.

Matters of *halakhic* import in the Conservative Movement have always been channeled through the Rabbinical Assembly Committee on Jewish Law and Standards (henceforth: the Law Committee). That Committee's composition and rules of procedure have varied considerably over the years, but it has consistently defined itself as a panel which primarily makes recommendations on the basis of legal scholarship; its decisions have binding power on Movement leaders only when a very strong consensus condition is met. For the past several years, the operating rule has been that only a position held by all but two or fewer members of the Committee is binding; a minority position with three adherents on the Committee becomes a legitimate option for Conservative congregations and rabbis.

Despite inevitable disagreements concerning one or another of the Law Committee's decisions, nearly universal respect has been accorded to the principle of legitimate option. Accordingly, in considering the proper course for the entire Conservative Movement on a matter such as the one under scrutiny, the history of the Law Committee's treatment of some of the related questions must be looked into.

The Law Committee published a majority decision in 1955 which allowed women the privilege of an *aliyah* at Torah-reading services. Although this practice is far from universal in Conservative congregations, it is a practice which is growing and which was legitimated by the 1955 decision. In 1973, the same committee issued a majority responsum which permitted congregations to count women as part of the *minyan* for public worship. This practice has likewise not nearly become universal, but the number of congregations which have been accepting it is steadily growing. Finally, a *minority* report in 1974 declared that women should be permitted to serve as witnesses in legal proceedings, including the signing of *ketubot* and *gittin*. Since that minority report was issued by six committee members, the rules of the Law Committee imply that it is a legitimate option for rabbis and congregations in the Conservative Movement. Thus, the Commission established that the practices referred to in points (3), (4), and (5) had already been declared by the Committee on Jewish Law and Standards of the Rabbinical Assembly to be *halakhically* acceptable options within the Conservative Movement. Hence the Commission determined that its resolution of the ordination issue could not lead to a possible contravention of a binding standard for the conservative Movement.

More important than the foregoing observations was the fact that irrespective of what one's *halakhic* view is on the matter of a woman performing these practices, they are strictly secondary to the issue of ordination. A wide variety of functions are viewed as part of the role of the rabbi today. Among these are teaching, preaching, counselling, officiating at religious ceremonies, representing the Jewish community, etc. Leading a prayer service as the *shaliah tzibur*, receiving an *aliyah*, or even signing a *ketubah* or *get* as a witness are not among these essential functions. A rabbi supervising divorce proceedings might be entitled to sign the *get* as a witness, and may on occasion do so as a matter of convenience, but surely it is not the rabbi's role qua rabbi to do so. Similar observations would apply to other forms of testimony and to the various roles associated with public worship which have been mentioned. The simple fact is that the rabbinate, as noted above, is not defined or circumscribed by *halakhic* strictures. Hence there can be no direct *halakhic* objection to the conferral of the title "rabbi" upon a woman, together with all the rights and responsibilities to perform the functions essentially connected to the office. In connection with this, the Commission noted that it is a commonplace to ordain *Kohanim*, even though officiating at a funeral, which can pose *halakhic* problems for a *Kohen*, is popularly viewed as a rabbinic function.

One objection raised against this analysis was given very serious consideration by the Commission. It was as follows: granted that the religious functions in question are logically distinct from the role of the rabbi, they are certainly connected closely enough in practice to be a serious cause for concern. Specifically, it is unreasonable, according to this objection, to ordain a woman, place her in a pulpit in a small community, and expect that she will not lead prayer services, sign legal documents affecting personal status, etc. The very inevitability of one event following on the heels of the other might make the two inseparable for the purposes of this discussion.

In the course of lengthy consideration of this objection, the Commission noted several things: (a) As indicated above, previous Law Committee decisions have resolved the problems concerning the practices in question for many members of the Conservative Movement. Indeed, there are already many congregations giving *aliyot* to women and counting them in a *minyan*, and there are Conservative rabbis who, in accordance with the minority responsum of the Law Committee, allow knowledgeable women to sign *ketubot* and *gittin*. (b) Even for those who do not accept the lenient positions on these issues (and this group is largest on the question of testimony, where a good number believe that a female serving as a witness is contrary to biblical law), the objection is still not connected to ordination itself, but rather to an assessment of what is quite likely to happen given a certain job situation in a certain place. The Commission decided that there was little point in speculating on such matters, particularly given the fact that with the increased education and activism of women in the Conservative Movement, the act of ordination itself would not be likely to significantly affect the prevalence of practices which are not universally accepted. Excessive concern over possible objectionable effects of an unobjectionable action (i.e., ordination), where those effects are objectionable to only part of the community, and are not caused solely by that action, can easily degenerate into an *ad infinitum* list of potential objections. (c) Observations (a) and (b) taken together make it clear that there is no cogent argument on *halakhic* grounds for denying a sincere, committed woman the opportunity to study for and achieve the office of rabbi.

In closing this section on *halakhah*, the Commission notes that in the medieval period, the spiritual leadership of women was not unknown. One bit of evidence for this is to be found in the fourteenth-century work of a Spanish rabbi, known as *Sefer Hahinukh*, which assumes that a woman is eligible to perform the most basic of the classical rabbinic functions, viz., deciding specific matters of law. Section 152 of that treatise, which deals with the prohibition of deciding matters of ritual law while intoxicated, notes that the prohibition "applies to males, as well as to a knowledgeable woman who is eligible to give such instruction."

To summarize, then: The *halakhic* objections to the ordination of women center around disapproval of the performance by a woman of certain functions. Those functions, however, are not essentially rabbinic, nor are they universally disapproved, by the accepted rules governing the discussion of *halakhah* in the Conservative Movement. *There is no direct halakhic objection to the acts of training and ordaining a woman to be a rabbi, preacher, and teacher in Israel.*

The problems associated with ancillary functions were deemed by the Commission to be insufficient grounds for denying a considerable and growing group of highly talented and committed Jewish women the access they desire to the roles of spiritual and community leaders.

B. Ethical Considerations

Although there was some discussion on the subject, there was no agreement among Commission members concerning precisely what the relationship is or ought to be between *halakhah* and ethics. One general observation was, however, agreed upon. In many areas of Jewish law, the developmental history of the *halakhah* exhibits a strong tendency to approach ever more closely an ideal ethical state within the parameters and constraints of the *halakhah*. Indeed, echoing the opinion of Rav that the *mitzvot* were given us in order to "refine us," the Commission accepted the view that the commandments have among their chief purposes the ethical perfection of the individual and of society. The basic ethical principle underlying the democratic society in which we live—a principle that has deep roots in our biblical-rabbinic tradition—is that each person should have at least a legally equal opportunity to pursue a chosen career. This principle should be followed within the Jewish community more especially where no specific *halakhic* violation is involved. Since there is no specific *halakhic* argument against ordaining women, denying a Jewish woman the opportunity to serve the Jewish community and the cause of Torah as a rabbi merely because she is a woman would be ethically indefensible.

One ethical objection considered by the Commission was actually rooted in sociology and economics. That objection invoked the possibility, or even the likelihood, considering the initial experiences of other movements which have ordained women, that female Conservative rabbis might at first face great difficulty in finding congregational positions. This argument then maintained that it is unethical to train people for a profession with the knowledge that they will find it extremely difficult to practice that profession and thereby fulfill their aspirations and earn a livelihood. The Commission dealt with this objection in several ways. First, it was noted that the results of the public hearings which were held in the fall of 1978 did not indicate that most congregations would be unreasonably reluctant to hire a female rabbi. On the contrary, there was growing evidence, gathered at the Commission's hearings and through the United Synagogue of America, that the receptivity to female rabbis in the communities was much higher now than it had been several years ago. Apparently, familiarity with the issues, as well as the presence and visibility of some ordained women over the last six years had taken effect. At any rate, the assumption of a bleak future in the job market seemed quite unjustified, particularly given the fact that the Conservative Movement is experiencing a shortage of rabbis to serve its congregations.

In addition, the Commission questioned whether job placement was a legitimate ethical issue. Many graduate and professional schools in all fields train students year after year despite wide fluctuations in the job market. While the size of an entering class should certainly not be excessively out of line with what the market can absorb, there is nothing unethical about providing an opportunity for a person to train for his or her chosen profession despite possible difficulties in locating a suitable job situation. What could be improper is withholding information about the realities of the job market, but that is certainly not a serious possibility.

A more serious ethical concern was voiced many times by many interested parties. This objection concerned the right of a minority to have its commitment to conscience respected. Specifically, it was argued as follows: when the Law Committee decided certain *halakhic* issues by means of majority and minority reports, those whose consciences directed them to the more traditional position could still feel comfortable and legitimate, while respecting their colleagues' right to choose the position which they felt was mandated by the relevant factors. Were the Seminary to begin ordaining women, however, it would be the first time that the central academic institution of the Movement would have entered the arena to take a public stance on an issue of *halakhah*, a stance which could *ipso facto* become the standard for the Movement. Those who opposed the ordination of women on religious grounds would then have no legitimate option but to silently acquiesce in the decision, or to leave the Movement.

The sincerity and the frequency with which this argument was raised led the Commission to consider it very carefully. Having done so, the Commission recognized that there would indeed be some unavoidable uneasiness whatever its recommendation would be. Nevertheless, there were three points which were found to mitigate some of the strength of this objection:

(1) This objection partially hinges on the assumption that there are serious matters of *halakhic* import connected with a decision by the Seminary to ordain women, and that these are serious enough to create difficult crises of conscience. Because of the analysis given in the previous section of this report, it was felt that this objection was overstated.

(2) The objection apparently is intended to argue that the Seminary faculty should not be taking a stance, so as to avoid foreclosing the legitimacy of the opposing view. It fails to take into account the fact that at this point, for the Seminary faculty not to vote to change the status quo would *in itself* be a stance on the issue. Moreover, it has been the observation of the Commission that there are commitments to conscience among those who favor the ordination of women which are as strong as those among opponents of that decision. The reality is that the Seminary faculty, irrespective of what it does, is going to give rise to some uneasiness in some quarters. This is not to say that one position is obviously better than another,

but it does obviate the force of this objection to action on the part of the Seminary faculty. The important issue which does arise out of this is the need to assuage the uneasiness and ensure that it is only a temporary reaction to a decision of great import.

(3) Finally, this objection reveals a bias, which has often been expressed to the Commission, against the Seminary faculty taking a stand on *any halakhic* matters affecting the Conservative Movement. This bias was of particular concern to the Commission, and was discussed on several occasions. It was ultimately the consensus of the Commission that on an issue such as the present one, one which will affect the very nature of the American rabbinate, and which manifestly will not go away if ignored, it is rather the unavoidable responsibility of the Seminary faculty to get involved and take a stand. The Commission assumes that the stand which the faculty will find it necessary to take on any *halakhic* issue will be a thoroughly informed stand, and that the decision which it now must of necessity make on the issue of ordaining women will be based not only on the careful study of this report, but on the examination of all other data available to it which relate to this issue.

The most compelling ethical argument heard by the Commission was one in favor of ordaining women, and it was heard from members of the Conservative laity in many different parts of North America. As noted in the previous section, the Conservative Movement has a proud history of educating females in Jewish Studies from the earliest ages on a perfect par with males. In fact, it is worth considering for a moment what it is like today for boys and girls to grow up in a committed Jewish home identified and affiliated with the Conservative Movement. Such a boy and girl would both be given the very same Hebrew or Day School education from the outset. Both would prepare for *Bar* or *Bat Mitzvah* ceremonies and in most cases perform the same functions in the service. Both would likely receive intense Judaic training at Camp Ramah. They would proceed to Hebrew High School, join LTF and/or United Synagogue Youth. In many congregations, they would participate in public worship equally through adolescence, building on their acquired Jewish skills. They would seek out the same reinforcement of their Jewish values while away at college, and form a more sophisticated intellectual commitment to Judaism. That commitment would in some cases be strong enough to generate a desire to study for the rabbinate at the Seminary of the Conservative Movement. Suddenly, discontinuously, at this point, the female is differentiated from the male in being unable to fulfill the education she was given and encouraged to pursue in the way she chose to fulfill it.

This scenario was not an abstract creation, but rather was the actual testimony of many parents who, confronted by the problem, were unable to explain the sudden differentiation to their daughters. In considering this increasingly common phenomenon, the Commission felt that it was morally wrong to maintain an educational structure that treats males and females equally up to the final stage, but distinguishes between them at that stage, *without a firm and clearly identifiable halakhic reason for doing so.* In such a case, the Commission felt that the secondary *halakhically* related issues dealt with in the previous section paled even further in significance. On balance, the ethical arguments *coupled with the absence of halakhic counter-argument* were considered by the Commission to constitute a strong case for the training and ordination of women as rabbis at the Jewish Theological Seminary of America.

C. *Other Considerations*

A good deal of other evidence came to the attention of the Commission and was discussed by it. Most of it tended to support a decision to recommend the training and ordination of women as Conservative rabbis. These blocks of evidence fall under a variety of rubrics and will be summarized in this section.

(1) Preliminary data from the survey commissioned by this body indicated that, in absolute numbers, a majority of the laity of the Conservative Movement was ready to accept women in the role of congregational spiritual leader.

(2) Those persons who testified at the regional hearings convened by the Commission represented an extraordinary range of backgrounds, talents, professions, and ages. In all, a considerable majority of these strongly favored the ordination of women in the Conservative Movement. Another fact which came to light as a result of the hearings was that there are more women interested in pursuing this career out of genuine commitment to the traditional Jewish community than had been assumed.

(3) Although the opinions of members of the psychological profession previously reported in the literature were mixed, those professionals in the field who made contact voluntarily with the Commission were overwhelmingly positive and encouraging on the issue of ordination.

(4) Two United Synagogue congregations are currently being served in some rabbinic or quasi-rabbinic role by a woman, and both communicated, through official leadership as well as through individual congregants, their satisfaction with that situation.

(5) The student body of the Seminary's Rabbinical School, when surveyed by the Student Government, expressed support for the admission of women to the Rabbinical School by an affirmative vote of 74 percent.

(6) It became clear as well that a decision not to ordain women would mean the neglect if not the rejection of a pool of talented, committed, and energetic women who could eventually represent 50 percent of the potential spiritual leaders, and who could play a major role in revitalizing Jewish traditon and values in the Conservative Movement. Indications are that the Movement cannot afford the cost of refusing to take advantage of that leadership talent at the present time.

There was one other major consideration which was voiced many times, and could best be classified under the category of "symbolism." This point was raised by many persons who believed on substantive grounds that the ordination of women was both correct and defensible, but who feared what they termed the symbolic break with tradition that such a move would represent. For exponents of this argument, the symbolic result of admitting women to the rabbinate would be a blurring of the ideological lines which have divided Conservatism from more liberal Jewish movements. That, it is claimed, would destroy the main attraction of the Conservative Movement, to wit, the coexistence of authenticity of tradition with a critical view aimed at developing that tradition within the framework of *halakhic* norms.

The Commission took this argument most seriously, but concluded that it was insufficient to militate against ordaining women. The reason for this conclusion was that, by the Commission's own commitments and chosen procedures, a recommendation in favor of ordination would be based on a thorough and predominant commitment to *halakhah*. In a case such as this, where a recommended development is consistent with *halakhah*, and manifestly to the advantage of the community, symbolic considerations must not be allowed to block that development. To be sure, the symbolic considerations must be taken very seriously, but rather as a challenge to educate the community to the extent that it is evident to all that the development is in consonance with the historical ideological commitments of Conservative Judaism, and does not represent an ideological shift. It is hoped that this report will constitute a first step in that process of education.

IV. Recommendations

Based on its overall commitment to *halakhic* authenticity, and all of the evidence and reasoning which have been summarized or alluded to in this report, the signatories to this majority opinion recommend that qualified women be ordained as rabbis in the Conservative Movement. Specifically, the recommendations are:

(A) That the Rabbinical School of the Jewish Theological Seminary of America revise its admission procedures to allow for applications from female candidates and the processing thereof for the purpose of admission to the ordination program on a basis equal to that maintained heretofore for males.

(B) That this revision of policy be accomplished as quickly as possible, preferably so as to allow applications from women for the academic year beginning in September 1979.

(C) That the Jewish Theological Seminary of America take steps to set up appropriate apparatuses for the recruitment, orientation, and eventually, career placement of female rabbinical students.

(D) That the major arms of the Conservative Movement immediately begin discussion of procedures to be followed to educate the community concerning issues raised in this report so as to ensure as smooth and as harmonious an adjustment to the new policy as possible.

In making these recommendations, the Commission is making no recommendation in regard to traditional practices relating to testimony, and no implications concerning such practices should be drawn on the basis of this report.

The following members of the Commission join in supporting the above majority report:

Gerson D. Cohen	Fishel A. Pearlmutter
Victor Goodhill	Harry M. Plotkin
Marion Siner Gordon	Norman Redlich
Rivkah Harris	Seymour Siegel
Milton Himmelfarb	Gordon Tucker
Francine Klagsbrun	

Minority Opinion

Although the signatories to this section are in sympathy with many of the arguments and sentiments expressed by our colleagues on the Commission, and embodied in the majority opinion given above, we remain opposed to the ordination of women as rabbis in the Conservative Movement. Since many of the reasons for this conclusion have already been discussed or at least mentioned earlier in this report, we shall simply list briefly our motivations for arriving at this recommendation.

(A) Our main thrust has to do with certain *halakhic* problems which cannot in our opinion be separated from the question of ordination but flow from it almost inexorably. Not all congregations accept the view that women may be counted in a *minyan*, receive *aliyot*, or lead the service in liturgical prayer as a surrogate for others. Many more congregations and many Jews outside our Movement may be affected by practices in connection with testimony relating to marriage and divorce, where the laws are restrictive in the case of women. You cannot, within the present climate of the Conservative Movement, ordain women and expect that they will not at some point infringe on these *halakhic* restrictions in the performance of their rabbinical duties.

(B) We fear the possible disruption of the unity of the Movement. One of the consequences of a decision to ordain women might very well be the violations of *halakhic* principles adhered to by others in the Movement, which in turn would result in the untenable position of individual rabbis being unable in good conscience to recognize the validity of marriages, divorces, and conversions supervised by one of their colleagues.

(C) A decision to ordain women would mark the first time in recent history that the Seminary had entered the arena of *halakhic* decision-making. The centrality and authority of the Seminary would perforce be a uniformizing influence which could have the unfortunate effect of foreclosing the options of minorities wishing to remain within the Movement.

(D) Finally, we are concerned that at a time when American Jewish youth seem to be turning more toward traditional values, and to an authentic *halakhic* life-style, this would seriously compromise the traditional image of the Conservative Movement, and the Jewish Theological Seminary of America as an authentic *halakhic* institution. We feel strongly that such matters of symbolism must be taken as seriously as possible, for a wrong decision on an issue of this magnitude will, in our opinion, alienate many more *halakhically* committed people than it will attract.

For these reasons, we recommend to the leaders of the Conservative Movement that appropriate roles be created for Jewish women short of ordination so that their commitment and talents may be a source of blessing and not of unnecessary controversy.

The following members of the Commission join in supporting the above minority opinion:

Haim Z. Dimitrovsky
Elijah J. Schochet
Wilfred Shuchat

Statement at Commission Hearing: December 3, 1978

JOSEPH A. BRODIE

As my friends know, I don't speak out publicly on political and/or religious issues frequently. In fact, for the record, in my 24-year association with the Jewish Theological Seminary, this will be the first time. Isn't it about time?

Why do I feel so strongly? To my mind, what's at stake for our Movement on this issue is the role of *halakhah* in the future of Conservative Judaism. To many, the question of granting women ordination appears to be a relatively non-complex *halakhic* issue of little significance. This is a misconception. For me, this issue is no less significant, no less a turning point for our Movement, than was the issue of Hebrew to our intellectual precursor, Zechariah Frankel.

The significance of this issue is whether *halakhah* and *halakhic* authority remain central to our Movement. Major *halakhic* ramifications will inevitably result from the ordination of women, and they require prior consideration.

Can women serve as *edim* witnesses? As *hazzanim* leaders of public prayer? Before ordaining women, *halakhic* decisions produced by *halakhic* authorities must be rendered in these matters.

To act now on ordaining women rabbis severely limits the possibility of genuine *halakhic* debate on these crucial *halakhic* issues. With all due respect to the Commission, to act now on the basis of a commission report, a commission the majority of

31

whose members are not *halakhic* authorities, would in effect be to institute a new format for rendering *halakhic* decisions.

Who could deny the woman rabbi the right to be a witness? To lead a public service?—after ordaining her. Obversely, who would want to create a category of second-class rabbis?

By not confronting these issues first, they will be decided de facto. We will be creating a new process for rendering what are essentially *halakhic* decisions, and will thereby be betraying the authentic *halakhic* process.

Any movement which calls itself *halakhic* cannot in good conscience allow non-*halakhists* in effect to decide *halakhic* issues and then post facto seek rationalizations for these decisions. Such a precedent could only be used by later commissions and committees to justify any and all deviations from the *halakhic* tradition. The very nature of our Movement, its historic direction, will have been irretrievably altered.

Let my position be clear. I am objecting specifically to the way in which this is being done. I *do not deny* that the ordination of women, and the resolution of the problems caused by the *halakhic* ramifications, might be possible within *halakhah*. I insist, however, that the decision should reflect our Movement's commitment to the primacy of *halakhah*. This means that while the Commission might counsel our *halakhic* experts, only our *halakhists*, can determine whether the ordination of women is permitted or forbidden, and only those *halakhists* can decide whether the ramifications of that decision would or would not cause irreparable harm to the *halakhic* process. The primacy of *halakhah* demands that *halakhic* decisions be rendered by bona fide *halakhists*, not to be made in effect by broad-based commissions!

Let me tell you a story. Eighteen years ago, I went to California for the first time, driving cross country with another rabbinical student. We couldn't wait for a good meat meal. Upon arriving in Los Angeles, we made a beeline for the Jewish section.

We saw a sign—a sign we had up until that time never seen back East. "Kosher-style." We argued. My friend maintained that "kosher-style" meant kosher. I responded that only kosher meant kosher. "Kosher-style," I contended, must be something else; it couldn't possibly be authentically, legitimately, kosher. We all know now that "kosher-style" is, in reality, *traif*.

I am appealing for the integrity of our Movement. Up to now we have had more right than any other group to call ourselves *halakhic* Jews. Let's not forfeit that right. Will we remain *halakhic*, legitimately and authentically so? Or, to coin a term, are we becoming "*halakhic*-style"?

By limiting our options for legitimate *halakhic* decision-making, there will be no question that we are becoming "*halakhic*-style." And, if we are "*halakhic*-style," what differentiates us from Reform? If so, let's drop the pretensions of being authentically *halakhic*.

Today the Conservative Movement is at a crossroads. As for me, no matter which road we take I will remain a Conservative Jew. I am too committed to Conservative Judaism to give up that identity. I refuse to do so.

I am an unabashed, old-fashioned, unrepentant *halakhist*. Perhaps to coin yet another term, those who share my view may be called "Classical Conservative Jews."

I pray that it may never be said that "Classical Conservative Jews" went out of style, together with *halakhah*, as "*halakhic*-style" became the trademark of the Conservative Movement in 1979.

Thank you.

On the Ordination of Women

ISRAEL FRANCUS

There are those, albeit very few, who claim that "it is a theological and moral imperative to grant women full equality in the religious sphere even if it violates the *Halakhah*." All that I can say to them is: you have read yourself out of the Conservative Movement, which was founded on, and continues to subscribe to, the primacy of *Halakhah* in Judaism.

We must turn our attention only to those among us who are committed to *Halakhah* and are searching for a way to make it halakhically possible to have women rabbis. The idea that we will ordain women with a proviso that will limit their rabbinic activities to what is tolerated by the *Halakhah* must be rejected outright. Not only is this impractical, but also unenforceable. It is nothing more and nothing less than plain and simple deceit. Once a woman is ordained and takes a position as a congregational rabbi, no one will be able to tell her what to do. She becomes the *Mara De-atra*—the authority in religious matters—and the Rabbinical Assembly will see to it that her rights are not violated.

Among the essential functions of a rabbi, especially in small communities where the newly ordained usually start their rabbinic careers, are that of serving as *shaliah tzibbur*—a cantor "leading the congregation in prayer"; *baal-koreh*—"reader of the Torah portion" on Sabbaths, Festivals, and other occasions; reciter of the *Birkat Hatanim*—the "benedictions recited at a wedding"; and that of being counted in the *minyan*. Unless we

35

can find a halakhic way to permit a woman to perform these functions, she will not be able to serve as rabbi. The average layman will find it very difficult to understand and even more difficult to accept the proposition that the religious leader of his congregation may not lead him in prayer (as a cantor) and that the marriage performer is not permitted to recite the *sheva brakhot*, "the seven benedictions" recited at the wedding, and may not even be counted as one of the required *minyan* for either occasion.

The halakhic reason why a woman may not perform the above functions is that she is halakhically exempt from these *mitzvot* and consequently cannot be *motzi*—she "cannot act as the agent to perform these *mitzvot*" in behalf of the men present on those occasions because the men are *hiyuvim*, "obliged" to perform the *mitzvot*. The question before us with regard to women is therefore twofold.

1. Can a woman acquire the status of a *hiyuvit*—of "one obligated" in relation to *mitzvot* from which she is exempt?
2. If the answer is yes, will the quality of her "obligation" be of such a nature as to qualify her to be *motzi*—"to act as an agent to perform *mitzvot*" in behalf of men?

After careful examination of the rabbinic sources, one must conclude that the answer to the first question is yes, and to the second question, it is absolutely no. A woman can never—not today, not tomorrow, not next year, and not next generation— acquire the status of a *hiyuvit*—of one "obligated" in relation to a *mitzvah* from whose performance she is now halakhically exempt, which would qualify her to act as agent in the performance of those *mitzvot* in behalf of men.[1] For there is a hierarchy among "obligations," and the status of a man's obligation, whether it is biblically or rabinically imposed, has greater *halakhic* weight than the self-imposed "obligation" of a woman. According to rabbinic law, the status of the *hiyuv* ("the obligation") of the *motzi* ("the one who is performing a *mitzvah* in behalf of another") must halakhically be at least equal to the status of the *hiyuv* ("the obligation") of the *yotzei* ("the one in whose behalf the *mitzvah* is being done"). Let me explain in as concise and clear a manner as possible.[2]

The Mishnah Rosh Hashana 3:8 states: "A deaf-mute, imbecile, or minor may not fulfill an obligation on behalf of the many.[3] This is the general rule. Anyone on whom an obligation is not incumbent cannot fulfill that obligation on behalf of the many."[4]

No *psak-halakhah* ("halakhically definitive pronouncement") on the matter of who can be *motzi* ("who can fulfill a *mitzvah* on behalf of whom") can be given on the basis of the above-cited Mishnah alone. We have to explore further the different kinds of *hiyuvim* ("obligations") in rabbinic law and their relation to one another. The distinction between a *hiyuv d'oraita* ("a biblically imposed obligation) and a *hiyuv d'rabbanan* ("a rabbinically imposed obligation") is made many times in the Talmud. It is also made clear in the Talmud that a *hiyuv d'rabbanan* cannot be *motzi* a *hiyuv d'oraita*. What this means is that a *hiyuv d'rabbanan* does not have the same halakhic "weight" as does a *hiyuv d'oraita*.[5] Hence even a *hiyuv* about which there is merely some doubt about whether it is *d'rabbanan* or *d'oraita*, can not be *motzi* a *hiyuv* that is unquestionably *d'oraita*.

Let me cite an example which deals with the question of a woman being *motzi* a man. On the basis of the Gemara in Brakhot 20b, the Rambam states in Hilkhot Brakhot 5:1:

> Women and slaves are also under the obligation of saying Grace after meals. It is doubtful, however, whether this obligation is imposed by the Torah, there being no set time for its fulfillment—or whether it is only imposed by the sages. Hence they [women and slaves] cannot, by saying it, discharge male adults from their obligation [of saying Grace].

Having noted the existence of two kinds of *hiyuvim* ("obligations") and the halakhic relationship between them, we turn to the question of whether a *hiyuv* of lesser status can by some voluntary act be changed into a *hiyuv* of higher status, so that a *hiyuv* which is only *d'rabbanan* may become equal to a *hiyuv* which is *d'oraita*—with all its implications of extra stringencies, greater punishment for transgressions, etc.—and then be able to be *motzi* a *hiyuv d'oraita*. The answer to the above questions is that one who is a *hiyuv d'rabbanan* may consider himself to be a *hiyuv d'oraita* and observe the *mitzvah* most scrupulously, but he cannot thereby be *motzi* a *hiyuv d'oraita*. This can be proved from many passages in the Talmud, but I shall limit myself to one *Sugya*.

In the tractate Pesahim 116b we read:

> R. Aha b. Jacob said: A blind person is exempt from reciting the Haggadah. . . . But that is not so, for Meremar said: I asked the scholars of the school of R. Joseph, Who recites the Haggadah at R. Joseph's? And they told me, R. Joseph; Who recites the Haggadah at R. Shesheth's? And they replied, R. Shesheth.[6] Apparently these Rabbis were of the opinion that the obligation to eat *matzah* [unleavened bread] nowadays [i.e., after the destruction of the temple] is *d'rabbanan* [a rabbinically ordained obligation.] Hence it follows that R. Aha b. Jacob is of the opinion that eating *matzah* nowadays is *d'oraita* [a scripturally ordained obligation]. But it was R. Aha b. Jacob himself who said: The obligation of eating *matzah* nowadays was rabbinically ordained. Rabbi Aha is of the opinion that whatever our Rabbis enacted, they enacted it similar to Scriptural law.

Can anyone doubt that R. Joseph and R. Shesheth would gladly have done whatever was required in order to be considered as *hiyuvei d'oraita* ("biblically obligated") if this were at all possible? The fact that the Gemara could find no way to justify their being *motzi* their household in the recitation of the Haggadah, other than by declaring the reading of the Haggadah to be *hiyuv d'rabbanan* ("rabbinically ordained") is proof that their *hiyuv* could never be more than a *hiyuv d'rabbanan*, as far as being *motzi* others is concerned.

We have thus far noted that there are two kinds of *hiyuvim* ("obligations"), *d'oraita* and *d'rabbanan*, and discussed their relationship to one another. What is common to both of them is that they are imposed upon us by either the Torah or the sages. We have no choice but to follow their commandments. There is, however, a third kind of *hiyuv,* a self-imposed one, that is basically different from the other two. According to the Gemara, the *Maariv* ("evening prayer") is not obligatory. However, according to the author of the *Halakhot Gedolot,* a Gaon of the ninth century, one may accept upon himself the evening prayer as a *hovah* ("obligation").[7] The Ravia, one of the universally recognized halakhic authorities of the twelfth and thirteenth centuries, follows the view of the *Halakhot Gedolot* and adds that the recitation of the Hannukah prayer in the Grace, which is voluntary, can be accepted by the individual as an obligation.[8]

It should be pointed out that the change from the voluntary to the obligatory that we just mentioned has halakhic implications.[9] At the same time we must also emphasize that the implications, found in both the *Halachot Gedolot* and the Ravia, are all *L'humra* (i.e., all make the observance of the *mitzvah* more stringent for the person who made it obligatory for himself). Anyone acquainted with the principles of rabbinic law knows that we may not apply what the Rabbis say in regard to *humrot* ("more stringent observance of a *mitzvah*") to *kulot* ("a *mitzvah* less arduous").[10] It should also be noted that neither the *Halakhot Gedolot* nor the Ravia, in the cases mentioned above, makes any reference to the *hiyuv* of women or addresses himself to the issue of being *motzi* others.[11] We could safely say, however, that the self-imposed *hiyuv* would not rank high in the established hierarchy of *hiyavim*. It must be considered as being of a lesser status than the *hiyuv d'rabbanan*.

We shall now proceed to examine what rabbinic law has to say about the obligation or nonobligation of women to observe *mitzvot*.

In the Tractate Bava Kama 15a we read:

> Rav Judah said on behalf of Rav, and so was it also taught at the school of R. Ishmael: Scripture states, "When a man or woman shall commit any sin" [Numbers 5:6]. Scripture has thus made

woman and man equal regarding all the penalties of the Law. In the school of Elazar it was taught: "Now these are the ordinances which thou shalt set before them" [Exodus 21:1]. Scripture has thus made woman and man equal regarding all the judgments of the Law. The school of Hezekiah and Jose the Galilean taught: Scripture says, "It hath killed a man or a woman" [ibid.,v. 29]. Scripture has thus made woman and man equal regarding all the laws of manslaughter in the Torah.

Unlike men, however, women are legally exempt from many *mitzvot*.[12] We have already noted that the *Halakhah* requires that one who is to be *motzi* a *hiyuv* must not only himself be a *hiyuv* ("obligated"), but also that the legal status of his obligation should be at least equal to that of the obligation of the one whom he is *motzi*. A number of questions then inevitably are raised.

1. May a woman choose to perform a *mitzvah* from which she is halakhically exempt?
2. If she is permitted to do so, may she also recite the blessing over the *mitzvah*?[13]
3. And if she may both perform the *mitzvah* and recite the blessing, is there also a way whereby she can change the status of her "voluntary" observance to an "obligatory" one?
4. And if she can change her status to "obligatory," will her "obligation" be equal to the "obligation" of men?

Only if the answer to all the above questions is in the positive, may she be *motzi* men in the performance of the *mitzvot*.

All the early authorities, with the exception of one,[14] agree that women may perform *mitzvot* from which they are legally exempt. The dispute among them centers around the question of whether these women are also permitted to recite the required blessing. Rashi,[15] Rambam,[16] and their followers hold that they may not recite the blessing. If she does recite it, she would be guilty of transgressing the prohibition of making a *brakhah l'vatala*. According to this view, women may perform but can not fulfill a *mitzvah* from which they are exempt. Hence, they cannot be *motzi* a man, who is a *hiyuv* and is therefore obliged also to recite a benediction as part of the *mitzvah*.

There is, however, a more liberal view. Rabenu Tam,[17] Raavan,[18] and many others[19] are of the opinion that women may not only perform a *mitzvah* from which they are exempt, but may also recite the appropriate blessing. According to this view, the act of a woman who chooses to perform such a *mitzvah* would be no different from the "act" of a man performing the same *mitzvah*.

Does this mean that a woman who chooses to obligate herself to perform a *mitzvah* from which she is exempt becomes a *hiyuvit* in relation to this particular *mitzvah?* The authorities cited above, that permit women to recite a blessing on such a *mitzvah*, are silent on this matter. Yet it is altogether possible to assume that her voluntary performance of the *mitzvah* should take on the status of obligation. We make this assumption on the basis of the view held by the *Halakhot Gedolot* and the Ravia, cited earlier, that the evening and the Hannukah prayer in the Grace after the meal can change from a *reshut* ("a voluntary act") to a *hovah* ("an obligatory act"). By combining the opinion of Rabenu Tam, with regard to a woman's reciting a blessing over a *mitzvah* from which she is exempt, with the view of *Halakhot Gedolot*, that a *reshut* can become a *hovah*, we conclude that a woman can become a *hiyuvit* in relation to a *mitzvah* from which she is exempt. This does not happen automatically. She would have to obligate herself to observe this *mitzvah* permanently, with all the related consequences. Such a woman would then be able to be *motzi* other women with similar commitments.

However, the question that remains crucial for our purpose is whether such a woman would also be able to be *motzi* men. Does there inhere in a self-imposed obligation halakhically valid authority to enable it to be *motzi* a rabbinically or a biblically imposed obligation? Reason alone would dictate a negative answer to this question. In the hierarchy of *hiyuvim*, a *d'oraita* comes first, a *d'rabbanan* second, and a self-imposed *hiyuv* third. We have previously pointed out that halakhically neither a rabbinically imposed obligation nor even a questionable biblically imposed obligation can be *motzi* an unquestionable biblical obligation. Hence, a self-imposed *hiyuv* cannot be *motzi* even a *hiyuv d'rabbanan*, let alone a *hiyuv d'oraita*.

Fortunately, we do not have to depend on our reason alone. In my opinion, this conclusion is corroborated by the same two authorities, *Halakhot Gedolot* and Ravia, upon whose opinions our previous conclusion that women can become *hiyuvot* was based.

The Tractate Megillah 4a records: "R. Yoshua b. Levi also said: women are under obligation to *read* the *Megillah* [the scroll of the book of Esther], since they also benefitted by the miracle then wrought." Hence, according to R. Yoshua b. Levi, in regard to the *mitzvah* of reading the *Megillah*, the obligation of the women has the same status as that of the obligation of the men. For both of them, it is a *hiyuv d'rabbanan*. It follows, therefore, that a woman may read the *Megillah* and be *motzi* male listeners.[20] However, the *Halakhot Gedolot* and the Ravia had a different reading in the Gemara. Instead of "to read," they had "to listen"[21] to the *Megillah*. According to their reading in the Gemara, women are obliged only to listen to the reading of the *Megillah*, while men are obliged to read it. That a man too can fulfill the *Mitzvat Megillah* by just listening to the reading of the scroll does not change the fact that the quality of his *hiyuv* is different from that of hers. She is not obliged to read it, only to hear the reading, while he is fulfilling his obligation of reading through hearing. According to the sages in this instance, hearing is equal to reading.

On the basis of this minor difference between the *hiyuv* of men and the *hiyuv* of women, even though the *hiyuv* of both is *d'rabbanan* and both fulfill their obligation of *Mitzvat Megillah* by just listening to the reading of it, the *Halakhot Gedolot*[22] and the Ravia[23] conclude that a woman cannot be *motzi* men with her reading of the *Megillah*. Now, if one *hiyuv d'rabbanan* cannot be *motzi* another *hiyuv d'rabbanan*, because of a comparatively slight difference in the quality of their obligations, then surely a self-imposed *hiyuv* cannot be *motzi* a *hiyuv d'oraita* or a *hiyuv d'rabbanan*.

To conclude: women who voluntarily obligate themselves to observe *mitzvot* from which they are exempt cannot be *motzi* men, whose obligation is imposed by the Torah or the sages. Consequently, a woman cannot act as a cantor or a reader of the Torah at a service, or recite the marriage benedictions, or be counted in a *minyan*. Without being able to perform the above-mentioned functions, she will not be able to carry out her duties as a rabbi in a congregation.

Hence, anyone who will contribute in any way towards enabling women to be admitted to the Rabbinical School will be transgressing the biblical injunction, "Before one who is blind, do not place a stumbling block" (Leviticus 19:14). He will also be violating the rabbinic prohibition to assist transgressors.[24]

NOTES

1. See also the paper of Dr. Roth, published in this collection, and the paper of Dr. Halivni, found in the Jewish Theological Seminary's xeroxed collection "On the Ordination of Women as Rabbis" (J.T.S. Library, Nr. Ref. BM, 726, J48, 1983) for different views. According to the former, it can be accomplished here and now, and according to the latter, only after a generation. I respectfully disagree with both.

2. The sources I am about to examine in this paper, plus some others, are already mentioned in the *Talmudic Encyclopedia*, vol. II, p. 250. See also *Sdei Hemed*, vol. V, p. 70.

3. The fact that women are not listed in this Mishnah among those that are not qualified to be *motzi* others, should not be interpreted that they may, under certain circumstances, be *motzi* men in the performance of a *mitzvah* from which women are now exempt. Women could not be included in this group, because this statement includes only those who are exempt from all *mitzvot*. It serves to illustrate the principle that follows in the Mishnah that "anyone on whom an obligation is not incumbent cannot fulfill that obligation on behalf of the man." Women, however, are obliged to observe all the negative commandments and most of the positive ones. They cannot, therefore, be included among those who are not obliged to perform any *mitzvot*.

4. "I.e., such a one may not blow the shofar at the New Year." Translation and note by Herbert Danby. See Brakhot 20b and parallels.

5. In connection with this, I wish to comment that the statement of R. Hanina in Kidushin 31a that "greater is one who is commanded to perform a

mitzvah and does so than one who is not commanded to do it and yet does so" has no bearing whatsoever on the subject of who can be *motzi* whom. His dictum is a purely aggadic-theological statement and has no bearing on the legal requirement for a *hiyuv* to be *motzi* another *hiyuv*. Proof for this can be found in the Yerushalmi Sheviit 6:1, 36b. From the statement of R. Elazar there with regard to tithes, we learn that he differs with R. Hanina. His opinion is that "one who is not commanded and fulfills is greater than the one who is commanded and fulfills." Yet it is inconceivable that R. Elazar differs from the Mishnah in Rosh Hashana and holds that one who is not obligated can be *motzi* one that is obligated. What is meant by "greater" might be a greater reward for fulfilling the *mitzvah*, but as far as being *motzi* others it is irrelevant.

6. R. Joseph and R. Shesheth were both blind, and were thus exempt from reading the Haggadah. Hence, how are we to explain the fact that they did read it and thereby were *motzi* the others participating in the Seder? The answer to this question is the assumption that R. Joseph and R. Sheshet were of the opinion that the obligation to read the Haggadah was rabbinically ordained. Hence, though they would not have read the Haggadah if it were biblically ordained and be *motzi* the others, they felt free to do so because it was only a rabbinic law and they too were rabbinically ordained to read it. The Gemara then goes on to say that since R. Joseph and R. Sheshet were of the opinion that nowadays (after the destruction of the Temple) reading the Haggadah is only a rabbinically ordained practice, R. Aha, who seems to differ from them, must have been of the opinion that it was a rabbinically established practice. How then explain his statement that a blind person is exempt from reading the Haggadah and therefore can not be *motzi* others? And the Gemara responds by saying that R. Aha was of the opinion that "whatever our Rabbis enacted, they enacted similar to the Scriptural law" (Soncino Translation).

7. See *Halakhot Gedolot*, ed. Warsaw p. 7, ed. Berlin p. 31, ed. Jerusalem, p. 29. R. Simeon Kayara is the author of *Halakhot Gedolot*.

8. Ravia, pt. 2, p. 284.

9. See the *Halakhot Gedolot* and Ravia cited in the previous two notes.

10. To be *motzi* others is a *kulah*, since the *yotzeh* does not have to perform the *mitzvah* himself.

11. In the cases they deal with, the evening and Hannukah prayers, the question of *motzi* doesn't arise, since everyone has the same kind of *hiyuv*.

12. See Mishnah Kidushin 1:7, which states that women are exempt from all positive commandments which are time-bound. There are exceptions to this rule. There are also some *mitzvot* from which women are exempt which are not time-bound. What is relevant to us here is that a woman who serves as a rabbi will have to perform *mitzvot* from which she is exempt and be *motzi* men who are obligated to observe them.

13. The blessing contains the name of God, and one is not permitted to use His name in vain. One might then argue, since she is not obliged to perform the *mitzvah*, that it is a *brakhah l'vatala* ("a useless benediction") and, therefore, a frivolous use of His name.

14. The Raavad, in his commentary to *Sifra*, Vayikrah, chap. 2 Halakhah 2,

ed. Weiss 4c. He forbids a woman to perform a *mitzvah* from which she is exempt, even without the blessing.

15. As testified by the *Or Zarua*, pt. 2, Hilkchot Sukkah and Lulav, 68d. The fact that Rashi in a responsum, ed. Elfenbein p. 80, no. 68, quotes a different view in the name of R. Yitzchak Halevi without comment, is not sufficient to doubt the *Or Zarua's* statement. As is well known, the responsa of Rashi did not reach us in the form they left his pen.

16. See Hilkchot Tzitzit 3:9.

17. A twelfth-century scholar in France, the grandson of Rashi. His opinion is found in Tosafot Eruvin 96a and parallels.

18. A twelfth-century scholar in Germany. See *Sefer Raavan*, responsum no. 87, ed. Albeck 66b.

19. See *Talmudic Encyclopedia* and *Sdei Hemed*, cited in note 2.

20. And this seems to be the opinion of the Rambam in Hilkhot Megillah 1:2. See also Magid Mishneh there, and Tosafot Megillah 4a, s.v. *nashim*.

21. This is also the reading of Rabenu Hananel, located in the margin of the Gemara.

22. Ed. Warsaw, p. 80, ed. Berlin p. 196, ed. Jerusalem p. 406.

23. Ravia, pt. 2, p. 292, no. 569.

24. Avoda Zarah 55b.

The Ordination of Women

ROBERT GORDIS

The issue of the ordination of women for the rabbinate, which has stirred a furor in American Jewry, has dimensions that go far beyond narrow religious concerns. The swirling controversy that has raged around the question makes it clear that there are far-reaching social and cultural implications, as well as deeply ingrained psychological attitudes, both on the conscious and the unconscious level.

Nevertheless, for those who value the Jewish religious tradition and grant it authority in their lives—and essentially it is only for them that the issue is significant—the broader social, ethical, and cultural aspects of the ordination of women enter into the picture only *after* the religious element has been dealt with.

Opponents of women's ordination have continued to proclaim that "the Halakhah is opposed to the ordination of women." Relying on the reiteration of the formula, they have rarely stooped to presenting evidence. Instead they have nurtured the implication that the material is too recondite and complicated for examination by generally intelligent laymen. They have insisted that it can be fathomed only by a handful of Halakhic experts, and whoever disagrees with their conclusions is, by definition, not a Halakhic expert!

This tactic is one more striking illustration of a phenomenon characteristic of contemporary Jewish life—the existence of a cultural, social, and ethical lag 20 or 30 years behind society at

47

large. Thus, precisely at a time when the doctrine of papal infallibility has encountered increasing opposition in Roman Catholic circles, the idea of rabbinic infallibility has become an increasingly popular doctrine in the Jewish religious community: "The law is thus and so because we say so." The old Talmudic principle *neitei sepher veneheze*, "Let us take the book and see,"[1] is largely ignored. Instead, there are pronouncements *ex cathedra* handed down in the name of an august authority who rarely deigns to disclose the basis for his judgment. In the past, the Talmud encouraged students and colleagues to disagree with their master so that the truth might emerge. Today, those who have had the temerity to question these august judgments are not being refuted but are attacked as lacking in respect for the Torah and in deference for its only true expositors.

The sincerity of those opposed to rabbinic ordination for women is not being questioned—only their right to arrogate to themselves the sole authority to decide the issue by fiat rather than by presentation of evidence. Actually, when the contention "The ordination of women is forbidden by the Halakhah" is examined in the light of the evidence, it becomes clear that the absolute judgments pronounced on the subject bear an uncanny resemblance to the Emperor's "new clothes" in Hans Christian Andersen's tale.

A preliminary observation is in order: rabbis today bear the oldest honorific designation in continuous use in human history. The title "rabbi" is far older than any honorary degree or academic distinction in vogue today.

At the same time, the rabbinate represents virtually a new calling, since the functions designated by this ancient title have undergone a far-reaching transformation. The term "rabbi" is an old label on a bottle of new wine. Elsewhere I have attempted to trace the five principal stages in the rabbinate from Talmudic times to the present, and the end of the development of the office is not yet in sight.[2] The modern rabbi, for good or for ill, and perhaps for good *and* for ill, is a *novum* in Jewish experience. It is therefore not at all astonishing that the subject of the ordination of women is not discussed in traditional sources, because past generations never contemplated the possibility. To offer an extreme analogy, nowhere do we encounter a discussion whether Martians are obligated to put on *Tefillin* or are required to observe the Noahide laws.

In the absence of any direct testimony on the subject, opponents of the ordination of women have had recourse to various rabbinic passages from which they have sought to draw inferences of their own, a procedure that is entirely legitimate. We need, however, to examine these passages in detail and discover whether in fact they have any bearing upon the issue. It is not without significance that, during the relatively brief history that the question has been actively discussed, many of the passages that were originally advanced with great assurance have now been tacitly abandoned and new texts offered instead.

Some arguments against ordination are homiletic rather than Halakhic in character. Thus one rabbinic scholar cited the Mishnah, *Hakol šōhatin ǔsehitátán kešérah hǔs mehéréš šōteh veqa-tán*, "Everyone is eligible to slaughter an animal, except a deaf mute, an insane person, or a minor."[3] This passage, it was argued, proves that the Rabbis permitted a woman to be a *shohet* but not a rabbi. The contention scarcely requires refutation.

One congregational rabbi in a letter to an Anglo-Jewish weekly declared, "The Halakhah is opposed to women's ordination," and then cited a Talmudic reference, *Sotah* 20a. While the uninformed reader might imagine that the text bears upon the subject under discussion, it actually deals with the biblical law regarding the ordeal undergone by a woman accused by her husband of adultery (Numbers, chapter 5).

In this connection, the Talmud quotes two diametrically opposed opinions of Mishnaic teachers: "On the basis of what has been said above, Ben Azzai says, 'A man is required to teach Torah to his daughter (so that if she should ever have occasion to undergo the ordeal of the accused wife, she would know that any merit she possesses would create a suspension of punishment for her).' Rabbi Eliezer says, 'Whoever teaches his daughter the Torah is teaching her obscenity (because from the Torah she would learn how to circumvent the law and hide her immorality).' "

Evidently, the writer of the letter wishes to infer from Rabbi Eliezer's statement that since it is forbidden to teach Torah to a girl, she obviously cannot be ordained as a rabbi. Even this view, however, is the opinion of only one sage and is contradicted in the very same passage by the view of another. What is more, Rabbi Eliezer was one of the most conservative and srong-willed of the scholars, who held highly individual views. Time and again, the vast majority of his colleagues did not hesitate to overrule his judgment, as in the famous case of the "Stove of Achnai" in *Baba Metzia* 59b. So, too, while virtually all his colleagues interpreted the famous phrase "an eye for an eye" in Exodus 21:24 to mean that monetary compensation is to be given for an injury, Rabbi Eliezer took the biblical phrase literally.[4]

Undoubtedly, in the Middle Ages, the restrictive opinion of Rabbi Eliezer regarding the education of women was adopted by some later authorities. However, I would be interested to learn whether the American rabbi would operate on the theory that the teaching of Torah to women is prohibited in the case of his own daughters and whether he forbids girls to be enrolled in his Hebrew school.

It may be added that the Talmud nowhere condemns Rabbi Hananya ben Teradyon for giving his daughter Beruriah an intensive education in the Written and the Oral Torah. On the contrary, as the wife of Rabbi Meir, her opinions are cited with respect and sometimes even prevail over the views of her male colleagues.[5]

Another proof-text has been found in Maimonides' Code, *Mishneh Torah*, where he repeats the substance of a Tannaitic midrash. Among the biblical laws regarding the qualifications of a king, the provision is included: "You may indeed set as king over you him whom the Lord your God will choose. One from among your brethren you shall set as king over you; you may not put a foreigner over you who is not your brother."[6] The *Sifre* comments: "A king, not a queen,"[7] a statement which Maimonides broadens to mean "every position of authority (*mesimot*) which shall be limited to one of your brothers (and therefore not a woman)." This decision would effectively rule out any appointment or election of a woman to a position in government, legislative, executive, or judicial, or in any voluntary agency in the community.

In view of an aggadic statement comparing rabbis to kings,[9] Maimonides' judgment that women cannot be kings is now used to declare them ineligible to serve as rabbis!

It is difficult to believe that this aggadic passage is being seriously offered for deciding the Halakhah. But if it is being advanced seriously, it may be pointed out that the Pharisees, who were the predecessors of the Tannaim in the fashioning of traditional Judaism, had no difficulty in accepting Shelom-Zion (Salome Alexandria), the widow of King Alexander Jannaeus, as legitimate queen during the Second Temple (76–67 BCE). Indeed, they praised her friendly relations with Simeon ben Shetah and her adherence to Pharisaic norms.[10] Similarly, in the first century of the common era, when the royal house of Adiabene adopted Judaism, Queen Helene is praised for her piety and philanthropy, and no word of censure is raised against her rule, though, to be sure, she may have sat on the throne with her husband King Monobaz.[11]

The argument is raised that the laws of *niddah* (the separation which the Halakhah enjoins for the period before, during, and after menstruation), would effectively preclude a woman's officiating as a rabbi. It may be granted that this consideration would be effective in a right-wing community of Hasidim, where all regulations of *niddah* are punctiliously observed and where women in general have no social contact with men outside their immediate families. Exclusive of these enclaves, there is scant evidence that the social segregation of women during their menstrual periods is observed, even in Orthodox circles.

I worship in an Orthodox synagogue that is militant in its

adherence to Orthodox interpretation of Halakhah and is at-
tended by very large numbers of women. After a decade, I
have yet to encounter one instance where a woman refrained
from shaking hands with a man who extended his hand in
greeting. Moreover, many, if not most, of these women, young
and old, are gainfully employed or attend college or are active
in the public sector. I doubt whether even those who observe
the regulations regarding the *mikveh* adhere to the other traditional prohibitions in their daily lives. I am not discussing the
rationale of the laws of *niddah*;[12] I am simply noting the fact that
in Conservative (and most Orthodox) practice these bans on
social intercourse play no part. On the other hand, if a woman
rabbi wished to observe these prohibitions, she would be as
free to do so in the rabbinate as in any other calling.

We now turn to what is generally recognized as the strongest
Halakhic argument against the ordination of women—the contention that the traditional Halakhah exempted women from
the obligation (*hiyyubh*) of prayer. This exemption in turn is
buttressed by the Talmudic principle that "women are free
from commandments that must traditionally be performed at
specific times" (*mitzvot aseh šehazman gerama*).

Before examining the implications that are being drawn from
this rule, it should be noted that the principle was far from
universally applied. Always there were exceptions. Time-
bound obligations, such as the kindling of Sabbath and festival
lights, was held to be obligatory for women. So, too, rabbinic
law commanded women as well as men to hear the reading of
the *megillah* on Purim, "since they, too, were involved in that
miracle of salvation."[13] It is therefore a reasonable conclusion
that the principle that women were excused from the obligation to observe *mitzvot* having a specific time-frame is a generalization from a few specific instances and not a universally
binding rule.[14] In other words, the Gemara, as is often the case,
observing a series of concrete statements of the Mishnah on
different subjects, seeks to evolve an underlying principle to
cover them all. The generalization, incidentally, may or may

not have been in the minds of the authors of the various passages in the Mishnah.

In our case, the rule is clearly descriptive and not prescriptive, as the many exceptions make clear.[15] With regard to prayer, the Mishnah (*Berakhot:3*) exempts women from reciting the *Shema* and putting on *tefillin*, but makes the recitation of the *tefillah* (i.e. the Amidah or Silent prayer) obligatory for them. The Talmud (*Berakhot 20b*) explains the exemption because women are free from time-bound mitzvot. In post-Talmudic Judaism down to our own day, women were not expected to engage in statutory prayer services or to attend the synagogue. The application of the rule exempting women from prayer in whole or in part is therefore a rationalization after the fact rather than the reason for its enactment. Apologetics aside, the retention of this rule is an expression of the inferior status of women and of their segregation from public life.[16]

The justification offered by the fourteenth century scholar David Abudarham for the exemption of women from the positive commandments that are time-bound, was that the husband has a prior claim on his wife's services at any time. This hardly comports with the realities of present-day life. It has also been explained that the manifold tasks devolving upon women as homemakers made it impossible for them to observe prayer and other time-bound obligations at the specified hour. The contention may have had a measure of validity in the past, when a woman's household duties were onerous and unlimited; it clearly has little justification today. In this age of labor-saving devices, a woman who is a homemaker, even if she takes care of a family, has at least as much free time available as her husband, who is a worker, a businessman, or a professional engaged in his occupation all day long. As for the woman who is gainfully employed outside the home, she is in exactly the same position as her male counterpart.

The American historian James Harvey Robinson once said that every event in history has a good reason and a real reason. In the case of the *mitzvah* of prayer for women and their exclusion from the *minyan*, the truth is that the real reason is not good and the good reason is not real.

Let us grant that the Talmudic principle cited above was originally established by the Sages out of a sense of genuine compassion for women, whose working day coincided with all their waking hours, with virtually no leisure at all. It would be ironic to invoke this principle, which the Sages established out of consideration for women in the past, to serve as a basis for discrimination against them in the present. However, even if all these considerations are brushed aside and the principle maintained that "women are exempt from the obligation of prayer," its bearing upon the ordination of women as rabbis is tenuous in the extreme. The major functions of the modern rabbi—preaching, teaching, conducting funeral services, serving as *mesadder kiddushin* ("officiant" at marriage ceremonies), personal counselling, and adult education—are none of them prohibited by extant rabbinic sources.

The speciousness of the argument becomes clear when it is recalled that it is the cantor and not the rabbi who is the *shaliah sibbur* (the messenger of the congregation). The rabbi may read some prayers in English or supplement the service, but the function of leading the congregation in prayer is essentially that of the cantor or laymen.

One may also question the logic of the contention that one who is not *obligated* to pray cannot fulfill the function for one who is. Obviously, a woman is not *forbidden* to pray, and if we were to accept the principle that a pray-er can exempt the non-pray-er, there would be no logical ground for denying this to the woman. When a fire breaks out in a building, the fireman is obligated by his occupation to rush in and save the life of a child. The general citizen has no such obligation, but he is not *prohibited* from leaping into the building and saving the child. *Me^cikkara dedina pirkhah*, "the original assumption is dubious."

The doctrine that the *shaliah sibbur* must be a person obligated to pray is subject to challenge from another direction as well. According to the Halakhah, the *shaliah sibbur* conducting a service is fulfilling the obligations for the worshippers who cannot pray for themselves. The provision stems from a time, before the invention of printing, when prayerbooks were scarce, so that many Jews could not pray on their own. So, too, the law had in mind pious and observant Jews who, because of the pressures of their work, were unable to read their prayers at the proper time. Today the situation is totally different. Prayerbooks are available everywhere. The majority of Jews who do not engage in prayer are not prevented by preoccupation but by indifference. To deprive a community of the service of a woman rabbi for these anachronistic reasons certainly argues a strange scale of values.

Another objection, more germane to our theme, has also been raised. Since according to rabbinic law, women are ineligible to serve as witnesses, a woman rabbi would be incapable of signing as an *edh* (witness) on a *ketubbah*. It is true that the Halakhah today excludes women as witnesses and places them on a par with minors and deaf-mutes with regard to testifying before a religious court.[17] The issue needs further analysis.

For many, if not for most people today, the principle of the exclusion of women as witnesses is morally questionable. In a society where women were sheltered and had little experience or contact with the world at large, there might perhaps have been some basis for regarding their testimony as inexpert and therefore inadmissible. To defend such a principle today is, for most people, morally repugnant and sexist. To bring the Halakhah in this respect into conformity with *our* ethical standards constitutes part of the unfinished business of contemporary Judaism. That the Halakhah in the past reflected the inferior status of women in a society where they played no role in general society is understandable; for modern Halakhah to perpetuate this status in a society where women participate in all areas of life is unconscionable. It is noteworthy that even in Israel, where right-wing religious authorities have a virtual monopoly in many areas of Israeli life, the exclusion of women as witnesses in the secular courts has not been proposed.

But even before the age-old doctrine of the inadmissibility of women as witnesses is modified, there is a striking precedent in Halakhah for making an exception for a woman rabbi acting as a witness at a wedding. The precedent is particularly impressive, because it occurs in an area dealing with the sanctity of the person and the inviolability of the marriage bond. If a woman's husband disappears, she is left an *agunah*, a chained wife, doomed to perpetual widowhood. The Rabbis of the Mishnah sought every conceivable method for ameliorating her tragic status. They went so far as to rule that if the woman herself had evidence that her husband had died, her unsubstantiated testimony to that effect was accepted.[18]

This ruling set aside no less than three *fundamentals in rabbinic jurisprudence:* the first, already referred to above, that a woman was ineligible as a witness; the second requirement, going back to the Bible, that two witnesses are required to establish valid testimony;[19] and the third, the rabbinic principle *adam karobh 'etzel ʿatzmo*, "Each person is close to himself," and therefore his testimony on an issue in which he himself is involved is invalid.[20] Thus, it is clear that the Rabbis did not hesitate to modify basic legal procedures in the case of a putative *ešet ʿiš* (a married woman), which represented an issue of the utmost gravity. Nevertheless, when considerations of humanity were at stake, the Rabbis were prepared to suspend the three fundamental principles out of a sense of compassion.[21] We should do no less in the interests of justice.

Strictly speaking, the entire issue of the ineligibility of women as witnesses is irrelevant to their ordination as rabbis. *There is no necessity for the rabbi, male or female, to serve as a witness at a wedding. The rabbi's role is that of a mesadder kiddushin,* the arranger of the marriage ceremony. Two other witnesses can be, and often are, co-opted for the *ketubbah.*

At this point the Halakhists who are opponents of the ordination of women become "sociological" and ask us to consider the position of a small community in which the rabbi is the only religious functionary. If the rabbi were a woman, she might be called upon to act as the *hazzan* (cantor). In the case of a marriage ceremony, she might need to serve as a witness for the *ketubbah*, especially because of the paucity of religiously observant witnesses.

The response, however, might be put as follows: The Rabbis of the Talmud *šaqedu ʿal taqqanat benot yisra'el*, "were diligent for the welfare of the daughters of Israel."[22] Surely in such special cases, where the happiness and welfare of a bride and groom are involved and they wish to be married "according to the Law of Moses and Israel," the entire thrust of the Halakhah and its underlying spirit suggest the approach to be adopted where no other proper witness is available: it is entirely appropriate that a woman, both religiously knowledgeable and observant, be recognized as a legitimate witness in special instances such as these, as happened with the Mishnaic ruling with regard to the testimony of an *agunah*.

In conclusion, it is clear that these objections, while ostensibly based on the Halakhah, are indirect at best and far-fetched at worst. In the face of major problems confronting the survival of Judaism, the role of women in contemporary society and the ethical issues involved, no Halakhic objections of substance have been adduced. *The truth is that the Halakhah neither sanctions nor forbids the ordination of women—it never contemplated the possibility.*

In the absence of clear-cut Halakhic sources against the ordination of women, opponents of the idea have advanced another argument—it is a matter of *minhag*, custom, and, as the popular saying has it, "a custom supersedes a law."[23] It is undeniable that custom plays a very important role in Jewish religious practice and is enshrined in Jewish literature; many customs are highly appealing because of the piety and ethical sensitivity they express or their colorful folk-character. It is, however, a far cry from this observation to the conclusion that *minhag* qua *minhag* is sacrosanct and not subject to analysis and critique. The customs, local and general, to be found in Jewish communities have different points of origin, serve diverse functions, and vary widely in their value and significance. Thus, authorities as eminent as Rabbi Solomon ibn Adret and

Nahmanides opposed the practice of *kapparot* on the eve of Yom Kippur,[24] and Rabbi Joseph Karo, the author of the *Shulhan Arukh*, called it a *minhag šetut*, a custom of folly, stupid custom.[25] In the history of Judaism, countless customs have arisen, flourished, and disappeared. To set up the *minhag* as the final arbiter is to violate the inner spirit of a religion that has produced the Talmud as a monument to rational discussion, the establishment of consensus, and the practice of justice and equity.

A study and analysis of the Halakhah throughout its history discloses two basic characteristics, which varied in importance in different periods but were never totally lacking: (a) a responsiveness to emerging religious and ethical insights; and (b) an awareness of new social, economic, political, and cultural conditions.[26] It is clear that these factors, far from being extra-Halakhic or anti-Halakhic, constitute an integral element in the Halakhic process. We have examined the passages in traditional Halakhic sources allegedly opposed to the ordination of women and have found that they neither favor nor oppose the idea. We are, therefore, not stepping outside the parameters of Halakhah in presenting the case for the admission of women to the rabbinate against the background of conditions prevalent in contemporary society in general and in the Jewish community in particular.

As the oldest living tradition in the Western world, Judaism began as a male-centered and male-dominated society, as was every other civilization up to and including our own age. It was, therefore, entirely natural—and requires neither apology nor apologetics—that women, though honored and loved, occupied a subordinate position in Jewish society. Their inferior status with regard to marriage, divorce, the levirate, inheritance, and many other aspects of life is clear and undeniable, and has been documented time and again.

Male domination was so all-pervasive that it often was unconscious. One instance will suffice. The Talmudic dicta *qol* (and *še ʿar*) *beiša ʿerwah*,[27] "A woman's voice (and hair) is sexually seductive," have their analogues in other cultures. The judgment was undoubtedly true in a society where a woman was sequestered and had no contact with any male outside her immediate family. Yet there is no corresponding statement, "A man's voice (and hair) is sexually seductive (to a woman)." But if the first statement is true, so is the second. The various regulations governing *seniyut*, modesty, apply in overwhelming measure to the behavior of women.[28] Yet the virtue is surely as applicable to males as to females!

The greatness of traditional Judaism lies in the fact that, originating in the ancient world, which was overwhelmingly male-dominated, the Halakhah was able to register so much progress during Mishnaic, Talmudic, Geonic, and even medieval times toward reducing the prerogatives of the male and increasing the rights of the female. Since the law always codifies the positions attained by society at an earlier period, it is no wonder that the process of conferring full equality upon women has not been completed. This is true in secular law and not merely in the Halakhah.

Nevertheless, the progress of women toward equality has been phenomenal. In our day, women have achieved positions certainly more advanced than the law codes would indicate. Each change in the status of women has inevitably brought not merely new opportunities but also new problems in its wake. That there are changes that should not be greeted with enthusiasm may be true, but it is beside the point—the overall process of women's liberation is irreversible. It may be hindered; it cannot be halted.

Except in ultra-rightist religious groups, few women in Western society would accept *Kinder, Kirche und Küche*, "children, church, and kitchen," as representing the boundaries of their world. Since the beginning of the century, women have greatly expanded their occupational roles. In the past, the only occupations open to them outside the home were as domestic servants and governesses or, a little higher in the social scale, as nurses and school teachers. Early in this century, women came into offices as clerical workers against strong opposition, and they literally fought their way into law and medicine. The battle for women's suffrage is still vividly recalled both in the United States and abroad. These women set a process in motion that now includes such formerly unlikely fields as the army, navy, trucking, contact sports, politics, and public administration—the trajectory is not yet spent.

It is undeniable that the entrance of women into independent careers has placed new strains on relations between husbands and wives, parents and children, and on the institution of the family as a whole. When both husband and wife pursue independent careers, there is no longer a full-time homemaker available, so both partners must shoulder additional duties after completing their day at the office. This is, of course, a permanent and universal problem.

More serious difficulties may also arise. The new interests and broader social contacts of the wife bring her new stimuli and new opportunities. They may also bring in their wake new temptations and relationships that may threaten the marriage bond. If either partner is offered a better job in a new community, the unity of the household is threatened: the "long-distance marriage" with weekends together is hardly a recipe for long-term happiness. On the other hand, if one or the other partner forgoes the new opportunity, the decision is bound to be painful. Obviously, some *modus vivendi* must be achieved in each individual case, but there is a price to pay.

Nevertheless, no one seriously suggests reversing the trend—as if that were possible—by expelling women from the labor market. Instead, the path of wisdom is to seek to cope with the new conditions, to overcome the problems, and to utilize the gains for the general welfare. In life, the solution of a problem offers not total ease and peace of mind, but rather the opportunity to face new problems and register new advances.

The ordination of women represents such a step in the movement for equal rights, the consequences of which will need to be faced in due course.

When women enter the rabbinate, it will surely appear strange and even uncomfortable at the beginning, but not as strange as it would have been in 1880 or 1780, when there was no public role for women in Judaism and little more in general society. In the world of our great-grandfathers, the role of women was governed by the rabbinic interpretation of the passage in Psalms: *kol kebudah bat melekh penimah*. The verse was taken to mean, "All the glory of a king's daughter lies within [the home]."[29] To have ordained women as rabbis in an earlier age would have been obviously counter-productive, since women had only a private role in society. Hence the appearance of a woman on a pulpit would have been a sensation that would have disrupted the traditional values of communal prayer and the study of Torah.

Today the situation is radically different. Undoubtedly, there will be a process of adjustment, painful at times, and the success of the process will vary with individuals and groups. In this connection, it should be kept in mind that the issue is not that women *must* be ordained and congregations *must* accept women rabbis, but that women may be ordained and congregations should be free to accept or reject them as their rabbis.

Nor is this an artificial issue. It has been reported that of the 240 students presently enrolled in the Reform and Reconstructionist seminaries in the United States, 25 percent, or 60, are women. It is also known that many of these 60 female rabbinical students are Conservative both in theory and in practice, loyal to Jewish tradition, observing the Torah and the *mitzvot*. By excluding them from rabbinical training at the Seminary we are driving some of the most potentially valuable human resources available to us out of the movement. This impoverishment of our potential spiritual leadership is a great loss not only for Conservative Judaism, but for Judaism as a whole. For I profoundly believe, with all due recognition of the virtues and achievements of our sister movements, that it is Conservative Judaism that holds the key to a vital and meaningful Judaism in the modern day.

The accession of women to the rabbinate will be particularly valuable in view of the shortage of dedicated and knowledgeable personnel in Jewish life. The rapid tempo of geographical and occupational mobility among American Jews has led to the decentralization of Jewish communities and the breakup of the large concentration of Jewish population into hundreds of smaller communities. Many, if not most of them, are totally bereft of competent Jewish leadership, and their survival is gravely imperiled.

In addition, there is an unmistakable movement in American Judaism today to overcome the impersonalization and mass character of our larger congregations. Many are mammoth institutions with memberships running into hundreds, even thousands, in which the individual, already stripped of much of his sense of personal worth in society at large, seeks in vain to recover a sense of identity. Differing widely in orientation, background, and interests, *minyanim*, *shtiblach*, and *havurot* have proliferated. They are united by this quest for a "do-it-yourself" Judaism with a large measure of personal participation and a warm feeling of community.

This evidence of renewed interest in Judaism deserves the enthusiasm with which it has been greeted. Yet the fact remains that the creation of small, independent groups completely unrelated to existing synagogues and therefore competitive with them is not the total solution to the problem of the survival of Judaism. The destruction of large synagogues and synagogue-centers would represent a substantial loss of the energies in the building of these institutions by dedicated men and women over many years.

Nor is this all. The creation and maintenance of well-staffed, properly graded, adequately housed Jewish schools, both on the elementary and the high school levels, requires substantial financial resources beyond the power of a *minyan*. Adequate adolescent and adult education programs also require substantial memberships and considerable funding. Attractive social and cultural programs for singles are a crying necessity today. Badly needed centers for personal counselling, particularly under religious auspices, would also be virtually impossible, if, for example, a congregation of 1,000 families were to be dissolved and in its stead 20 independent groups of 50 families apiece were to emerge.

The solution, I believe, is to be sought in the retention and the restructuring of the synagogue so that it will serve as the base for all these activities and as the source and center for smaller "special interest" groups, such as *havurot*. All too often, the high hopes reposed in these groups have not been realized, primarily because they need properly trained personnel to work with them. Women rabbis would help fill the need for a far larger number of rabbis on congregational staffs than is now available. If the recent experience, admittedly brief, of some Christian churches is any indication, many ordained women rabbis will gravitate to the fields of childhood, youth, and adult education and personal counselling.

The past half century has witnessed the opening up for rabbis of many non-congregational positions in such fields as academics, communal organizations, and professional counselling. As a result, the number of Conservative congregations has continued to increase. An expansion in the number of available rabbinical students and graduates would, therefore, help meet the current needs of American Judaism—we can use all the help we can get.

The needs of the Jewish community constitute only one element in the picture. The other includes the broad ethical dimension. To continue to exclude women from this area of service when they are admitted to virtually all others will surely alienate many ethically sensitive men and women, particularly among our youth, and drive potentially creative members of the Jewish community out of Jewish life. Judaism has always prided itself on being in the vanguard of ethical progress, whether it be in the areas of personal rights, universal education, political freedom, social justice, or international peace.

Today the Jewish community is acutely conscious of the threat to its survival posed by the defection and alienation of many of its youth, often the most creative and sensitive members. The agonizingly difficult task of winning their loyalty and commitment to Judaism would become far more difficult if the ordination of women were to be denied. They would regard it as a sign of the petrifaction of Judaism, a betrayal of its pretentions to ethical significance. The youth might well be reinforced in their estrangement from their spiritual roots if Conservative Judaism, which carries the mantle of a living Jewish tradition, were to deny equality to women at a time when there is both a deep desire to serve and a crying need for the service. That there is no substantive objection from the area of Halakhah would aggravate the situation.

What possible considerations are there against the ordination of women? It is noteworthy that it is no longer being argued that women are intellectually inferior and therefore incapable of pursuing the course of study. Our experience with women students at the Seminary demonstrates their intellectual capacities.

Nor can it be maintained that the admission of women to the Rabbinical School would be a frivolous expression of sensationalism, or, as some have elegantly expressed it, a "gimmick." I know several women who are enrolled as rabbinical students or have been graduated and are serving as rabbis. They are serious people who know full well what difficulties lie ahead. Undoubtedly, many women who undertake such a course of study may fall away, in view of the obstacles they will encounter. It will require determination, dedication, and courage of a high order for a woman to go through the course of study and then run the gauntlet of prejudice and discrimination still rife in the community at large. The ordination of women will need to be accompanied by a campaign of education for the laity.

Another contention that has been advanced against the ordination of women runs as follows: "Each sex has its specific role. The roles of men and women are separate but equal. We do not want women to act like men." The first contention is partially true, but misleading; the second completely untrue. Advocates of the ordination of women are not asking that women act like men, only that they act as rabbis. There is nothing specifically masculine involved in teaching, preaching, counselling, or engaging in any other aspect of the rabbinate. If Deborah and Huldah could take their place among Israel's prophets, women can take their place among Israel's rabbis.

As for the threadbare doctrine of "separate but equal," one would imagine that two decades and more after the historic Supreme Court decision of 1954, it would be clear to all that "separate but equal" means "separate and unequal." That is the nub of the question.

In sum, both on ethical and on pragmatic grounds, taking into account the crying needs of Jewish life and the call for equal opportunity to serve on the part of Jewish women, we must conclude that their ordination is highly desirable, indeed a necessary element in any program designed to advance the health of Judaism and strengthen the survival of the Jewish community.

One may hope that when passions cool and calm consideration of the issues prevails, those who have been doubtful on the issue or opposed to it, like those who favor it, will recognize that the goal to which all energies must be directed is *lehagdil Torah ulha 'adir*, "to magnify the Torah and make it glorious."

NOTES

1. *B. Sanh.* 6b.
2. Cf. "The Rabbinate—Its History, Functions and Future," reprinted as Chap. 16 in R. Gordis, *Understanding Conservative Judaism* (New York, 1978).
3. *B. Hullin* 1:1.
4. *B. Baba Kamma* 84a.
5. *Tos, Kelim, Baba Metzia* 1:6.
6. Deut. 23:20, 21.
7. *Sifre, Shofetim,* sec. 157/ Cf. *alia, B. Ber.* 49, "Rab said, 'The convenant, Torah and royal rule . . . do not apply to women.' "
8. *Mishneh Torah, Hilkhot, Melakhim I:4.*
9. *B. Gittin* 62a.
10. *B. Betzah* 48a; *Midrash Berešit Rabba* 91:3.
11. See *B. Baba Batra* 11a; *P. Peah* 1:1, 15b; *Tos. Peah* 4:18 and Josephus, *Antiquities* 21:17.
12. A sophisticated argument for the laws on *niddah* on mystical-philosophic grounds is offered by Rachel Adler, *Tumah and Taharah, End and*

Beginnings, with an appendix, comment, and response in Elizabeth Koltun, ed., *Jewish Women* (New York, 1976), 63–71.

13. *B. Meg.* 4a.

14. That the generalization is not a hard-and-fast rule becomes even clearer from a careful examination of the sources. Of eight time-bound *mitzvot* from which women are ultimately exempted, only three are based on incontrovertible Talmudic law: *sukkah, lulav,* and *shofar* (*B. Suk.* 38a; *B. Kid.* 33b), while there is substantial debate on two others, *ṣiṣit* and *Tefillin* (*B. Erub.* 96b; *B. Kid.* 35a; *Men.* 43a). On the *omer,* there is no Talmudic exemption; on the *Shema,* the Babylonian Talmud exempts women (*Ber.* 20a, b), but the Palestinian Talmud implies the existence of dissenting opinions (see *Ber.* 25b). Nevertheless, Maimonides lists all of them among time-bound positive commandments from which women are exempt (*Sepher Hamitzvot,* end of "Affirmative Precepts"). Out of 60 positive commandments listed by him as incumbent on the individual, women are exempt from 14: eight affirmative precepts limited by time; *Shema, Tefillin* (head and arm), *ṣiṣit,* the counting of the *Omer,* living in a *Sukkah,* taking the *lulav,* hearing the *shofar;* and six are not limited by time. These include the study of Torah and the commandment to procreate children.

On the other hand, there are more affirmative precepts equally linked to time from which women are *not* exempt, listed in the Talmud: *Kiddush* (*B. Berakhot* 20a), fasting (*B. Sukkah* 29a), *matzah* (*Kidd.* 34a), rejoicing on festivals (ibid.), *haqhēl,* "assembling once in seven years" (see Deut. 31:12, ibid.), sacrificing and eating the Paschal lamb (*B. Pesahim* 91b).

Finally, there are four affirmative precepts of rabbinic origin limited in time that are obligatory for women: lighting Hanukkah lights (*Shabbat* 23a), reading *Megillat Esther* (*Meg.* 4a), drinking the four cups of wine (*Pes.* 108a), and reciting *Hallel* on Pesah night (*B. Suk.* 38a).

15. This judgment coincides with that of Rabbi Saul J. Berman, "The Status of Women in Halakhic Judaism," *Tradition,* Fall, 1973, who writes, "So the Mishnah is descriptive of *some* of the laws regulating the status of women, but is inaccurate as a general description and is certainly not a useful prediction principle."

16. Rabbi Berman (*ibid.*) argues that only the motive for keeping women out of the public sphere explains their ineligibility to serve as witnesses and their exclusion from many *mitzvot.* But this motive incorporates a conception of the inferiority of women not applied to their male counterparts.

17. See Rambam, *Edut* 9:1, 2, who bases the disqualification of women on the Bible's use of the masculine in referring to witnesses (*Sifre Deut.* 190; *M. Rosh Hashanah* 1:8; *B. Shevuot* 30a). However, this argument is rejected by Joseph Karo "since the Torah always uses the masculine" (*Keseph Mishneh* on *Yad Edut* 9:2). Nonetheless the Rambam's view has prevailed in practice.

18. *Yebamot* 16:7, where the stricter opinions of Rabbi Eliezer and Rabbi Joshua, who insist on two witnesses and of Rabbi Akiba who does not wish to accept the woman's testimony, are overridden by the majority of the Sages. Cf. *M. Yeb.* 15:8; *B. Yeb.* 13b, 114b, N. 6.

19. Deut. 19:15.

20. *B. Sanh.* 10a.

21. It is noteworthy that Barukh Halevi Epstein, *Torah Temimah, Devarim,* 126a, col. 2, declares that the ineligibility of women as witnesses *lav kelal gamur hu,* "is not a fixed principle" and proceeds to give instances where their testimony is accepted. For the Responsa literature, see *Encyclopaedia Judaica,* vol. 16, 586.

22. *B. Kethubbot* 10a and parallels.

23. *P. Yeb.* 12:1; *P. Baba Metzia* 7:1, *Sopherim,* chap. 14.

24. Adret opposed it because of its similarity to the Azazel rites on Yom Kippur (Lev. 16:5–22) and he called it a "heathen superstition" (*darkhei ha 'emori, Responsa,* part 1, no. 395).

25. *Shulhan Arukh, Orah Hayyim,* sec. 605. His language was later toned down to read, "It is best to avoid the custom." The Rama, however, declares that it has been practiced "in these lands" (i.e., the Polish-German communities) and therefore defends its retention. See J. Z. Lauterbach's study of the rite in his *Rabbinic Essays* (Cincinnati, 1915), 354–76.

26. The evidence in all areas of Jewish law is presented in R. Gordis, "A Dynamic Halakhah: Principles and Procedures" (*Judaism,* vol. 28, no. 3, Summer, 1979, pp. 263–282). A symposium by 17 scholars representing every school of thought in contemporary Judaism, and a "Reply to the Responses" by the author of the original article, appears in the Winter, 1980 issue of *Judaism,* under the title "Jewish Law: Eighteen Perspectives."

27. *T. Ber.* 25a; *Kid.* 70a.

28. See L. M. Epstein, *Sex Laws and Customs in Judaism* (New York, 1948), 25–66.

29. Ps. 45:14. See *B. Gittin* 12a and *Rashi ad loc.*

On the Question of the Ordination of Women as Rabbis by the Jewish Theological Seminary of America

SIMON GREENBERG

The following is in part a paraphrase, in part a translation, in part an abbreviation of the Hebrew paper which was submitted to the meeting of the Senate of the Seminary held in January 1980 and appears as the last essay in this volume.

In presenting the paper to the Senate, I noted that it was not a "final draft" and that "notes and an epilogue dealing with additional relevant consideration will probably be added." An "epilogue" has not been added, but notes have been. The epilogue was to have dealt with the question of whether the action of the Faculty of the Seminary conformed to the requirements of the "halakhic process." This subject turned out to require a far lengthier treatment than could be included in an epilogue to this paper. I am attempting to deal with it in a separate essay.

The question before us has many aspects. I shall comment upon three of them.

    I. The halakhic aspect.
    II. The sociological and the psychological aspects.

III. Its impact upon the future of the Conservative Movement.

I. THE HALAKHIC ASPECT

The Conservative Movement has repeatedly affirmed recognition of the centrality of the role of the *Halakhah* in determining the pattern of behavior that a Jewish community or a committed Jew should follow. The Committee appointed by the Chancellor to study the question of the ordination of women, therefore, decided at the very beginning of its deliberations that if it found that the ordination of women was unequivocally contrary to the *Halakhah* it would not recommend it.[1] However, the Committee also noted that the Conservative Movement always took into consideration the fact that there were in the past and that there are today major as well as minor legitimate differences of opinion among those committed to the *Halakhah* regarding the interpretation or the applicability of one or another of its specific requirements. The Committee therefore decided that in its deliberations it would take into account the decisions of the Committee On Jewish Law and Standards of the Rabbinical Assembly and the practices in vogue among the majority or a substantial number of the congregations associated with the United Synagogue of America.

Among the members of the Committee there were rabbinic scholars the profoundity and comprehensiveness of whose knowledge of the *Halakhah* was universally recognized. It is of particular importance, therefore, to note that all members of the Committee agreed, even the three who did not sign the final report, that the *Halakhah* does not prohibit the ordination of women per se, since the ordination does not obligate the ordained to do anything forbidden by the *Halakhah*. Their refusal to sign the report was based rather upon their fear that ordination would well-nigh inevitably result in the performance by the ordained of acts customarily performed by Conservative rabbis in the normal course of their functioning, but forbidden by the *Halakhah* to women, such as acting as a witness on a *ketubah* (marriage document), or acting as a *hazzan* or a Torah reader, or being counted as a member of a *minyan*.

Hence, this paper will not deal with the halakhic aspects of the act of ordination per se. Nor will it deal with the specifically halakhic aspects of those acts forbidden to women but which are customarily but not necessarily performed by a Conservative rabbi.[2] It shall deal, rather, with the historical and sociological setting within which these halakhic prohibitions were formulated. It is altogether "fitting and proper" that a statement purporting to reflect a Conservative view regarding the meaning or applicability of any text—halakhic or non-halakhic—should include some discussion of the historical setting within which it came into being, for the Conservative Movement was in the beginning usually referred to as the Historical School. It was thus designated because its founders and later expounders maintained that in studying, interpreting, and applying a traditional text one should take into account not only the literal meaning of its content, but also its history—the relationship of the content to the time when and place where it came into being and within which it functioned.

The following is not an exhaustive presentation of all historic aspects of the questions before us. Nor is it assumed that the circumstances which brought a law into being necessarily determine its present validity. The role of history or sociology—or any factors which are not specifically legalistic—in determining the present validity of a law or the meaning of a legal text has been a subject of endless difference of opinion among legal theoreticians.

Each one of us inevitably decides for himself what weight to give to sociological and historical factors when called upon to pass judgment on the validity of a law or the meaning of a text. What follows, therefore, is presented as a possible contribution to our understanding of the historical setting within which there were formulated the halakhic provisions which it is feared will be unavoidably violated by women who will be acting as Conservative rabbis. These considerations played a dominant role in determining my own decision to favor the ordination of women as rabbis.

II. THE SOCIOLOGICAL AND PSYCHOLOGICAL FACTORS THAT UNDERLIE MANY OF THE PROVISIONS OF THE HALAKHAH REGARDING WOMEN

The *Humash*—the Five Books of the Torah—which is the universally recognized, ultimate authoritative source of the *Halakhah,* contains no specific, clearly formulated law or opinion or myth or narrative which enjoins the *halakhot*—the specific laws which it is feared will inevitably be violated by women who will be acting as rabbis. Nowhere is there a specific statement in the *Humash* that forbids women to act as witnesses or as judges or as cantors. Two questions, therefore, inevitably come to mind. (1) Why did the Rabbis feel impelled to find biblical sanction for them? (2) If these prohibitions are not specifically spelled out or even clearly implied in the *Humash,* how did they become part of the *Halakhah?*

1. *Why did the Rabbis seek biblical sanction for the* halakhot *they formulated?*

All laws involve the curbing of some biologically or psychologically or sociologically rooted impulse or desire. Underlying Judaism's view of man is the proposition that no man or group of men has inherent right to enforce his or their will on another human being. Only God Himself or those specifically authorized by Him have that right.[3]

In the Jewish tradition, therefore, only law which can in some sense be viewed as having been ordained by Him, or by those who were in some sense authorized by Him to do so, is authoritative. The judges, the kings, and the priests of the biblical period were chosen by God. The courts derived their authority from the biblical injunction to "appoint magistrates and officials for your tribes, in all the settlements that the Lord your God is giving you, and they shall govern the people in due Justice" (Deuteronomy 16:18). Moreover, the people are enjoined to "repair to the place which the Lord your God will have chosen and appear before the levitical priests, or the magistrate in charge at the time . . . and act in accordance with the instructions given you and the ruling handed down to you" (ibid. 17:8–11).

Though the tradition views the whole of the *Tanakh*—the Hebrew Bible—as having been divinely inspired, nevertheless, in matters affecting the *Halakhah,* the *Humash* has special status. The tradition is unequivocal that it was the only book revealed to Moses and the Israelites during their forty years sojourn in the Sinai desert.

But the *Humash* does not contain specific reference to all the laws, customs, and rituals practiced by the people. Hence, for a law or custom or practice not specifically formulated in the *Humash* to be considered as obligatory, it had in some generally acceptable manner to be associated with or derived from a Pentateuchal text, or with a divine oral communication to Moses at Sinai.

2. *If the present halakhic provisions prohibiting women from doing certain things are not specifically formulated or even hinted at in the* Humash *how did they become part of the* Halakhah?

Though the Jewish people "dwelt apart" (Numbers 23:9), they could not and did not reject all opinions or practices which were universally held by all of their contemporaries and were not specifically proscribed by the *Humash*. There were four opinions about the nature of women which until very recent times were, to the best of my knowledge, well-nigh universally considered to be "self-evident truths."[4] Available evidence seems to indicate that they continue even unto our own day to be thus considered by the majority of "civilized" mankind. These "self-evident truths" are not specifically formulated in the *Humash*. But since the narratives of the *Humash* usually reflect generally accepted standards of behavior of the place and time of their occurrence, where a generally accepted standard is not specifically proscribed one can detect its presence in some biblical narrative.[5]

The specific *halakhot* limiting the role of the woman not only in the religious but also in many other aspects of life have their roots in such universally considered "self-evident truths." They are expressed in rabbinic dicta which are quoted as the rationale, but not as the *legal* sanctions, for the specific *halakhot*. The legal sanctions are supplied by the Rabbis, who, by ingeniously interpreting Pentateuchal texts, find in them the legal concretizations of these dicta. The ingenious and, from our point of view, often incredibly far-fetched interpretation of a biblical text in order to give biblical status to a widespread pattern of behavior was viewed as being eminently rational not only within the rabbinic universe of discourse, but also within that of their non-Jewish contemporaries. Just as Maimonides and all Jewish and non-Jewish philosopher-theologians who preceded and followed him found Aristotle's or Plato's or Plotinus' ideas, and the current science of their day, embedded in the Scriptures, so the Rabbis found in them universally accepted "self-evident truths" involving behavior which were not specifically proscribed in the Scriptures. And by and large the Rabbis frequently were more justified in their interpretations than were the philosopher-theologians. I shall mention four rabbinic dicta reflecting universally accepted opinions regarding the nature of women and refer to but a few of the instances in which they are quoted as the rationale for a specific *halakhah* which directly or indirectly limits the scope of a woman's activities.

I. *Nashim daatan kallah aleihen*—"women's intellect is *kallah*."[5a]

The term *kallah* has no precise English equivalent. It is derived from the Hebrew root from which terms signifying "lightly esteemed" and "held of little account" and "treated with contempt" are derived.[6]

The Mishnah states: "A man may not be alone with two women, but a woman may be alone with two men."[7] The Gemara ad locum then asks: "What is the reason for this difference?" and answers: "In the school of Eliyahu it was taught that this was due to the fact that the intellect of woman is *kallah*.[8] How do we know this? Rabbi Johanan said in the name of Rabbi Ishmael that this *halakhah* is hinted at (or suggested) by the verse 'If your brother, your own mother's son, . . . entices you' [Deuteronomy 13:7]. Does a mother's son entice and the son of a father not entice? But since the verse is thus worded,[9] we may derive from it that a son may be alone with his mother but not with any other woman forbidden him by the Torah."

This general principle is also the rationale for the *halakhah* that women should not or need not be taught Torah. The Rabbis find this *halakhah* implied in the verse (Deuteronomy 11:19) which states: "And teach them *livneikhem*," generally translated as "to your children." But because *livneikhem* is masculine the Rabbis interpret it as referring to "your sons" and as excluding "your daughters,"[10] even though the masculine form is widely used in the *Humash* to include both men and women. This rabbinic interpretation thus became the biblical basis for what was the widespread practice in all contemporary societies to offer only minimal educational opportunities to girls. The rationale for this *halakhah* is the opinion that the intellect of women being *kallah,* they will misuse what they learn.[11]

This is also one of the reasons given for the widespread practice of prohibiting women from acting as ritual slaughterers[12] even though the Mishnah specifically states that they may do so.[13]

The most serious prohibition which is thus rationalized is the *halakhah* that women, except in a very limited number of specified instances, may not act as witnesses.[14] That women are not dependable as witnesses the Midrash finds implied in the question addressed by Manoah, the father of Samson, to the angel (Judges 13:12). Manoah asked the angel to repeat what he had said to his wife because "women are not dependable that they will accurately report what was told them."[15]

The Rabbis found biblical sanction for this widely practiced prohibition only by using their interpreter's license to its utmost limit. They had recourse to the logically most questionable of the thirteen principles of interpretation, the *gezeirah shavah,*[16] in order to establish that the words *shnei ha-anashim,* "the two parties to the dispute (Deuteronomy 19:17) refer to witnesses, and since *anashim* is in the masculine, the witnesses may be only males. Again I must stress the fact that what may appear to us to be farfetched interpretations of a biblical verse were altogether proper and rational in the universe of discourse of the Rabbis and their gentile contemporaries. But this particular interpretation was seriously questioned even by some who were part of that universe. [17]

II. *Ha-ishah meshuabedet le-baalah*—"The wife is subservient to her husband."

a. One can easily muster a wide range of biblical and rabbinic quotations to support the opinion that the lot of the Jewish woman in society and especially in the home was a generally happier one than that in most contemporary societies from antiquity until modern times. Maimonides summarizes the widely scattered rabbinic statements:

> The Sages commanded that one should honor his wife more than himself and love her as he loves himself. If he is rich he should bestow benefits upon her in accordance with his wealth. He should not intimidate her excessively. He should talk gently with her, and not be wrathful or impatient. [18]

Despite the husband's moral, economic, and conjugal obligations towards his wife, the general principle that she is subservient to him holds sway. Thus the Mishnah states:

> Everywhere Scripture speaks of the father before the mother. Does this imply that the honor due to the father exceeds the honor due to the mother? But Scripture says "Ye shall fear every man his mother and his father" [Leviticus 19:12]. [In this verse] the mother precedes the father to teach that both are equal. But the Sages have said: Everywhere else Scripture speaks of the father before the mother, because both a man and his mother are bound to honor the father. [19]

And Maimonides adds:

> And thus they [the Sages] enjoin the woman to honor her husband as much as possible. She should be in fear of him and

do everything according to his directions. She should view him as an officer or a king, complying with the desires of his heart, and eschewing all that is hateful to him. This is the way for the holy and pure daughters and sons of Israel to follow in their marital relations, and thus all their relationships will be pleasant and praiseworthy.[20]

b. The Rabbis formulated the legal dictum that women are exempt from *mitzvot* which are to be performed at specific times. They derived this principle as follows:

1. Women are exempt from the study of Torah.[21]
2. From the juxtaposition of the command for men to study Torah and to put on *Tefillin* (Deuteronomy 6:7–8), the Rabbis deduce that women are exempt also from putting on *Tefillin*.
3. The *mitzvah* of putting on *Tefillin* has to be performed every weekday before 10 A.M. This, therefore, is a time-bound *mitzvah*.
4. Since they are exempt from this time-bound *mitzvah*, they are exempt from every other time-bound *mitzvah*, except where there is some identifiable reason for obligating them to observe it.[22]

But it is obvious that from the fact that women are exempt from putting on *Tefillin*, which happens to be a time-bound *mitzvah*, it does not necessarily or logically follow that they are exempt from all other time-bound *mitzvot*. What is it, therefore, which led the Rabbis to generalize from *Tefillin* to other time-bound *mitzvot*? Abudraham suggests that

> The reason why women are exempt from the time-bound *mitzvot* is because *ha-ishah meshuabedet le-baalah* [the woman is subservient to her husband] to do his bidding. And if she had to fulfill all positive, time-bound *mitzvot*, the occasion would arise when her husband would ask her to do something for him at the time when she would be engaged in the performance of a *mitzvah*. If she would persist in fulfilling the command of her Creator, she would incur the displeasure of her husband, and if she would do

his bidding and forsake the command of her Creator, she would incur His displeasure. Therefore her Creator excused her from some of His commandments, in order to preserve peace between wife and husband.[23]

c. This general dictum is clearly implied in the wedding ceremony. Maimonides states:

The words spoken by the man at the wedding ceremony must clearly state that he takes possession of the woman and not that he gave himself to her. Thus if he said, or wrote in a document to her, "I am your husband, I am your betrothed," or anything similar to this, it does not constitute a marriage. But if he said or wrote to her, "You are my wife, you are my betrothed," or something similar, she becomes his wife.[24]

d. The most obvious manifestation in the *Halakhah* of the woman's generally subservient position in society is found in the halakhic passages which group together women and slaves. "There are three ways in which the divorcing of a woman and the emancipation of a slave are alike . . ."[25] "All *mitzvot* incumbent upon a woman are incumbent upon a slave, and all *mitzvot* from which the woman is exempt the slave is also exempt, for we deduce the responsibilities of the slave from those of the woman."[26]

e. The spiritually most painful implementation in the *Halakhah* of the principle that the wife is subservient to her husband is the *halakhah* that the *get* (the document recording a divorce) must be given by the husband or his appointed agent to the wife. The tragedies and ruthless blackmail, the humiliations that have resulted from this *halakhah* are too well known to require documentation.[27]

III. *Kol guf haisha ervah*—"Every exposed part of the woman's body is seductive."[28]

Though the *Humash* lists in considerable detail those women with whom men are forbidden to have any sexual relations (Leviticus 18:6–20), and though Proverbs (chapters 5 and 7) warns against the seductive blandishments of the "strange woman whose lips drop honey," nowhere in the *Humash* is there any specific or even vague injunction to isolate women from the daily activities of the society of which they were a part or from the rather free intermingling of men and women in the course of their normal activities. Indeed the "woman of valor" is one who is "like the merchant-ships, she bringeth her food from afar, she considereth a field, and buyeth it . . . she maketh linen garments and selleth them. And delivereth girdles unto the merchant" (Proverbs 31:5, 7, 24).

Moreover, no tradition known to me assigns to women as central a role in determining the course of its history as does the Jewish tradition, beginning with the earliest period and continuing to the destruction of the first Temple.

No matter how we may today judge the acts of Sarah and Rebecca, it was Sarah whose action determined that Isaac rather than Ishmael should be heir to the Covenant that God had made with Abraham. Sarah's insistence on excluding Ishmael "distressed Abraham greatly," and he had to be reassured by God and told to do "whatever Sarah tells you" (Genesis 21:9–12). And it was Rebecca who saw to it that Jacob, not Esau, should get the blessings that were part of the birthright, and it was she who saved him from his brother's wrath (ibid. 27:1–17, 42–46). Miriam plays the central role in saving the infant Moses (Exodus 2:1–9) and leads the Israelite women in dance and song after the safe crossing of the Sea of Reeds (ibid. 15:20–21). The five daughters of Zelaphad, whose names have been immortalized in Scripture, are the first women known to history who dare to speak up for their rights and are responsible for the revelation that fixed the *halakhot* involving inheritance (Numbers 27:1–11). Deborah the prophetess, who "sat under the palm tree" and "judged Israel," gave the indispensable spiritual support to Barak, who led the hosts of Israel in one of the decisive battles for the conquest of the land (Judges 4:4–9). It was a woman who in the midst of battle cast the millstone upon the head of the ruthless usurper (ibid. 9:50–54), and the angel of the Lord announced the forthcoming birth of Samson to his mother, who was obviously wiser than his father (ibid. 3:2–23). It was Hannah who purposefully nurtured her son Samuel as a forthcoming leader of his people (I Samuel, chap. 1). The tradition places him in the same class as Moses and Aaron (Psalm 99:6). And King Josiah asks the prophetess Hulda to interpret the message of the Book that had been found in the Temple. Her message to the king leads to one of the greatest of religious reformations recorded in Jewish history (II Kings 22:12–20).

In preparation for the Sinaitic theophany, Moses is commanded: "Thus shall you say to the house of Jacob and to the children of Israel" (Exodus 19:3). The Midrash understands "the house of Jacob" as referring to women. Rabbi Tahlifa of Caesarea taught: "God said, 'when I created the world I first commanded Adam and then Eve, and she transgressed and blemished the world. Now if I do not call the women first they will nullify the Torah. Therefore 'say to the house of Jacob' first."[29]

Before his death Moses, in renewing the Covenant, says: "You stand this day, all of you, before the Lord your God . . . all men of Israel, your children, your wives . . . to enter into the Covenant of the Lord your God" (Deuteronomy 29:9–10). He further enjoins them that "every seventh year . . . you shall read this teaching aloud in the presence of all Israel. Gather the people—men, women, children and the strangers in your communities—that they may hear and so learn to revere the Lord your God and to observe faithfully every word of this teaching" (ibid. 31:10–12). Nehemiah records: "On the first day of the seventh month, Ezra the priest brought the Teaching [Torah] before the congregation, men and women, and all who could listen with understanding. He read from it . . . from the first light until midday, to the men and women and those who could understand" (Nehemiah 8:2–3).

All of this does not necessarily prove that the position of the Israelite woman was equal to that of the man in biblical days, but it would indicate that women were not isolated from the company of men and were not forbidden to mingle with them on occasions of public gatherings.

The only specific reference found in the *Tanakh*, the Hebrew Scriptures, that men and women were to gather separately in the observance of some public occasion is found in Zechariah: "In that day, the wailing in Jerusalem shall be as great as the wailing at Hadad-Rimmon in the plain of Megiddon. The land shall wail, each family by itself: the family of the House of David by themselves, and their women folk by themselves . . . and all other families, every family by itself with their women-folk by themselves" (12:11–14). Modern scholars tend to assign the passage to the third century B.C.E. The Rabbis assumed that the prophet here stresses the separation of the sexes lest the mourning he speaks of should be turned into a bacchanalia. The Rabbis then drew the altogether plausible conclusion that if the sexes are to be separated at a time of mourning because of fear of lasciviousness, how much more so does it apply to times of celebration.[30]

It is this passage which serves as the biblical sanction for the tendency that developed during the post-biblical period to keep men and women from mingling with one another not only on public occasions but on any occasion whether private or public. The Rabbis, for what many would agree were and are good reasons, viewed the sex instinct as the most persist-ent, ubiquitous, and powerful single factor leading men to sin. Indeed the term *averah* ("sin") as used by them was generally understood to refer to some sexual transgression. "Sinful (i.e., involving sexual transgressions) thoughts" were among the sins which every one committed every day.[31] The *yetzer hara*, man's "evil urge," was identified primarily with the sex in-stinct, and the woman, by her sheer presence, inevitably roused and stimulated this evil urge, so that she was identified with Satan. "Woman and Satan were simultaneously cre-ated."[32]

The earliest rabbinic statement specifically cautioning men to avoid the company of women is found in the first chapter of The Ethics of The Fathers. Rabbi Jose son of Yohanan (third century B.C.E.), cautions against engaging in "lengthy conver-sations" even with one's wife. Those who came after him drew the inevitable conclusion that one should all the more so avoid conversing with another man's wife or with any woman.

Maimonides summarizes the extremist's position by stating that a woman by her very physical presence is seductive. "Hence one should not look at a woman, even not at his own wife, while reciting the Shema, and if even a handbreadth of any part of her body is uncovered he should not recite the Shema in her presence,"[33] apparently whether he is looking at her or not.

Thus man's need to protect himself against his "evil urge," and to protect the woman against her propensity to be seduced,[34] constitutes the underlying rationale of many a *halakhah*, and of many of the practices that rigorously isolate women from the society of men among fundamentalist Mohammedans, and only somewhat less rigorously among "fundamentalist" Jewish groups.

IV. *Kol kevudah bat malekh penimah* (Psalm 45:14).

The new JPS translation of the Psalms notes that "the meaning of the Hebrew is uncertain." It translates it as "The royal princess . . . is led inside to the King." The previous JPS translation has: "All glorious is the King's daughter within the palace." The word *penimah* ("inside, within") suggested to the Rabbis that the psalmist here reflects the dictum that women were not to become involved in activities that would take them out of the home.

The religiously deep-felt need[35] to protect both man and woman against the importunities of the "evil urge" most likely contributed greatly to the formulation and the wide acceptance of the dictum that woman's place is in the home or even more specifically in the kitchen. I shall note briefly its use by the Rabbis as the rationale for one of their most radical halakhic interpretations.

Scripture states: "No Ammonite or Moabite shall be admitted into the congregation of the Lord; none of his descendants even in the tenth generation, shall ever be admitted into the congregation of the Lord" (Deuteronomy 23:4). The story of Ruth, the Moabite woman who was "admitted to the congregation of the Lord" and became the progenitor of David, (Ruth 4:10–22), thus obviously seems to be in violation of this commandment. The Midrash explains that the *Beth Din*, the court of the prophet Samuel, who anointed David as king at the behest of the Lord, interpreted the Hebrew term *Moavi*, the masculine form for "Moabite," and *Ammoni*, "an Ammonite," to refer to men only but not to Moabite or Ammonite women. They may be admitted into the congregation of the Lord. But a few verses later (Deuteronomy 23:5–9), Scripture says that in the case of an *Adomi*, an Edomite, and a *Mitzri*, an Egyptian, "children born to them may be admitted in the congregation of the Lord [only] in the third generation." In this instance the Rabbis did not interpret the verses as referring only to male Edomites and Egyptians but not to females. Both are excluded unto the third generation. Why this difference? The Rabbis find this difference indicated in the reason given in the *Humash* for the total exclusion of male Moabites and Ammonites. "Because they did not meet you with food and water on your journey after you left Egypt, and because they hired Balaam son of Beor . . . to curse you" (ibid., v. 5). Men were obligated to go out and meet the Israelites with food and water. Women were not so obligated because their place is in the home. Moreover, men "hired" but women are not supposed to be involved in such transactions. Ammonite and Moabite women were not obligated to "meet" (the Israelites) with food and water. Hence, they did not share in the transgressions for which the men were to be forever excluded from the congregation of the Lord.[36] This interpretation of the biblical text, ingenious as it undoubtedly is, could probably never have occurred to the Rabbis if it were not for the widely accepted "self-evident truth" that women's place was in the home. That "truth" explained to the Rabbis why the *Humash* in this instance does what it otherwise rarely does, it states the reason underlying the legislation, and thereby offers an acceptable rationale for the rabbinic interpretation that only male Moabites and Ammonites may not be admitted into the congregation of the Lord, but females may be admitted.

A number of other halakhic limitations upon women's activities are associated by the Rabbis with biblical texts, but that association is at best tenuous. These limitations flow directly or indirectly from the preceding universally accepted four dicta.

a. Thus the statement "You shall be free to set a king over yourself. . . . You must not set *ish nakhri* [a foreign man] over you" (Deuteronomy 17:15) is interpreted to imply that they may set a king over themselves but not a queen—*ish* (a man), but not a woman. From which they further concluded that a woman is not to be appointed as the head of the community.[37] Maimonides goes further. He states unequivocally that "among Israelites only men are appointed to any kind of a communal, responsible office."[38]

b. The question of whether a woman may act as a judge was at first easily disposed of, "since every one who is permitted to act as judge may also act as a witness, and since women may not act as witnesses,[39] they may not act as judges."[40] But the Rabbis were troubled by the fact that Scripture specifically states that "Deborah, a prophetess, . . . judged Israel at that time" (Judges 4:4). It would take us too far afield to follow the discussion of this problem among the Rabbis.[41] Suffice to say that the discussion reflects more than a modicum of uneasiness about the solutions offered to the problem.

c. The Rabbis also prohibit a woman from doing certain things even though they are halakhically permitted to her because it would reflect upon the *kvod hatzibur*, the dignity of the congregation. Thus, even though a woman may be called to the Torah as one of the seven called on the Shabbat,[42] the Sages nevertheless said that a woman should not read from the Torah because it reflects on the dignity of the congregation.[43] Considerations for the dignity of the congregation are given as the reason for prohibiting a woman to do a number of other things which she is halakhically permitted to do.[44]

VI. "Custom is (often) as binding as *halakhah*."[45]

But even assuming that many of the halakhot regarding women are based on what were once universally accepted dicta about the nature of women rather than on biblically rooted *halakhot*, the fact remains that this was the accepted Jewish practice for more than two millennia. Have we the right to change such long-established practices? We know how pervasive is the regard the Rabbis had for long-established practices, particularly for those that had been formulated into *halakhot* and included in widely accepted codes. They hesitated to violate a long-established custom of any Jewish community even though they knew that it had no halakhic basis. The Commission which was appointed by the Chancellor was fully aware of the sensitivity with which one should approach religiously sanctified practices. They therefore noted how widespread and in how many ways the traditional practices relating to women have already been irrevocably breached.[46] I shall add but one incident that occurred when I was in Jerusalem in the summer of 1979. It occurred in the Park of the Bell (a replica of the American Liberty Bell). The wife of Rabbi Jungreis, an Orthodox rabbi, attired and made up in most modern and attractive fashion and supported by a hasidic "rock" band, appeared before a mixed audience and delivered a rousing Torah-filled address urging her listeners to return to the ways of the Torah. She was sponsored by the religious education department of the World Zionist Organization. To the best of my knowledge, none of the religious leaders expressed a word of protest. With the exception of a minuscule minority, Jewish men and women, many of whom consider themselves as being Orthodox and are in fact observant of the Sabbath, dietary laws, etc., nevertheless mingle freely, attend theater and opera, dance with the opposite sex, send their children to co-educational schools, teach their daughters Torah and do practically all that custom and halakhah at one time prohibited. The kind of rigid separation of the sexes fixed in the past by custom or by halakhah, today reflects the practice of a diminishing minority of the Jews of the world and particularly of the Jews of the West. To withhold ordination from women because of a pattern of behavior which has been extensively and as far as one can see irrevocably breached is to give precedence to a largely discarded custom over our growing sensitivity to our moral obligation to apply to women the admonition of the arch-conservative Rabbi Eliezer ben Hyrcanes: "The honor or dignity of your fellow man should be as precious to you as your own."[47] To do so especially in our society is to declare the pervasive presence of women in every walk and on every level of human endeavor to be morally evil, and hence a threat to the society's welfare. Withholding ordination from women cannot restore the breached custom, nor stem the onrushing events that unconcernedly pass it by. It can only delay or impair the healthy integration of the Jewish woman into the Jewish society of the future.

III. THE IMPACT UPON THE FUTURE OF THE CONSERVATIVE MOVEMENT

There are those who predict that the question of the ordination of women at present agitating the Conservative Movement will inevitably result in the dissolution of the Movement. For if the Seminary decides to ordain women, it will signal the beginning of a process that will end with the merger of the Conservative and the Reform Movements. If the decision is to deny ordination to women, the Conservative Movement will be on the way towards merging with the Orthodox.

To be sure, the action which will be taken by the Seminary in regard to ordination of women will have a most significant effect upon the future development of the Conservative Movement, but it will in no way presage its dissolution. On the contrary, it may well mark the beginning of an era of renewed spiritual and intellectual vigor during which its influence on the course of the development of the Reform and the Orthodox wings of Judaism will be even greater than it has been in the past.

For the ordination of women will not eliminate the differences between us and the Reform Movement on basic matters of ritual, such as dietary laws, Sabbath observance, Hebrew in the liturgy, conversions, divorce, intermarriage, patrilineal descent, and the role of the *Halakhah* in our lives. Where there fortunately has been rapproachment between the Conservative and the Reform Movements, as in the case of the attitude towards Zionism and Israel, it was the Reform Movement that underwent radical change.

Insofar as our merging with the Orthodox, that would require us to renounce our intellectual integrity, our commitment to the scientific study of our tradition and history, our determination not to withdraw into either a geographic or an intellectual ghetto, and our conception of the *Halakhah* as authoritative but not as fossilized.[48] Nor do we subscribe to the frequently articulated presumption that if we change one *halakhah* it will inevitably be followed by our changing many more *halakhot,* for how will we know where to stop changing? Changes in the *Halakhah* are not made by the Committee on Law and Standards of the Rabbinical Assembly merely because they are enamored of change. Individuals may act irresponsibly, but the national institutions of the Conservative Movement do not. The fact that twenty-three amendments have been made to the Constitution of the United States has not resulted in a plethora of amendments which destroyed the Constitution. On the contrary, the amendments (some of which annuled previous provisions of the Constitution) reinforced the authority of the Constitution and made it viable.

It is our contention that in a society constantly undergoing change, the refusal to make any changes in a legal system of any kind will of necessity lead to the fossilization not only of the legal system but also of the society that strives to live by it. A fossil can continue to exist indefinitely, even as a fossilized society, but neither Judaism nor the Jewish people were ever fossilized. Both constantly underwent change, sometimes radical, sometimes hardly perceptible change, as the Jews and Judaism have continued not only to exist but to live both as a dynamic creative people and as an ever richer spiritually life-affirming tradition.

Moreover, our study of Jewish history has established the indisputable fact that neither the Jewish people nor Judaism ever constituted ideologically or legally monolithic structures.

We are not that today, and we cannot, even if we deemed it desirable, become that tomorrow. No individual or group can guarantee that the change they advocate is the best possible response to the need of the time or place. But to oppose change merely because it is change is to ask mankind to stop thinking, inventing, aspiring. And the Jewish people is part of mankind.

The indisputable fact that faces us today is that within the ranks of the Conservative Movement there is probably no one who would publicly or even in private subscribe to the dicta regarding the nature of women which underlie the *halakhot* that govern the status of women within the halakhic structure. Surely no one in the Western democracies today accepts them as valid. Moreover, the present status of women in American society in particular has its theological roots in the biblically grounded conceptions of the dignity and sacredness of the individual regardless of race or gender.[49] It is, therefore, altogether congenial to our biblically rooted tradition and can be integrated into the *Halakhah* in accordance with halakhically valid principles. We ought not to be among those who would impede such integration, but rather among those who encourage it.

Should the Seminary decide to ordain women, an awesome responsibility will rest upon it and upon the Conservative Movement. It shall be incumbent upon us as individuals and as a Movement to be patient towards those within our Movement who differ from us, to do all in our power not to alienate them, and to be tireless in our efforts to articulate and disseminate the considerations that led us to this decision. Above all, however, it shall be doubly incumbent upon us to demonstrate that piety, modesty, study of Torah, uprightness in human relations, love of God, love of Israel, and love of mankind are nourished and flourish in our midst.

NOTES

1. See p. 13.
2. They are very fully discussed in this volume in the papers by Francus, Gordis, Rabinowitz and Roth.
3. See S. Greenberg, *A Jewish Philosophy and Pattern of Life* (The Jewish Theological Seminary of America, 1981), p. 203

4. As is well known the authority of Aristotle's writing was for millenia well nigh universally considered to be on a par with that of Scripture. Maimonides' monumental philosophic work "The Guide to the Perplexed" was intended to prove that there is no conflict between Aristotle's writings and the teachings of the *Humash*. His opinions on the nature of women are therefore relevant to our discussion. The following quotations are from his Politics as found in The Basic Works of Aristotle edited and with an Introduction by Richard McKeon—Random House, N.Y. 1941.

"The male is by nature superior and the female inferior; and the one rules and the other is ruled. This principle of necessity extends to all mankind" (Bk 1, ch. 4 McKeon p. 1132). "For although there may be exceptions to the order of nature, the male is by nature fitter for command than the female." "A question may indeed be raised whether there is any excellence at all in a slave . . . whether he can have the virtues of temperance, courage, justice and the like . . . A similar question may be raised about women and children, whether they too have virtues; ought a woman to be temperate and brave and just . . . The slave has no deliberative faculty at all, the women has but it is without authority. Clearly, then, moral virtue belongs to all of them; but the temperance of a man and of a woman, or the courage and justice of a man and of a woman, are not, as Socrates maintained the same; the courage of a man is shown in commanding, of a woman in obeying" (Bk 1 ch. 11, 13 pp. 1143–1144). "All classes must be deemed to have their special attributes, as the poet says of women "Silence is a woman's glory" but this is not equally the glory of man (Bk 1. ch. 13 p. 1145).

5. Thus Abraham's response to the question "Where is your wife Sarah"— that she is "there in the tent" (Genesis 18:8) is taken as indicating where a good wife should always be. Yevamot. 77a

5a. Shabbat 33b.

6. Gesenius—Brown-Driver-Briggs—Hebrew and English Lexicon of the Old Testament s.v. Kallah II

7. Kiddushin 80b

8. Rashi explains that "because the intellect of women is kallah both of them are easily seduced and the one does not fear the other because she will do as the other one does." But two men can be alone with one woman "because each one is ashamed of the other."

9. So that the words 'mother' and 'son' are juxtaposed.

10. Kiddushin 29b

11. Sota 21b. Rabbi Baruch Ha-Levi Epstein, one of the very greatest universally recognized traditional Talmudic scholars of the twentieth century, is the author of the *Torah Temimah*. It is composed of selections of rabbinic comments on Penteteuchal verses and his commentaries on these rabbinic comments. The biblical text (Deuteronomy 11:19) reads "And teach them to your sons." The Rabbis deduce therefrom that no one is obligated to teach Torah to women. (Kiddushin 29b) On this rabbinic statement the *Torah Temimah* comments ad locum note 48 as follows: "From this it would appear that one is merely not *obligated* to teach a woman Torah, but that if he wants to he *may*. But the truth of the matter is that we are forbidden to teach Torah to women". He then quotes the statement of Rabbi Hisda that "the Lord endowed women with greater *binah* than men. (Niddah 45b). This seems to

contradict the prevalent rabbinic opinion that the *daat* of woman is *kallah*. To obviate this seeming contradiction, Rabbi Epstein proceeds to differentiate at length between *binah* and *daat* thus validating both the opinion that the woman is more abundantly endowed with *binah*, but that her *daat* is *kallah*. Since *daat* is the basis of *binah*, where the *daat* is *kallah* the *binah* can come up with *deiot nifsadot ve-kozvot*, with "defective and false opinions."

12. Hulin 2a Tosafot "Hakol Shohatin"

13. Zevahim 3:1

14. Shevuot 30a. See also Sefer Ha-hinukh, Mitzvah 122.

15. Bamidbar Rabbah ch. 10 para. 5

16. "However, in the official hermeneutic rules the term *gezeirah shavah* was applied not to analogy of content, but to identity of words (i.e. verbal congruities with text) a manner of comparison which sometimes appears to be without logical basis." Saul Lieberman, *Hellenism in Jewish Palestine* (New York: Jewish Theological Seminary, 1962), p. 61.

17. For an extended presentation of the rabbinic discussion of this interpretation see pp. 149–52.

18. Hilkhot Ishut, 15:19

19. Kerithoth 6:9 (Danby translation)

20. Hilkhot Ishut 15:20

21. See above p. 75.

22. Kiddushin 34a

23. Abudraham Hashaleim—Hozaat Usha—Jerusalem 5719 p. 25

24. Hilkhot Ishut 3:6

25. Gittin 9a

26. Hagiga 4a

27. For a lengthy discussion of this subject see chapter 3 of *The Ethical in the Jewish and American Heritage* by Simon Greenberg.

28. Maimonides Hilkhot Kriat Shema—3:16

29. Shemot Rabba ch. 28:2

30. Succah 52a

31. Baba Batra 164b.

32. Bereshit Rabba 17:6

33. See note 28

34. See p. 74.

35. The achievement of "holiness" is generally associated in the tradition with the curbing but not with the total suppression of the "evil urge." See Ramban's comment on Leviticus 19:2.

36. Ruth Rabbah chap. 4 para. 9, *"Va-yomer Boaz Le-naaro"*

37. Sifre Piska 157. Yet we know that Salome Alexandra, widow of King Alexander Jannaeus, ruled as Queen (76–67 B.C.E) and we have no record of any one of the Rabbis, her contemporaries or their successors who raised any objection to her rule.

38. Hilkhot Melakhim chapter 1 paragraph 5

39. See above p. 75.

40. Niddah 49b

41. See Sefer Hahinukh—Mitzvah 77 and Tosafot Shevuot 29b "Shevuat ha-edut."

42. Tosefta Megillah chapter 3 paragraph 11.

43. Megillah 23a. There is considerable discussion regarding the statement that a woman may be called to the Torah as one of the seven. But that too would take us too far afield. Originally each one of the seven called to the Torah would read before the congregation from the Scroll the section over which the blessing was made.

44. See pp. 204–206.

45. J. T. Sheviit Chapter 5, halakhah 1. B. Betza 4b Baba Metzia 86b

46. See p. 17–25, 57, 98.

47. Ethics of the Fathers Chapter 2:15

48. For a lengthy discussion of what is meant by the statement that "The Halakhah is authoritative but not fossilized" see Greenberg S. *Foundations of a Faith*, pp. 59–69 and *A Jewish Philosophy and Pattern of Life*, pp. 435–446 and pp. 449–464.

49. Simon Greenberg, "Pluralism and Jewish Education," *Religious Education Magazine*, vol.81 no. 1, Winter 1986. The original title of the essay was "Pluralism—Its Theological Bases."

On the Rabbinic Ordination of Women

DR. ANNE LAPIDUS LERNER

INTRODUCTION

We stand on the threshold of the 1980's, embroiled in a controversy the ramifications of which touch our religious, scholarly, professional and personal lives. We are being asked to make a change, a change which is perceived by some as a radical break with tradition; by others, as a long-overdue extension of the rights and responsibilities of Judaism to its women, the majority of the Jewish people. Individually and collectively, we have all grappled with the question. Now, we are faced with a decision on an issue which cannot be compromised and will not go away. Even delay, the absence of a decision, will be perceived as a decision, a negative one. Positions have been taken, and often hardened and there are few among us whose positions are not known to all. I do not know if there is anyone among us who is still entirely undecided.

The question of the ordination of women which has so exercised us as a faculty for the past year is not a new one. When Henrietta Szold asked to study at The Jewish Theological Seminary of America in 1903 she was admitted to classes "only after she had assured its administration that she would not use the knowledge thus gained to seek ordination."[1]

Clearly, the idea of rabbinic ordination of women was not a complete impossibility in the first decade of the century. In fact, the issue of ordaining women was probably first directly raised in this country in 1922 when the Central Conference of American Rabbis passed a resolution declaring that "women cannot justly be denied the privilege of ordination."[2] In our own movement, the issue was joined much later in the wake of both the appearance of Ezrat Nashim at the Rabbinical Assembly Convention in March, 1972, and a *takkanah* by the Committee on Jewish Law and Standards of the Rabbinical Assembly in September, 1973, allowing women to be counted in a *minyan*. In 1973, the United Synagogue, at its biennial convention, adopted a resolution on "The Role of Women," including the following statement on "Admission of Women in the Rabbinical School of the Jewish Theological Seminary of America": "Recognizing the growing role of women in the life of our congregations, the United Synagogue of America, in convention assembled, wishes to note that it looks with favor on the admission of qualified women to the Rabbinical School of the Jewish Theological Seminary of America."[3] It was proposed at various Rabbinical Assembly conventions that women be admitted to the Rabbinical Assembly and/or to the Rabbinical School.[4] Finally, at the 1977 convention, after such a resolution had been proposed, Chancellor Gerson D. Cohen was asked to appoint a Commission for the Study of the Ordination of Women as Rabbis to investigate the matter thoroughly and to make its recommendations to the 1979 Rabbinical Assembly Convention. The recommendation to ordain women was presented first to the Rabbinical Assembly and then to the faculty. The Rabbinical Assembly, not wanting to force the hand of the Seminary, decided to allow the faculty to consider the Commission report first. That we did, having the date for a vote changed from February, 1979 to May, 1979, to January 1980.

The preceding brief review of the history of the women's ordination issue makes it clear that we have been given ample time to consider the matter. We can no longer claim that the ramifications of a decision to ordain women have yet to be considered, that these things must be done slowly, that we need more time to come to a decision. Not only do we have no excuse for a delay, but a delay would be counter-productive.

Further delay would be seen as an indication of the cumbersome and halting nature of the halakhic process. It would serve to strengthen the hand of those who feel that the Halakhah cannot deal with current issues. If, as a result of our delay, the Rabbinical Assembly should take action either to admit women rabbis ordained elsewhere or to ordain rabbis itself we would be abdicating to it our position of primacy in the movement. Furthermore, for the women who are hoping to be admitted to the Rabbinical School, delay will serve only to embitter a group of supporters of Halakhic Judaism who will feel that their lives are being left hanging by a faculty which is not sensitive to their commitment and abilities.

To my knowledge the only other time our Faculty was involved in a halakhic issue, was during the forty year attempt to ameliorate the situation of the *agunah*. The repeated delays, the appointment of committee upon committee, served not only to allow time for two more generations of *agunot* to arise while the men involved in the decision deliberated, but also to reduce the respect accorded the Halakhah. As Rabbi Ralph Simon said in 1951, "When I first joined the Rabbinical assembly, the *agunah* already was present at our conventions. Since that day, the *agunah*'s daughter has grown up, and now *she* is an *agunah*. We still have not done anything about the problem, and I now have fears for the *agunah*'s granddaughter."[5] Do we dare allow the women's ordination issue to follow the same path? Like the *agunah* it will not go away.

THE HALAKHAH

To my mind, there would be no way in which we could make this innovation were it halakhically indefensible. The halakhically formulated argument made by our colleague, Professor Joel Roth, in support of the ordination of women is most persuasuve. Our concern for Halakhah must be demonstrated not only in the decisions we make but also in the way we make them. The issues should be considered, as Rabbi Roth proposes, in logical, halakhic sequence, with responsibilities pre-ceding rights. Nor would the growing number of female candi-dates for Rabbinical School with whom I have spoken want it any other way. The respect for halakhah evinced by the women I know, their own concern for halakhic legitimacy, is manifest in the group which regularly participates in the daily services here. This only supports my contention that ordination is not at all a left-right issue, but cuts across those lines.[6]

At the same time I am concerned that the Committee of the Conference on Halakhic Process seems to have arrogated ex-clusively to the anti-ordination rabbis the concern for preserv-ing the authority of the Halakhah. Surely there are those on both sides of the ordination issue who are equally deeply concerned. But such concern yields and has always yielded differences of opinion rather than unanimity. Respect for Jew-ish law, scholarship or the rabbinate is not enhanced when valid differences of opinion on a halakhic issue are turned into attacks on the fidelity of proponents of ordination of women to our sacred tradition.[7] If there is as there often is, more than one halakhic answer, let us admit that this is so and try to explain why one position or another is preferable to us. Since each of us believes that this controversy is "for the sake of heaven", each of us ought to behave in as upright a manner as possible. Only in this way will we be able to enhance the prestige of the Halakhah.

Although the Halakhah may allow for the ordination of women, it does not require it. What does require it is justice, a consideration often outside The Halakhah when narrowly de-fined. The woman of today is different from the woman of the second, or even the nineteenth, century. Generally speaking, women's religious or intellectual capabilities are no longer called into question. Due to a longer life expectancy, lower birth-rate and lower infant mortality, child-bearing and nurs-ing no longer occupy as large a portion or proportion of a woman's life. "Parenting," involving both parents, is replacing "mothering" as a description of the child-nurturing role. Women hold high positions in virtually all areas of public life.

Their goals, like those of men, include careers of service to God and fellowpersons. If, as has been argued, there is no halakhic barrier, on what grounds can we exclude capable, committed women from the rabbinate?

THE SEMINARY

There has been some talk that the admission of women into Rabbinical School would irrevocably split our faculty. While opinions run strong on this issue, it is important to remember that they run strong in both directions, and that whether or not women are admitted to the Rabbinical School there will be a need for a period of healing for the faculty. The first step in such a process must be taken before the issue is resolved, by refraining from personal attack, and trying to conduct our-selves as befits a community of religiously concerned scholars. It helps no one to have persons on each side impugn the decision-making qualifications of individuals on the other side. We must not lose our respect for each other.

One salutary result of a positive decision on ordaining women is that the issue would then "go away" and we could get on with our major business, producing Jewish scholarship and educating committed Jews. A negative decision is, even in the opinion of some who are opposed to ordaining women, merely a temporary one, one which will be appealed repeat-edly until, in our lifetime or thereafter, it is overturned. Such a prolongation of the process, while it might serve to free from responsibility those of us who will retire in the interim, will not serve the Seminary well. It will only contribute to a further diversion of precious resources of time, energy, talent, and, alas, even money, from our major goals.

I have been asked what questions one might ask a female candidate for admission. I think that the answer to that ques-tion is implicit in Rabbi Roth's paper. I think that the questions should be the same for men and women. We must accept only those candidates of either sex who are willing to guide their lives by Halakhah, and to help their congregants or students lead lives so guided. If a woman is to act as a *sheliah tzibbur*, a cantor, we must expect her to have undertaken the obligations of daily prayer, just as we expect the men to do. We should expect that the women, too, have embarked on a religious quest, though theirs has certainly been complicated by the absence of role models. In short, they ought to be potentially worthy of ordination.

CONSERVATIVE JUDAISM

If the concept "justice" seems a bit vague as a basis for instituting change, the history and dynamic of the Conservative movement are not. We have seen within the Conservative movement in the United States, a slow, but steady, extension of rights and responsibilities to women. As Moshe Davis notes, even in the initial phase, the Conservative movement was concerned with enhancing the position of women:

> Of all the changes and reforms adopted internally by the members of the Historical School, the most profound was the recognition that women deserved a more significant role in the life of the synagogue. Although that role was not easily or quickly defined, the very acceptance of women as participants in synagogue life wrought a quiet revolution at the time and subsequently changed the character of the traditional synagogue in America.[8]

Improved education for Jewish women was a major concern of Isaac Leeser's. The introduction of the mixed pew or family seating was a dramatic break with religious tradition, in the wake of which all subsequent steps, including the ordination of women, are but a logical consequence. Further innovations of the movement regarding the religious life of women include Jewish education for women; the bat-mitzvah, first on Friday night and now, increasingly on Saturday morning; aliyot for women; and a takkanah permitting the counting of women in a minyan.[9] In addition, the agunah problem has been resolved by the new *ketubah*, the antenuptial agreement, and a willingness to perform, when necessary, *hafka'at kiddushin*. Intentionally or unintentionally, the movement toward equalizing the position of women has strengthened Conservative Judaism. In contrast, "perhaps the single most disruptive force, or strain to American Jewish Orthodoxy has been the subordination of women."[10] The enhanced position of women has proved and continues to prove to be a beacon in our movement to attract persons who are disenchanted with the position of women in Orthodoxy.

The women who want to become Conservative rabbis are, almost exclusively, products of the Conservative movement, of our Ramah camps, of our synagogues, of our Seminary. They have been raised in a movement which offered them equal education. They were encouraged to pursue Jewish learning and, at the same time, not to close themselves off from the world around them. It comes as no surprise that these women, having been raised like their "brothers," want, like their "brothers," to pursue a career in the rabbinate. What is surprising is, rather, the negative reception these women often receive.

It is of little use to admit women to the Rabbinical School if, in so doing, we are to alienate our lay membership. The 1973 United Synagogue resolution previously mentioned indicates that the lay leadership was then in favor of opening the Conservative rabbinate to women. It is reasonable to assume that they are now, with the passage of another six years, even more strongly in favor. The younger membership, which is the future membership, is heavily in favor of ordaining women. Using *Liebman-Shapiro* Table II, one can easily calculate that, while 15.1% of the members under 35 responding think that they would be disappointed or leave the Conservative movement if women were ordained, 38.6% of the respondents think that they would be disappointed or leave the movement if women were NOT ordained.[11] Why risk alienating such a high percentage of the movement's future? Table I of the survey indicates that of the respondents 28.3% would be alienated (leave or be disappointed) if women were *NOT* ordained, 20.8%, if they were. Thus, despite the preponderance of re-

spondents in the upper age brackets, a significantly larger
proportion favors ordination of women, than objects to it. In
terms of denominational identity (Table III), the only group
significantly opposed to ordaining women is the one which
identifies itself as Orthodox. Those people, by their own admission, do not really consider themselves part of the Conservative movement. Although they constitute only 3.4% of the
respondents they constitute one tenth (10.1%) of those opposed to ordaining women, and a quarter (24.1%) of those who
would leave if women were ordained.[12] Although we are
certainly grateful for their participation, we should remember
that some of them are doubtless with us by default, because
there is no Orthodox synagogue in the area. Were there one
they would probably join it. We cannot permit fear of their loss,
which may well come about for other reasons to lead us to
disregard the bulk of our membership. As this survey con-
firms, the bulk of the membership is prepared for the ordination of women.

SUMMARY

The ordination of women is a move for which Conservative
Judaism is ready. The halakhic analysis has been done, the laity
has been polled, our sense of ethics compels it. The move will
benefit Conservative Judaism. In the first instance, the discussion over the past few years has aroused a great deal of interest
in the halakhic process. While there is a long road from interest
to observance, the interest comes first. A decision to ordain
women will prove that, faced with a complex problem, the
Halakhah can come up with an answer within a reasonable
length of time. We will have opened to us a new source of
capable, committed and talented rabbinic leadership. The
problem will have been finally resolved, allowing us to turn
our attention to other important tasks which lie before us. We
must face the need to convert our nominal membership to a
meaningful membership. To do this we must show them that
the Halakhah has credibility, that it can function in this time

and on this continent. The admission of women to the Rabbinical school will give a signal to the young committed products of our movement, many of whom are involved in *havurot* and *minyanim* outside of synagogues, that we are open to change, to diversity, and finally to offering once again a dynamic program for traditional Judaism.

Appendix A

Proceedings of the Rabbinical Assembly
Volume XXXVII, 1975, p. 278

XIV. RESOLUTION REGARDING WOMEN AS RABBIS

The Rabbinical Assembly, in Convention assembled, hereby declares its desire to admit to membership in the Rabbinical Assembly, qualified applicants regardless of sex.

It further calls upon its members to work toward an end to discriminatory treatment in their individual synagogues.

It was duly moved and seconded that this proposal be adopted as a Convention resolution. During the discussion of this proposal, Rabbi Yaakov Rosenberg made the following amendment: "The Rabbinical Assembly, in Convention assembled, instructs its administration to do everything in its power to bring our influence to bear upon our alma mater, to make sure that the Jewish Theological Seminary of America admits qualified applicants to the Rabbinical School." Rabbi Rosenberg's amendment was duly seconded. After further discussion, during which opinions were expressed both in favor of and in opposition to the proposal and the amendment, Rabbi Herschel Portnoy moved that

the discussion of the proposal concerning the acceptance into member-
ship of women rabbis be tabled until a time when the entire member-
ship of The Rabbinical Assembly will first have been notified that the
discussion will take place, and that a vote will be taken, so that all of
our colleagues may carefully consider the matter and exercise their
vote. This motion to table was duly seconded, and passed.

Appendix B

Proceedings of the Rabbinical Assembly
Volume XXXVIII, 1976, pp. 322–323

XII. MEMBERSHIP

BE IT RESOLVED that the Rabbinical Assembly direct its Committee on Membership to consider applications for membership in the Rabbinical Assembly of otherwise qualified candidates regardless of their sex.

BE IT RESOLVED that the Rabbinical Assembly call upon the
Jewish Theological Seminary of America to admit otherwise
qualified candidates to the Rabbinical School regardless of sex.

The Rabbinical Assembly calls upon the United Synagogue
of America and its affiliated congregations to move with expe-
dition to bring about full equality, regardless of sex, within the
Synagogue.

This resolution was tabled.

Appendix C

Proceedings of the Rabbinical Assembly
Volume XXXIX, 1977, p. 139

I. THE ROLE OF WOMEN

The Resolutions Committee has revised its resolution as follows:

WHEREAS the Conservative movement initiated educational policies of equal intensive Jewish education for our daughters and our sons, and

WHEREAS the Conservative movement pioneered the ceremony of Bat Mitzvah to accord ritual expression to women, and

WHEREAS the Rabbinical Assembly has supported equal status of women within the synagogue, and

WHEREAS two major rabbinic seminaries now ordain women, and

WHEREAS we recognize the enormous potential for enhancing our people by utilizing the wisdom and commitment of our people, regardless of sex, and

WHEREAS Article III of the Constitution of The Rabbinical Assembly provides that all "upon whom the title of Rabbi has been duly and properly conferred by a recognized rabbinical seminary or by Semikha; provided, however, that they have the secular training equivalent to the requirement for a college degree" shall be eligible for membership.

BE IT RESOLVED that The Rabbinical Assembly encourages the Jewish Theological Seminary of America to consider and to admit to the Rabbinical School all qualified candidates regardless of their sex.

After discussion, the following substitute resolution was presented from the floor, was duly seconded and adopted.

BE IT RESOLVED that The Rabbinical Assembly respectfully petitions the Chancellor of The Jewish Theological Seminary of America to establish an interdisciplinary commission to study all aspects of the role of women as spiritual leaders in the Conservative movement.

BE IT FURTHER RESOLVED that this study commission, whose membership shall reflect the pluralism and diversity of the Conservative movement, shall be responsible for a progress report on its findings to be presented to the Executive Council of The Rabbinical Assembly in the spring of 1978 and for a final report and recommendation at the 1979 convention of The Rabbinical Assembly.

Appendix D

Attitudes toward Ordination of Women among Respondents under Age 35

Based on Liebman-Shapiro Table II
Respondents under 35 = 963 respondents
    588 women
  + 375 men
    963

273.4 women (46.5% of 588 women) would probably leave or be disappointed if women were NOT ordained

 97.9 men (26.1% of 375 men) would probably leave or be disappointed if women were NOT ordained

371.3 Total disappointed or probably leave if women NOT ordained is 38.6% of 963 respondents

68.2 women (11.6% of 588 women) would probably leave or be
disappointed if women were ordained
77.2 men (20.6% of 375 men) would probably leave or be
disappointed if women were ordained
_____
145.4 Total disappointed or probably leave if women were
ordained is 15.1% of 963 respondents.

Appendix E

The Orthodox-Identified and the Ordination of Women

Based on Liebman-Shapiro Tables III and I
138 women (2.9% of 4765 women) identify as Orthodox
178 men (3.8% of 4618 men) identify as Orthodox
316 respondents (3.4% of 9383) identify as Orthodox

Orthodox identified disappointed or probably leave if women
were ordained
87.1 women (63.1% of 138)
110 men (61.8% of 178)
197.1 respondents who are Orthodox-identified disappointed or probably leave if women were ordained

1951.7 respondents (20.8% of 9383 total respondents) disappointed or probably leave if women were ordained
10.1% of respondents (197.1 of 1951.7) who would be disappointed or probably leave if women were ordained are
Orthodox-identified

Orthodox-identified who would probably leave if women were ordained

52 women	(37.7% of 138)
61 men	(34.3% of 178)

113 respondents who are Orthodox-identified and will probably leave if women were ordained.

469.1 respondents (5% of 9383 total respondents) would probably leave if women were ordained

24.1% of respondents (113 of 469.1) who would probably leave if women were ordained are Orthodox-identified.

NOTES

1. Susan Dworkin, "Henrietta Szold," *Response* #18, p. 43.
2. Sally Priesand, *Judaism and the New Woman* (New York, 1975), p. 62.
3. *Proceedings of the 1973 Biennial Convention of the United Synagogue of America, November 11-15, 1973*, pp. 108–109.
4. See Appendices A, B, C.
5. *Proceedings of the Rabbinical Assembly, 1951, #15*, p. 140.
6. It may be of passing interest that one of the women ordained at another Seminary is reputed to observe *taharat ha-mishpachah*. Stephanie Dickstein, in an unpublished paper on "Feminism, Jewish Observance and Jewish Womanhood: A Study of Joint Program Women," concludes "that when women are committed to a Judaism which they respect, feminism does not lessen their observance. It does, in fact, have the opposite effect on these women who confront the issue of equality in ritual practice and decide they will take on equal responsibilities."
7. See S. Y. Agnon, "Shnei Talmidei Hachamim. . . ."
8. Moshe Davis, *The Emergence of Conservative Judaism* (Philadelphia: JPS, 1963), p. 124.
9. Rabbi Samuel Rosinger recalling his reactions to seeing Henrietta Szold participating in Professor Louis Ginzberg's class in 1904 said: "Yet, even in these ultra-modern days, it was certainly a unique experience to behold a Jewess, and an American product at that, attending one of the most abstruse courses which a theological institution can offer young men preparing themselves for the ministry." *Lives and Voices*, ed. Samuel F. Chyet (Philadelphia: JPS, 1972), p. 126. Seventy-five years later, the participation of knowledgeable women in Rabbinical school courses is commonplace. One might hope that seventy-five years is long enough an apprenticeship.
10. Marshall Sklare, *Conservative Judaism: An American Religious Movement* (Schocken, 1972), pp. 86 ff.
11. Appendix D
12. Appendix E

An Advocate's Halakhic Responses on the Ordination of Women

MAYER E. RABINOWITZ

The question of the ordination of women by the Jewish Theological Seminary of America has been debated within the
Faculty and the Movement for nearly ten years. Proponents of
both sides have written extensively on this issue, using both
halakhic and non-halakhic arguments.[1] The purpose of this
paper is to address some of the halakhic problems raised by the
opponents of women's ordination.

The halakhic objections raised relate exclusively to functions
that a rabbi is commonly but not necessarily expected to
perform, such as acting as a *mesadder kiddushin, sheliaḥ tzibbur*, a
witness to a *get* or *ketubah*, or to be counted in a *minyan*.

The opponents to ordination claim, on the basis of the fact
that the *Halakhah* presently prohibits women from performing
these functions, that ordaining them would place them in an
equivocal position, tempting them to transgress the law.[2]
Those who ordained them would thus be violating the biblical
injunction of "Before one who is blind [in a certain matter] do
not place a stumbling block" (Lev. 19:14) and the rabbinic
prohibition against assisting transgressors.[3]

Before addressing the more substantive objections, one may
question the validity of the charge of "misleading the blind."
How could anyone be "blind" in this matter when so much has
already been said and written? In regard to the substantive
objections, the tradition records various opinions concerning

the status of women vis-à-vis these functions. To claim that one's own interpretation of halakhic tradition is the *only* tenable one is to close one's eyes to the realities of the historic development of the *Halakhah*.

A study of the sources dealing with the aforementioned functions reveals that while it was customary to have men perform them, it does not follow that their performance now must be restricted to men.

This paper will seek to demonstrate that from an authentic halakhic point of view, a woman—

1. may be a *mesadderet kiddushin;*
2. may be counted in a *minyan;*
3. may serve as a witness; and
4. may serve as what is now designated as a *sheliah tzibbur.*

Anyone having even a minimum knowledge of the history of the legal codes of any known society knows that legal definitions and applications are influenced by time and place, no matter what transcendent authority may be involved. The *Halakhah* was no exception to this universal experience of mankind. When the Rabbis defined a term or structured an institution, they did so both as interpreters of a historic tradition and as contemporary leaders mindful of the social realities of their own time. Hence, in some cases long-established halakhic procedures were dramatically changed because of significant changes in social conditions. Hillel's well-known institutionalization of the *prozbul,* as well as the less-well-known changes made in the requirements for questioning of witnesses in monetary cases, come to mind.[4] As will be indicated later, in other cases the concept or the institution was retained, but the definition of the one and the function of the other were substantively changed.

I. MESADDER KIDDUSHIN (WEDDING OFFICIANT)

One of the arguments raised for prohibiting a woman from serving as a *mesadderet kiddushin* is that the *Halakhah* requires the presence of a *minyan* for the recitation of the *birkhat hatanim* (the wedding benedictions). It is argued theoretically that it is the community at large which is bestowing the blessing. The one who actually recites them is but the *sheliah tzibbur* (the emissary of the community), and a woman may not act in that capacity.[5]

It is also claimed that intimations of this idea are found in Genesis (24:60) and Ruth (4:2, 10), and that *Massekhet Kallah* attributes biblical origin to *birkhat hatanim*.[6]

An analysis of these arguments and sources reveals, however, that (1) the biblical sources quoted do not refer to *birkhat hatanim* at all; and (2) the reciter of the *birkhat hatamin* is not conceived as the emissary of the community and is, therefore, not a *sheliah tzibbur*.

The Biblical Sources

The verse in Genesis 24:60 reads: "And they blessed Rivkah and said to her, "O sister, may you grow into thousands of myriads." It was a blessing given by the family to a sister and daughter before she left their home. Indeed it could in no way be similar to the *birkhat hatanim* because the groom, Isaac, was not present. The Tosafot refer to this verse as but an *asmakhta*, as being but a tenuous biblical support for the rabbinic enactment regarding *birkhat hatanim*.[7] The clear literal meaning of the verse does not indicate that it can in any way be construed as the prototype for the present-day *birkhat hatanim* or *birkhat erusin*.[8]

Nor do the verses in Ruth refer to *birkhat hatanim*. They refer, rather, to the witnessing of a legal transaction. Boaz collected ten men (4:2) in order to witness legal arrangements relating to the sale of Elimelekh's property. Verse 9 clearly states: "and Boaz said to the elders and to the rest of the people, you are witnesses today that I am acquiring from Naomi all that belonged to Elimelekh."

According to the Talmud, the verses from Ruth seem to indicate that a quorum of ten is required for *birkhat hatanim*.[9] However, since the Talmud also accepts the fact that the bridegroom can be counted as one of those ten,[10] why did Boaz gather ten men rather than nine plus himself? Obviously, the verse was not dealing with *birkhat hatanim* but, rather, with a legal transaction. The Tosafot state that this verse is only an *asmakhta*.[11]

Is the Mesadder Kiddushin a Sheliah Tzibbur?

Before answering this question some terms must be defined. (1) *Birkhat erusin* is recited before betrothal takes place. There is no talmudic source that indicates that a *minyan* is required. In fact, there is a dispute among the codifiers concerning this issue.[12] According to Freiman,[13] the reason that the requirement of a *minyan* was instituted by R. Ahai (680–752 C.E.) was to publicize the betrothal. This need arose to help overcome malpractice and secret marriages. (2) *Birkhat hatanim* or *sheva berakhot* (seven blessings) is recited after the betrothal takes place and at the conclusion of meals for a period of seven days following the wedding. The Talmud requires a *minyan* for the recitation of these blessings, and the *hatan* himself may be counted in the *minyan*.[14]

Birkhat erusin is recited by the *mesadder kiddushin*, while *birkhat hatanim* may be recited by other individuals as well. Since there is no talmudic source for requiring a *minyan* for *birkhat erusin*, and it may be recited without a *minyan*, it follows that the reciter of the blessings is not representing a community or serving as *sheliah tzibbur*. In fact, most codes permit the *hatan* himself to recite the blessing.

The Rambam states: "Anyone who betrothes a woman, whether he does it himself or through an agent, either he or his agent must recite a blessing before the *kiddushin*."[15] The *Tur* also states that the *hatan* may recite the blessing.[16] The *Shulhan Arukh* concurs with the Rambam, and the Rema adds: "Some say that someone else recites the blessing, and that is the custom."[17] Rabbi Moses of Coucy (13th century) says:

> In the West it is customary for the man who betrothes to recite the blessing himself before he betrothes—unlike the practice in these countries [where Rabbi Moses lived] where the betrother

himself does not recite the blessing but rather someone else does.[18]

Rav Sar Shalom (died ca. 859) says that if there is no one competent to recite the blessing except the *hatan*, then the *hatan* recites the blessings for himself.[19] Obviously, the *hatan* is not serving as a *sheliah tzibbur*.

None of the reasons given for having someone other than the *hatan* recite the *birkhat erusin* is related to the concept of *sheliah tzibbur*. Rav Sar Shalom says: "If there is someone else who can recite the blessing, the *hatan* should not recite it, for it makes the *hatan* look like an arrogant person."[20] Rabbi Avraham ben Nathan Hayarhi (1155–1215) is of the opinion that the *hatan* cannot recite the blessings with the proper concentration or intention.[21] Still others say that the custom was instituted in order not to embarrass a *hatan* who cannot recite the blessings.[22]

Clearly, then, the *mesadder kiddushin* who recites the *birkhat erusin* is not acting as a *sheliah tzibbur* representing the community. The purpose of the blessing is similar to all other *birkhot mitzvah*, i.e., to recite a blessing before performing an act. Since the *mesadder kiddushin* may recite the blessings for the *hatan* (though he himself is not betrothing), the *mesadder kiddushin* is representing, at most, the *hatan* alone.

Rabbi Tzvi Hirsch Eisenstadt quotes the following discussion concerning *birkhat erusin:*

> It is clear that if both the bride and groom are deaf, the *birkhat erusin* may not be recited, since neither one of the couple would hear it and the blessing would be recited in vain. However, if only the *hatan* is deaf, there are grounds to permit the blessing to be recited. The reason is that the bride would hear it and, therefore, the blessing would not be recited in vain.[23]

Obviously, according to this reasoning the bride is considered as a party to the *birkhat erusin*.

This approach is most suggestive of the conditions we find today. The bride and groom are both involved in, and considered partners in, all aspects of the decision to marry. And since the *birkhat erusin* is being recited on behalf of the woman as well as the man, there is no reason to restrict the performance of this function to men alone.

Birkhat hatanim or *sheva berakhot* are blessings of prayer and praise.[24] The fact that they are recited at the conclusion of meals for seven days following the wedding indicates that they are not *birkhot mitzvah*, blessings to be recited before performing a specific act. Since women are not prohibited from reciting blessings of prayer and praise, there is no reason to prohibit them from reciting *birkhat hatanim*.[25]

To summarize, a woman can be a *mesadderet kiddushin* because: (1) there is no *sheliah tzibbur* involved; (2) the bride is equally a part of *birkhat erusin*; (3) *birkhot hatanim* are blessings of prayer and praise which may be recited by women; and (4) there is no biblical basis for either *birkhat erusin* or *birkhat hatanim*.

II. MINYAN

Another objection that is sometimes raised against ordaining women involves counting women in a *minyan*. According to some, a *minyan* consists of people sharing the same *hiyuv*, (obligation of prayer). Since women's obligations in prayer are different from those of men, it is argued that women cannot be counted in a *minyan*.[26] According to this argument, women should not be ordained because it would be inappropriate to exclude a woman rabbi from the *minyan* in her synagogue.

An analysis of the sources dealing with *minyan* reveals that equality of obligation in not a consideration for being counted in a *minyan*. Other criteria were used to define who could be counted in a *minyan*, and we maintain that these very criteria, when applied today, would support the counting of women in the *minyan*.

Biblical Sources

The requirement of a *minyan* for acts of sanctification (*devarim shebekedushah*) is found in *Megillah* 23b. Commenting on the

Mishnah which lists those acts requiring a quorum of ten persons, the Talmud states:

> From where do we derive the rules? Rabbi Hiyya bar Abba said in the name of Rabbi Yohanan, "Scripture says: 'That I may be sanctified in the midst of the Israelite people' [Lev. 22:32]. All matters of sanctification require no less than ten." How do we derive this from this verse? As Rabbi Hiyya taught, we derive it from the fact that the term *the midst* occurs both here [in Leviticus 22:32], which reads: "That I may be sanctified in *the midst* of the Israelite people," as well as in Numbers 16:21, which reads: "Stand back from *the midst* of this community." And just as in Numbers 14:27, which states: "How much longer shall that wicked community . . ." The term *community* refers to the ten wicked spies, so in Numbers 16:21 the term *community* refers to ten adults.[27]

The Rabbis thus derive the requirement of the presence of a *minyan* (ten adult Jews) "for acts of sanctification" in two steps.

a. They equate the term "the Israelite people" which occurs in Leviticus 22:23 with the term *edah* ("community") which occurs in Numbers 16:21, by noting that the Bible uses the term *tokh* ("the midst") in connection with both of them.
b. They arrive at the definition of the term *edah* ("community") as referring to ten adult Israelites by interpreting the phrase "that wicked community" as referring to the ten spies who brought evil reports regarding the Promised Land.[28]

The requirement of ten is, thus, based upon a tenuous connection established among three distinct verses—none of which is in any way associated with prayer or a quorum. This point was recognized by the Ran, who said that these verses are merely an *asmakhta*, since prayer itself was introduced by the Rabbis and therefore could not be biblical.[28a]

The main thrust for the requirement of ten for acts of sanctification, however, is based upon Leviticus 22:32: "That I may be sanctified in the midst of the Israelite people."[29] This verse, which follows rules and regulations concerning sacrifices, states their purpose: "You shall not profane my Holy name, that I may be sanctified in the midst of the Israelite people." Disobeying these laws profanes God's name, while obeying them sanctifies God's name. That is all that the *pshat* (literal meaning) of the verses conveys.

The verse does not state that a quorum is necessary, nor did the Rabbis rule that the rituals mentioned in the prior verses require a *minyan*. Nor does the term "Israelite people" as used in the verse exclude women. Since women were neither prohibited nor exempt from bringing sacrifices, this verse might well be understood to include women. In fact, the Mishnah simply states "less than ten."[30] It does not specify "ten males," nor does it specifically exclude women as it does in other cases.[31] The only ones specifically excluded are "slaves and minors." Thus also the early codifiers, when noting the requirements of a *minyan*, state merely *asarah gedolim u-vnai horin*—"ten adults who are free" (i.e., not slaves).[32]

Some opponents to the ordination of women base their position on the following sources: (a) Rabbi Joseph Caro (d.1575) states: "It [the *kaddish*] cannot be recited with fewer than ten adult free males."[33] (b) Rabbi Mordekhai Yaffe (d.1612) states that the most common meaning of *b'nai yisrael* ("Israelites," as used in the verse "so that I may be sanctified amongst the Israelites") is "adult males."[34] He also adds that slaves, women, and minors do not count in the quorum because they are not "obligated" to recite the Shema and to pray. But Rabbi Joseph Caro does not explain why he felt it necessary to add the term "males" when the Mishnah and the codifiers who preceded him did not deem it necessary to do so.

Rabbi Mordekhai Yaffe does not deem it necessary to validate his position that equality of obligation is a requirement for being counted in a *minyan*. In fact, there is no basis for this requirement in the Talmud. It is a relatively late rabbinic addition to the *Halakhah* based not upon a Scriptural text but upon "reason" alone. Indeed, this very fact moved Rabbi David Feldman to try to validate this notion rationally.[35]

As we have seen the basic criteria qualifying one to be included in a *minyan* are: (1) *gedolim*—belonging to the class of adults, and (2) *b'nai horin*—being free individuals. In the rabbinic period women were at a certain age classified as adults, but never as being completely free, because they started life as being legally subservient either to father or brother, and, when married, to their husbands. No one in our society today can reasonably argue that a woman is not as legally free as a man. Nor would any one today challenge her status as an adult. The criteria for eligibility to be counted in a *minyan* have therefore not changed. What has changed is the reality which now enlarges the number of those who meet the criteria.

III. SHELIAH TZIBBUR

Another objection to the ordination of women is based on the opinion that a woman cannot serve as a *sheliah tzibbur*. According to this view, since only one who is "obligated" can fulfill the obligation of others (*lehozi aherim yedai hovatam*), women—who are not obligated in the same manner as men to pray—cannot serve as *sheliah tzibbur*. Accordingly, women should not be ordained, since a rabbi is often called upon to lead services.[36]

An analysis of the sources reveals that the historical function of the *sheliah tzibbur* has changed. Fulfilling the obligations of others is no longer the function of what we call the *sheliah tzibbur*. It is rather to ensure that the congregation prays together, and generally to enhance the service.

There are two terms used in rabbinic literature for the person who leads a congregation in prayer: *hazzan* and *sheliah tzibbur*. Although these terms are often used interchangeably,[37] they represent two distinct institutions,[38] and reflect the different functions which developed for different reasons.

Hazzan is used in tannaitic literature to indicate several functions. He was responsible for removing the Torah from the ark,[39] for giving instruction to the participants in the service,[40] and for determining the abilities of the prospective Torah readers.[41] He was not necessarily the Torah reader, although he decided who would read and, on occasion, he himself might read.[42] In the rabbinic period the *hazzan* was a synagogue official whose functions were similar to those of a sexton or an elementary school teacher in our day.[43] *Sheliah tzibbur* was and is used to describe the person who actually leads the service and who may fulfill the prayer obligations of others (*lehozi et harabim yedei hovatam*),[44] who are present at the service but who for various reasons could not themselves fulfill their obligations.

When does a *sheliah tzibbur* fulfill the obligations of others? According to the Rambam, when the people listen to the *sheliah tzibbur* and answer "Amen" after every blessing, it is as if they are praying themselves (i.e., he has enabled them to fulfill their obligation).[45] But, continues the Rambam, he who knows how to pray cannot have his obligation fulfilled by anyone other than himself. The *Tur* agrees.[46] However, the *Beit Yosef* defines the term *aino yodeah le-hitpallel* ("does not know how to pray") as referring to an individual who does not know how to recite the prayers, but who understands what the *sheliah tzibbur* is saying.[47] For him the *sheliah tzibbur* cannot fulfill his obligation.

While the *Shulhan Arukh* states that any individual can prevent a particular person from serving as a *sheliah tzibbur* by insisting that he does not consent to being "represented" by him, the *Magen Avraham* qualifies this statement by saying that it refers only to those times (*bizmaneihem*) when the *sheliah tzibbur* would fulfill the obligations of others by means of his own prayers. In those cases, says the *Magen Avraham*, the *sheliah tzibbur* is functioning as an agent, and must have everyone's consent. But now (*attah*), when everyone knows (*bekiim*) the prayers, the *sheliah tzibbur* serves not as the public agent, but, rather, for the recitation of *piyyutim*.[48] Note the change that has taken place in the concept of the function of the *sheliah tzibbur*. It is no longer that of "fulfilling the obligation of others," but rather that of leading in the recitation of prayers which in no way involve the concept of obligation.

The *Arukh Hashulhan* refers to a number of views regarding the manner in which one may fulfill his prayer obligations.[49]

One may do so: (1) by reciting the prayers in Hebrew whether or not one understands Hebrew; (2) by reciting the prayers in another language which one does understand; or (3) by listening to and understanding every word which the *sheliah tzibbur* recites[50] and, some say, by reciting every word with the *sheliah tzibbur* even if one does not understand what he is saying.

Today, when all of our congregants have prayerbooks with translations for those who cannot read Hebrew, and often with explanatory notes, we are in the category of competent worshippers (*bekiim*), and our obligations cannot be fulfilled by a *sheliah tzibbur*.

The *Shulhan Arukh* does indeed stipulate that the *amidah* should be repeated by the *sheliah tzibbur* even if the entire congregation has prayed and is competent.[51] But the reason given for this practice is not that of fulfilling the obligation incumbent upon any of the congregants, but rather that of *lekayem takkanat hakhamim*—to preserve an ordinance promulgated by the sages.[52] Obviously the repetition does not serve as an opportunity to have one's obligation fulfilled by the *sheliah tzibbur*. In today's synagogue the office of the *sheliah tzibbur* does not involve any concept of "agency." He is a *hazzan*, a leader of the communal prayer service, who ensures that the *minyan* prays *together*,[53] and who enhances the service by the manner in which he leads it. Hence the claim that a woman may not serve as a *hazzan* or *sheliah tzibbur* because she may not fulfill the prayer obligations of a male congregant has no halakhic validity today.

IV. EDUT

A major objection to the ordaining of women as rabbis is the fact that the *Halakhah* prohibits women from serving as witnesses in most cases. Since a rabbi is often called upon to serve as a witness to a *ketubah* or a *get*, a woman rabbi would be expected to serve in a presently halakhically prohibited role.

It has been demonstrated elsewhere that even if we assume that the prohibition of women as witnesses is biblical (*deoraita*),

the Rabbis have themselves formulated the principle that under certain circumstances *yesh khoah beyad hakhamim la-akor
davar min hatorah*, "the sages are empowered to abrogate even a
biblically rooted norm."[54] But, while this can be a rabbinically
valid solution, it is by no means clear that the prohibition is, in
fact, biblical. The sources indicate that even as the determining
factors in the case of the prohibition of counting women to a
minyan were not biblical verses but rather the social and func-
tional realities of earlier times,[55] so also were these realities
determinative in the case of the prohibition of having women
act as witnesses.

To be sure the *gemara* derives the prohibition from biblical
verses,[56] but the fact that the *gemara* cites biblical verses in
answer to the question *menah hanei milei* ("how do we know
. . .") is not proof that the injunction is biblical. It is often,
rather, an attempt by the Rabbis to associate an existing practice with biblical verses. The rabbinic affirmation *adam dan
gezeirah shavah lekayem talmudo*—that "one may have recourse to
a *gezeirah shava* in order to validate a tradition or a practice"—
indicates that the Rabbis were aware that a law or a widespread
practice whose origin was unknown was by them at times
"derived" from, or associated with, biblical verses by means of
the principle of *gezeira shava*,[57] the logically most questionable
of Rabbi Ishmael's thirteen principles by which the Torah was
to be interpreted.[58]

The Rambam considers as biblical the law prohibiting
women from acting as witnesses. However, he rejects the
proof-texts used by the *gemara*. Instead, he bases the prohibition upon the fact that the verse "by the mouth of two witnesses" (Deut. 17:6) is stated in the masculine and thus specifically excludes women.[59] The *Kesef Mishneh* ad loc. is unhappy
with this proof, since the Torah generally uses the masculine
form when it wishes to include both men and women.[60] Thus,
while the prohibition was generally accepted, its origin or
source was not clear. Perhaps that is why the Rambam wanted
to strengthen the prohibition by stating that it was biblical. The
Shulhan Arukh simply states that a woman is unfit to serve as a
witness without attributing this rule to the Bible.[61] It seems

clear, therefore, that some halakhic authorities recognized by the tradition did not consider the prohibition against women serving as witnesses to be indubitably biblical.

Moreover, the rabbis did permit women to serve as witnesses in certain cases. Commenting on the statement in the Mishnah that "any testimony for which a woman is not fit, those persons enumerated in the Mishnah also are not fit," the *gemara* says, "But if a woman is fit, they are also fit."[62]

The areas from which they were excluded are those in which they were considered as not being knowledgeable or reliable due to their lack of experience or interest. For example, their material status depended upon their husbands or fathers and, therefore, women were not conversant with, or interested in, monetary matters. The social reality was that women did not fit the definition of *gedolim u'venai horin* ("free adults").[63] This is no longer the case. Contemporary women have careers, are involved in all kinds of businesses and professions, and have proved to be as competent as men. Therefore, we must reclassify the status of women vis-à-vis *edut* based upon the realities of our era. The general criteria established by the Rabbis whereby one is to be adjudged qualified to serve as a witness may very well remain the same. What has changed is the reality which now enlarges the number of those who meet the criteria.

It may well take time before the acceptance of women's testimony will be legitimatized in traditional Jewish law. In any event, the politicized religious establishment in Israel would negate any position and denounce any action by the Conservative movement in the field of *Halakhah*. This fact has not stopped Conservative Judaism from acting in such areas as conversion and divorce. It should not stop us in the area of *edut*—or in the area of women's ordination.

NOTES

1. "On the Ordination of Women as Rabbis—Position Papers of the Faculty of the Jewish Theological Seminary of America," henceforth referred to as *Faculty Papers*.

2. Dr. Israel Francus, "On the Ordination of Women, *Faculty Papers*, p. 35.

3. *Avodah Zarah* 55b.

4. For discussion on *Prozbul,* see Mishnah Sheviit 10:2–3 and Gittin 36a–b. For questioning of witness see Sanhedrin 32a.

5. Dr. David Weiss Halivni, "On the Ordination of Women," *Faculty Papers*, pp. 3–7.

6. Chapter I.

7. See *Ketuboth* 7b, *Tosafot* s.v. *she-ne'emar*. See also *Bayit Hadash, Tur Even Haezer* 34, s.v. *hamekadesh*.

8. *Bayit Hadash,* loc. cit. The *Bah* (*Tur Even Haezer* 62, s.v. *ein mevarkhim*) states that *birkhat hatanim* is only a rabbinical enactment (*takkanat hakhamim*). According to the Rambam (*Hilkhoth Ishuth* 10:6), the blessings *einan meakvot* are not a necessity for the validity of the marriage. See also *Arukh Hashulhan, Even Haezer* 62:12.

9. *Ketuboth* 7b.

10. Ibid. 8a and *Megillah* 23b.

11. See *Prisha, Even Haezer* 62, note 11.

12. *Rosh, Ketuboth,* chap. 1, 12; *Tur, Even Haezer* 34; *Shulhan Arukh,* Even Haezer 34, 4; The Rambam does not mention any requirement of a *minyan* for *birkhat erusin.*

13. *Seder Kiddushin ve-Nissuin,* pp. 16 ff.; see also I. Klein, *Guide to Jewish Religious Practice,* pp. 394–95.

14. See above notes 9, 10.

15. *Hilkhot Ishuth* 3:23.

16. *Even Haezer* 34.

17. Ibid.

18. *Sefer Mitzvot Gadol* (SEMAG) *Hilkhot Kiddushin,* p. 125a. See also *Hagaot Maimoniyot Hilkhot Ishut* 3:23, note 40.

19. *Ozar Hagaonim,* B. M. Levin, *Ketubot,* p. 16.

20. Ibid.

21. *Sefer Hamanhig,* ed. Y. Rafael, vol. II, p. 540: "Even though in all the commandments the person who performs the commandments recites the blessing, the bridegroom, since he is harried and nervous, will not be able to concentrate on the blessing."

22. *Turei Zahav, Baer Haitev, Beit Shmuel Even Haezer* 34. For a full discussion of the reasons given for having someone else recite the blessings, see *Sedei Hemed Hashalaim,* vol. VII (*maarekhet hatan v'kallah*) p. 39, par. 18.

23. *Pithei Teshuvah, Even Haezer* 34, note 1.

24. See, for example, *Ketuboth* 8a, Rashi s.v. *sameah.* See also *Mahzor Vitry* (chap. 472, p. 590) and *Siddur of R. Solomon Ben Samson of Garmaise* (ed. M. Hershler, p. 248). The *Abudraham,* Wertheimer edition (Jerusalem, 5723), pp. 359 ff., has a complete discussion of all of these blessings. See also *Arukh Hashulhan, Even Haezer* 34, 2 ff.

25. For an example of the present-day debate on this issue, see Joel Wolowelsky in *Amudim,* Kislev 5743, pp. 86–88.

26. Weiss-Halivni, op. cit., pp. 8–9.

27. See *Berakhot* 21b for variants in this quotation both in names and in the text itself.

28. Numbers 14:27 obviously does not refer to the ten spies but, rather, to the community that accepted the report of the spies. This community must have included women as well.

28a. Ran to *Megillah* 23b, s.v. *ve-ein nosin*. See also E. Urbach *Hahalkhah-mekorateha Vehitpathutah Yad la-Talmud*, 1984, p. 80, where Urbach shows that laws derived by *midrash* were not considered biblical if another interpretation of the verse was possible.

29. *Berakhot* 21b. This verse is used to prove the opinion that the *kedushah* (which is recited during the repetition of the *amidah*) cannot be recited by an individual but requires a community. This opinion became the accepted *halakhah*. The opposing opinion does not consider this verse as a proof that the *kedushah* requires ten.

30. *Megillah* 4:3.

31. See, for example, *Mishnah Berakhot* 3:3, 7:2; *Hagigah* 1:1; *Kidushin* 1:7.

32. Rambam, *Hilkhot Tefillah* 8:4. See *Kesef Mishneh, Hilkhot Berakhot* 5:7, and Rambam, *Hilkhot Berakhot* 2:9, where it is specified that the *minyan* cannot contain slaves or minors. The *Tur (Orah Hayyim* 55) states that these ten must all be free people and adults who have signs of puberty.

The *Beit Yosef, Orah Hayyim* 55, discusses the different points of view regarding the inclusion of one minor to complete the quorum. The *Kol Bo* 11 cites cases where even three minors could be counted. The proof-text of this is *Mishnah Megillah* 4:6, which prohibits a minor from fulfilling the obligation of others but does not prohibit a minor from being counted in a *minyan*.

Even though most authorities do not permit counting a minor, the fact that some authorities would include minors who are not obligated proves that the equality of *hiyyuv* is not a consideration for being counted in a *minyan*. The reason given that it is permissible to count minors is that the *shekhinah* requires a minimum of ten. Therefore, any group of ten conforms to the requirement "that I may be sanctified in the midst of the Israelite people."

The *Kol Bo* 11, quoting the *Sheilthoth* of *Rav Ahai*, states that ten people who have completed their prayers and have heard *kedushah, kaddish, barkhu,* and the whole order of the service, can be counted in another *minyan* to help one person who has not recited the prayers. If equality of obligation is a consideration, then people who have completed their obligation should not be eligible to be counted. Since they are counted, it follows that a *minyan* can be composed of people, some of whom are obligated and some of whom are not.

A person who is under a ban *(menudeh)* cannot be counted in a *minyan*. (Rambam *Hilkhot Talmud Torah* 7:4, *Tur, Yoreh Deah* 334). Even though a *menudeh* is obligated to pray, he cannot be counted. Once again, we see that equality of obligation is not a consideration for being counted in a *minyan*.

33. *Shulhan Arukh, Orah Hayyim* 55:1.

34. *Levush Hatekhelet* 55:4.

35. "Women's Role and Jewish Law," *Conservative Judaism*, XXVI, 4:36. He uses the case of an *onen* as proof. For a refutation of his argument, see *Birkhei Yosef* (the Hida), *Orah Hayyim* 55:5.

36. See above, note 26.

37. For example, *Arukh Hashulhan*, entry *hazzan*, and *Ikar Tosafot Yom Tov* to

Mishnah Shabbat 1:3 and *Tur Orah Hayyim* 124. The *Abudraham*, p. 126, says that the *sheliah tzibbur* is customarily called the *hazzan*.

38. See *Rosh, Berakhot* chap. 5, 17; *Mordekhai, Megillah* 817; *Tosafot Berakhot* 34a, s.v. *lo*.

39. *Mishnah Yoma* 7:1; *Mishnah Sotah* 7:7.

40. *Tosefta Sukkah* 4:6, *Tosefta Taanit* 1:14.

41. *Mishnah Shabbat* 1:3, See *Shabbat* 11a and Rashi ad loc., s.v. *ha'hazzan*.

42. *Tosefta Megillah* 3:13 and *Tosefta Kifshuta* ad loc., p. 1196.

43. Salo Baron, *A Social and Religious History of the Jews*, vol. II, p. 367.

44. See, for example, Rambam, *Hilkhot Tefillah* 8:4, 9–10; *Tur Orah Hayyim* 128; *Shulhan Arukh Orah Hayyim* 53:19; 124:1; *Arukh Hashulhan Orah Hayyim* 124.

45. Rambam, *Hilkhot Tefillah* 8:4, 9–10, and 9:3, 9.

46. *Orah Hayyim* 124.

47. Ibid., s.v. *u'leahar*.

48. *Orah Hayyim* 53:19, note 20. *Kaddish* is recited by mourners who are not acting in the capacity of *sheliah tzibbur*, and the congregation can be a respondent to the doxology. It may be recited only if a *minyan* is present but that does not mean that it requires a *sheliah tzibbur*. It is widely accepted that women may recite *kaddish* and the congregation may respond. Professor Saul Lieberman permitted it in The Seminary, and he listened and answered Amen.

49. *Orah Hayyim* 124.

50. Commenting on the word *yekhaven* used by the *Tur* and *Shulhan Arukh* (*Orah Hayyim* 124, 1), the *Beit Yosef* and *Magen Avraham* interpret it to mean "understand," for otherwise *yekhaven* is an inappropriate word.

51. *Orah Hayyim* 124, 3.

52. The reason why this repetition will not be considered a *berakhah le-vattalah* is precisely because of the *takkanah*. The rabbis did not want to differentiate between various *minyanim* and, therefore, decreed that the *amidah* should always be repeated. Similarly, in the case when there is no one benefitting from the public recitation of *kiddush* and *berakhah ahat me-ein sheva*, the reciter is not acting as a *sheliah tzibbur*. To omit any of the above would result in a rule that varies according to circumstances (*natatah devarekha lesheiurin*), and the rabbis refrained from doing that.

A different reason for the repetition of the *amidah* in a congregation that is competent is to enable the congregation to recite *kedushah* (*Arukh Hashulhan, Orah Hayyim* 124:3, quoting the *Tur*). Once again, the person leading the service is not acting as an agent to fulfill the obligations of others.

53. With regard to *kaddish*, see note 48. In the recitation of *barkhu* the leader is not serving as an agent who fulfills the obligation of the congregation, but, rather, offers the congregation the opportunity to respond. This is exactly what occurs when a person recites the blessing before the Torah reading. It is interesting to note that the Codes refer to fulfilling one's obligation only in the case of the repetition of the *amidah*. Concerning *kaddish* and *barkhu* the Codes talk about responding (*onim*). In addition, it was customary for the congregation to recite a prayer while the leader recited *barkhu* (see *Tur, Orah Hayyim* 57). If one must listen in order to have his obligation fulfilled, the

leader in this case would not be fulfilling the obligation of the congregation, since the congregation is reciting a prayer at that time. As far as *kedushah*, there is no talmudic requirement to say it (*Kol Bo, Hilkhoth Tefillah* 11).

54. Dr. Joel Roth, "On the Ordination of Women as Rabbis," p. 160.

55. See above, p. 112.

56. *Shevuot* 30a.

57. T. P. *Pesahim* 33a (chap. 6:1). In this case we do not have to worry about the possibility of misusing this rule of hermeneutics due to the fact that the outcome is already known.

58. S. Lieberman, *Hellenism in Jewish Palestine* (New York: Jewish Theological Seminary, 1962), p. 61.

59. *Hilkhot Edut* 9:2. See also SEMAG, *Lavim* 214. However, the SEMAG does not say *min hatorah* in the case of women, but he does say *min hatorah* in the case of *reshaim*. It is noteworthy that the *Tur, Hoshen Mishpat* 35, omits women from the list of incompetent witnesses.

60. Similar objections are raised by the *Kesef Mishneh* and *Lehem Mishneh* concerning the proofs used by the Rambam for prohibiting slaves and fools from serving as witnesses.

61. *Hoshen Mishpat* 35:1, 14.

62. *Rosh Hashanah* 22a. See *Torah Temimah, Devarim* 19:15, note 44, and *Encyclopaedia Judaica*, vol 16, 586, for a list of cases where women are admitted as competent witnesses.

63. See above p. 55. It is interesting to note that the *Encyclopedia Talmudit* (s.v. *ishah*), when discussing the status of women as witnesses, uses the term "trustworthiness" as the topical subheading rather than *edut*.

A Brief Position Paper on the Ordination of Women

DAVID G. ROSKIES

What is it that we wish to renew? Is it Judaism, ossified after centuries of enforced isolation, or is it Americanism, grown fat and self-indulgent after decades of untrammeled growth?

And how shall renewal be wrought? Shall we take the neo-classical stance of the Mitnagdim and uphold the old values of Torah and discipline; shall we, like the Hasidim, perpetrate a "creative betrayal" of an earlier tradition by reappropriating its vocabulary, dress, code, stories, and songs; or shall we engage in the subversive tactics of the Haskalah?

In our day, Orthodoxy, be it in the guise of Lubavitsh, Gush Emunim, or Lincoln Square, is making a comeback by exploiting a sense of apocalypse, of the Decline of the West, our fear of the chaos that reigns in the political and moral spheres. We return to strict segregation, ritualism, an image of pre-industrial society, *Gemeinschaft*, and unabashed Jewish patriotism to demonstrate our rejection of the modern world.

At the other extreme is Jewish secularism, which has so clearly played itself out that it is fitting for Irving Howe and others to wax eloquent over it. Things have gotten so bad that hardly anyone will own up to being a cosmopolitan anymore.

Which leaves us with the strategy of "creative betrayal," a term coined by Gershon Shaked to designate the free adaptation of the classics into Hebrew. It is very much an ongoing process. Just as Hasidism reshaped Lurianic Kabbalah in its

125

own image, so Peretz, Berdichevsky, Buber, Wiesel, and Havurat Shalom reshaped Hasidism in their own image. What makes this approach so Jewish is that it seeks to legitimate the new in the name of the old. It is the dialectical tension out of which Conservative Judaism was born and continues to thrive.

Creative betrayal is essentially midrashic, for it tries to relate the unrelated, to reconcile irreconcilables. Feminism and Judaism are two such polarities. The time has come to mediate between them, and of all the movements in Jewry, ours, I think, is uniquely equipped for the task.

If we adopt a non-apocalyptic view of the world, and if we assume, as I do, that on the specific issue of women, it is Judaism that has been lax and unresponsive while Feminism has unleashed a vast reservoir of creativity and commitment, then what follows is a creative betrayal of tradition in the name of this new and vital force. If we believe, furthermore, that the Synagogue, not the golf course, not the community center or the B'nai B'rith lodge, is the dynamic focus of Jewish life, then the Synagogue must be an arena for women to assume leadership positions. To channel this energy into the pulpit rabbinate is not to subvert Judaism but to Judaize Feminism.

Bra-burnings are a thing of the past. The movement as a whole is now concerned with ERA* and other complex legal, educational, and essentially *constructive* tasks. The women contemplating the Conservative rabbinate are deeply committed to *Halakhah* and Jewish learning. They come with a new sensitivity, a new perspective, perhaps even a new language with which to reinterpret the Jewish experience. To dress this exotic creature in a *tallit* and *tefillin* and to place her on the pulpit is to my mind as potentially exciting a role model as Maimonides' rabbi-as-philosopher and the Baal Shem Tov's rabbi-as-zaddik.

Creative betrayal is an ongoing process. It is undertaken by those who believe that a living tradition must be violable to be viable.

---

*Equal Rights Amendment to the Constitution of the United States.

On the Ordination of Women as Rabbis

JOEL ROTH

The question of the ordination of women can be analyzed halakhically either narrowly or broadly. A narrow analysis would confine itself to the issue of ordination per se, while a broad analysis would consider as well the ancillary issues which might be involved.

One who undertakes a broad analysis of the question must deal with two crucial ancillary issues: (1) the status of women vis-à-vis *mitzvot* from which they are legally exempt, and (2) the status of women as witnesses. These issues are crucial because they involve matters which are widely considered to be either necessary or common functions of the modern rabbinate. These two issues apply to all women, not only to those who might seek ordination.

This paper will be divided into four parts: (1) Women and *mitzvot*; (2) Women as witnesses; (3) Women and ordination per se; (4) Conclusions and recommendations to the Faculty of the Seminary.

SECTION ONE

There are many *mitzvot* from which women are halakhically (legally) exempt. Those *mitzvot* are generally categorized as "positive commandments which are time-bound" in that they have to be performed at a specific time of the day or on specific days of the year.[1] This categorization is, however, imperfect.

127

There are positive time-bound commandments which women are obligated to observe,[2] as well as positive non-time-bound commandments from which they are legally exempt.[3] The *gemara* itself was aware of the problem, and resolved it by recourse to the dictum of Rabbi Yohanan, *Ein lemeidin min ha-kelalot*—general principles are not to be understood as definitive.[4]

However, the imperfection of the principle is legally insignificant.[5] Even if one could demonstrate that the principle is totally insufficient to explain which *mitzvot* women must observe and from which they are exempt, each specific case, either for obligation or for exemption, has the clear weight of precedent to support it.

The *gemara* plausibly resolves the inconsistency between the stated principle and the actual law by pointing out that the literary style of the *mishnah* in which the principle appears dictates a phrasing which will be parallel to the other principles in that *mishnah*, which are accurate. To reverse either specific rabbinic decisions vis-à-vis certain *mitzvot* from which women are now exempt, or to abolish the principle in its entirety, requires a presentation in each case of the *legal grounds* and justification for overturning precedent. To do so solely on the basis of the imperfection of the principle would be totally insufficient, since the promulgators of the norms themselves recognized that the precedents they were setting were not absolutely consistent with the principle.

The affirmation that women are exempt from certain *mitzvot* necessitates analysis of four issues.

1. May women perform those *mitzvot* from which they are exempt, and may they recite the appropriate blessings? (These are two distinct questions. However, most of the sources which will be quoted deal with both questions at the same time. The two will therefore be treated as one question.)
2. If women may observe *mitzvot* from which they are exempt, is their observance of these *mitzvot* governed by the

same rules as is the observance by men of those same *mitzvot*? Thus, men are permitted to violate some Sabbath prohibitions in order to observe certain *mitzvot* which are obligatory upon them but not upon women. Are women who observe such a *mitzvah*, though legally exempt from its observance, also entitled to violate that Sabbath prohibition?[6]

3. Can the voluntary observance of a *mitzvah* ever become in some significant sense religiously obligatory?
4. If it can, can that self-imposed obligation have the same legal status as the obligation of men which, legally speaking, is "other-imposed" either by the Torah or by rabbinic authority?

The most restrictive position regarding the right of women to observe *mitzvot* from which they are exempt is expressed by the Ravad (1125–1198).[7] The *Sifra* records a disagreement between Rabbi Yose and Rabbi Shimon, who allow women to lay their hands on the head of the burnt-offering,[8] and an anonymous view which forbids women to do so. The Ravad attributes the anonymous view to Rabbi Meir and Rabbi Yehuda.[9] He states:

In any case, the law is not according to Rabbi Yose. For Rabbi Meir and Rabbi Yehuda disagree with him, and the anonymous *mishnah* in Rosh Hashanah[10] reflects the view of Rabbi Meir and Rabbi Yehuda. The *mishnah* in Rosh Hashanah states: "We do not prevent children from blowing the *shofar*."[11] This implies that we do prevent women from doing so—i.e., because to them the *shevut* of sounding the horn applies.[12] Therefore, we do not agree with Rabbi Yose. This opinion we also find in Erubin, chapter 10.[13] The *mishnah* in Sukkah[14] states: "A woman may accept [the *lulav*] from her son or her husband [and put it in water]." On this passage the *gemara* comments:[15] "Obviously! What might you have thought? [One might have thought that] since she is not obligated [to observe the *mitzvah* of pronouncing the blessing over the *lulav*], she should also be forbidden to carry it."[16] If we accepted the position of Rabbi Yose, she would be as entitled as men to use the *lulav* for its ritual function, and if she could be so entitled, there would be no grounds for the assumption that she should be forbidden to handle it. . . . Therefore we may deduce [on the basis of these sources] that we accept the view of Rabbi Meir and Rabbi Yehuda [that a woman may not observe the *mitzvot* from which she is exempt]. As a result, it goes without saying that we would not permit women to wear a *tallit* the *tzitzit* [fringes] of which are made up of mixed species, even though men may, for this involves a biblically enjoined prohibition [Deuteronomy 22:11, Leviticus 19:19]. [Hence, women who wear such a *tallit* are violating a biblical commandment]. We also do not permit them [women] even to recite the benediction over the *lulav*. But sitting in the *sukkah* or holding the *lulav* are permitted to women since they involve neither chance of mishap [*kikul*] nor denigration of the *mitzvah* [*zizul mitzvah*].

The Ravad forbids women from performing any of the *mitzvot* from which they are exempt except those like sitting in the *sukkah* in which their physical presence itself is fulfillment of the *mitzvah*. The handling of the objects involved in the performance of *mitzvot* is not included in the prohibition, so long as she does not handle them for the sake of performing the *mitzvah*. Thus, she may not recite the benediction over the *lulav, esrog*, etc., while she holds them.

One step less stringent is the view codified by Maimonides. He wrote:[17]

Women, slaves, and minors are exempt by the law of the Torah from *tzitzit*. . . . Women and slaves who wish to enwrap themselves in *tzitzit* [i.e., in a *tallit*] may do so without reciting the blessing. And similarly, all other positive commandments from which women are exempt may be performed by them, without blessings—and they should not be prevented from doing them [*ein memahin be-yadan*].

Maimonides allows the actual performance of the actions which constitute the *mitzvah*, but those actions must remain free of any intimation that the act is performed qua *mitzvah*. Since the act could not be described as compliance with a commandment without the recitation of the requisite blessings, forbidding the recitation of the blessings clearly indicates that women are not actually fulfilling *mitzvot*,[18] even though they may be performing acts which might otherwise be so interpreted.[19]

The passage which was quoted above from the tractate *Sukkah* is quoted, as well, by the *Or Zarua* (1200–1270). He interprets exactly as does the Ravad, but adds the following appendix:[20]

> Nonetheless, Rashi [1035–1104], consistent with his own view which forbids women to recite blessings, interprets this passage thus, as I have explained in *Hilkhot Rosh Ha-shanah*.[21] But Rabbenu Tam [ca. 1100–1171], who permits them to recite the blessings,[22] explains that passage thus: [The *gemara's* hypothesis is] that a woman, who is not obligated to perform the *mitzvah*, might be considered forbidden to handle the *lulav* except for her own need.[23] Therefore, the *mishnah* informs us that since she is entitled to handle it and recite the blessing, the *lulav* acquires for her the legal status of a vessel.[24] Nonetheless, the view of Rashi [which forbids women to recite the blessings] seems more plausible.

Two points raised by the *Or Zarua* are worthy of emphasis: (1) He affirms that the *sugya* in *Sukkah* provides no incontrovertible proof that women may not perform the *mitzvot*, even with blessings. Though he himself prefers the view of Rashi (which forbids women to recite the blessings), the *sugya* does not constitute a clear refutation of the view of Rabbenu Tam, who does permit them to recite the appropriate blessings. (2) He quotes Rashi as denying women the right to recite the blessings, thereby making Rashi's view the same as the view of Maimonides.

However, the following passage[25] indicates that the view that Rashi prohibited women from reciting blessings is not certain.[26]

> Rabbi Yitzhak Ha-levi has rendered a decision that women are not to be prevented from reciting the blessings on *sukkah* and *lulav*. For the statement[27] that women are exempt from all posi-

tive time-bound commandments is meant only to indicate that they are not obligated. But, if they wish to bring themselves under the yoke of the commandments, they are entitled to do so, and should not be prevented. For they are not to be more disadvantaged than "those who fulfill *mitzvot* even though they are not commanded."[28] And if they wish to observe the *mitzvot*, it is impossible to do so without the blessing.[29]

Since the responsum includes no indication that Rashi disagreed with the decision of Rabbi Yitzhak Ha-levi, it would be fair to assume that he agreed. Thus, there are two attested, but contradictory, indications of Rashi's view on the subject. Be that as it may, this responsum deduces the right of women to observe the time-bound *mitzvot* from the very principle which the *mishnah* uses to designate the general category of *mitzvot* from which they are exempt. The principle implies exemption, not proscription. Given the class of "those who observe though not commanded," and the absence of any clear and explicit prohibition, there are no grounds for asserting that women may not observe *mitzvot* qua *mitzvot*. Furthermore, since the blessings are integral to the *mitzvot*, there can be no justification for denying them the right to recite the appropriate blessings as they perform the *mitzvot*.

Thus far, then, there are three positions: (1) Women are forbidden even to perform the time-bound *mitzvot*. (2) They are allowed to perform the *mitzvot*, but forbidden to recite the appropriate blessings. (3) They are allowed both the observance and the recitation of the blessings.

The dispute among *posekim* has persisted until modern times, with the division generally along Ashkenazi-Sephardi lines. The former usually adopt the third position, and the latter generally follow the second—the Maimonidean position. Thus, Caro (1488–1575) states in his code:[30] "Although women are exempt, they may blow the *shofar* . . . but may not recite the blessing." Isserles (1525–1572) added: "Our custom is for women to recite the blessings on positive time-bound commandments. In this case, too, then, they may recite the blessing for themselves."

A short responsum of the Rashba (ca. 1235–1310) epitomizes the view which seems most logical. He wrote:[31]

> You already know of the dispute among the *rishonim* and their proofs. I agree with those who claim that women may observe and recite the blessings on all the positive commandments, based upon the precedent of Michal bat Shaul,[32] who used to wear phylacteries, and the Sages did not stop her. Rather, she acted with their approval. And obviously *[ustama de-millata]*, if she put them on she recited the blessing.

That position has even "heavenly" approval. Rabbi Yaakov Ha-levi, in one of his *Teshuvot Min Ha-shamayim* ("Responsa from Heaven"),[33] wrote

> I asked concerning the women who recite the blessing over the *lulav*, and concerning those who recite the blessing over the sounding of the *shofar* for women, whether there is a transgression involved, and if it is a "purposeless benediction" since they are not obligated. And they answered . . . "Whatever Sarah says, obey her" [Genesis 21:12]. Go and say to them: "Return to your tents, and bless your Lord." . . . If they wish to recite the blessing over the *lulav* and the *shofar*, they may.

There is, therefore, ample halakhic precedent to allow women to observe positive time-bound commandments, and to recite the appropriate blessings.

The other theoretical problem involved in the recitation of the blessings by women is the appropriateness of their saying ve-tzivvanu ("and He commanded us"), which is integral to blessings recited before performing the *mitzvot*. If women are exempt, how can they be "commanded"? Both the Ritba (1250–1330) and the Ran (ca. 1310–1375) have dealt with this problem. Interestingly, each of them deals with it after having "disproved" all of the purported proofs of Rabbenu Tam that women may recite blessings.[34] Having done so, both the Ran and the Ritba nevertheless agree with him that they may recite the blessings, and each for the same reason, namely, that the assertion that "he who is commanded and performs *mitzvot* is greater than one who performs though not commanded"[35] implies only that the former class is greater than the latter. It does not imply that the latter class receives no reward for the observance of the *mitzvot*. It implies only that it receives a lesser one. The Ran then adds:[36]

And do not say: "Since they were not commanded, how can they say *ve-tzivvanu?*" That is no problem. Since the men were commanded, and the women also receive "reward," they clearly may say *ve-tzivvanu*.

The Ritba puts it this way:[37]

And they are entitled to say *ve-tzivvanu*, since they are included in the class of "Israel" which is commanded to perform *[the mitzvot]*. Therefore, to them, too, who have the right [to observe] and receive reward, *ve-tzivvanu* is applicable as members of the class of "Israel."

One further issue regarding the right of women to observe *mitzvot* from which they are exempt remains to be addressed. Admittedly, it is an infrequent occurrence. On occasion, the observance of one *mitzvah* involves the violation of another *mitzvah*. Sacrifices which are offered on Shabbat are one example. One might theoretically argue that the right to violate *mitzvah* A in the performance of another *mitzvah*, B, is restricted to those who are obligated to perform *mitzvah* B and does not extend to those whose observance of *mitzvah* B is voluntary.

A direct and unequivocal response to this question is found in the Yerushalmi.[38] "Rabbi Lazar said: 'The Paschal sacrifice by women is voluntary,[39] but takes precedence over Shabbat.'" Though women are legally exempt from the sacrifice, and though it may involve a violation of Shabbat, the sacrifice takes precedence over Shabbat even for women who choose voluntarily to observe it.

A similar response is found in the Ravad. He wrote:[40]

There are those who claim that according to the view of Rabbi Yose and Rabbi Shimon [who claim that *nashim somekhot reshut*—

"on a sacrifice brought during a festival women may lay their hands voluntarily"], even *semikhah gedolah* [the laying on of the hands in full force] is permissible to women.[41] [Since in this case] the Torah permits women voluntarily to observe in the same manner as men what men are obligated to observe, hence we may deduce that in regard to positive time-bound commandments women may observe them as do men even if it involves a violation of a biblical commandment. [This then would permit] a woman voluntarily to observe the *mitzvah* of *tzitzit* [the wearing of a tallit] even though the tzitzit violate the prohibition of *sha'atnez* [Deuteronomy 22:11–12).[42]

The Ravad seems here clearly to maintain that once the voluntary assumption of *mitzvot* by women is recognized as valid, no distinctions can be made between men and women regarding the nature of the observance. What is mandatory or permissible for men is permissible for women as well. To the extent that the mandatory observance of a man may either allow or dictate the violation of another *mitzvah* in the process, the voluntary observance of a woman similarly allows or dictates.

By and large, women have refrained from the observance of most of the *mitzvot* from which they are exempt. That tendency is particularly true of commandments which require daily observance, such as *tallit* and *tefillin*. The codes reflect the idea that women who choose to observe the *mitzvah* of *tallit* may be guilty of *yoharra*, "arrogance."[43] However, the sources quoted thus far indicate quite clearly that women who choose to observe *mitzvot* have ample, though not universal, support and ought not to be considered in violation of the law.

Mitzvot which do not require daily observance are not in the same category as those which do. The frequent mention even in the sources quoted thus far of *mitzvot* like *lulav* and *shofar* offers testimony to the fact that women did observe those commandments, and in large enough numbers to warrant their being dealt with seriously by the *posekim*. As will become clear, the number of such *mitzvot* is not restricted to two. Furthermore, *mitzvot* of this category raise the question whether there can be any element of *hiyyuv* (obligation) applicable to women who voluntarily observe *mitzvot* from which they are exempt. This question also involves the question whether a state of obligation can in general be created by voluntary observance, even for men.

In the latter third of the seventeenth century the following comment appears in the writings of Rabbi Abraham ben Hayyim Ha-levi Gumbiner, the *Magen Avraham*:[44] "Women are exempt from counting the Omer, since it is a positive time-bound commandment. Nonetheless, they have already made it obligatory upon themselves [by having voluntarily decided to observe it]."

Almost two hundred years later, perhaps realizing the potential significance of the *Magen Avraham's* statement, Joseph Babad, the *Minhat Hinukh*, reacts with startled amazement. He wrote:[45]

> Women and slaves are exempt from this *mitzvah* [counting the Omer], since it is a positive time-bound commandment. Yet note that *Magen Avraham* has written that now they have made it obligatory upon themselves. That view, indeed, requires further investigation. The view that women, if they accept upon themselves to observe a commandment from which they are exempt, should be considered obligated by virtue of their having accepted it upon themselves as an obligation, is a *davar hadash* [novel view]. I have not seen such a claim made anywhere.[46] . . . Nor do I know the source of the view here expressed by the *Magen Avraham*.

In essence, Babad is claiming that the view of Gumbiner is unprecedented. But even if Babad were correct, the fact remains that Gumbiner is among the most widely recognized halakhic authorities. His view could itself set a precedent which later *posekim* might follow. However, Gumbiner's view is not without precedent. It can be traced back at least to the *Halakhot Gedolot*, which, in turn, attributes it to the *gemara* itself. The *Halakhot Gedolot* reads:[47]

> When an individual forgets to mention Rosh Hodesh during his recitation of the evening *amidah*, he should not repeat it, for Rav

Anan said in the name of Rav:[48] "If one erred and did not mention Rosh Hodesh during the evening *amidah*, he should not repeat it, since the month must be consecrated during the day." But if one erred and forgot to mention either Shabbat or Yom Tov or Hol Ha-moed during his recitation of the evening *amidah*, we do make him repeat it. For even though we have clearly established that the evening *amidah* is voluntary,[49] that applies when one has decided not to recite it all. But if one has already made the effort and prayed and thus accepted the recitation of the evening *amidah* as an obligation, if then he has erred by forgetting to mention [the special occasion] he must pray it over again. For if it were not so, why was it necessary to offer the reason that the month must be consecrated during the day as the ground for not repeating the evening prayer on Rosh Hodesh? This could have been deduced from the fact that even on Sabbaths and Yamim Tovim he should not repeat, since the evening prayer is voluntary. The obvious conclusion is that the statement that the evening prayer is voluntary refers to the option not to recite it at all. But, having recited it, he accepts it upon himself as obligatory, and we enjoin him to repeat it because he had forgotten to mention Shabbat or Yom Tov.

The thrust of the comment of the *Halakhot Gedolot* is quite clear. The recitation of the evening *amidah* is *reshut*, "voluntary," the same as the status of a woman's observance of positive time-bound commandments. Yet, once one begins to recite it, one has changed its legal status from voluntary to obligatory, with whatever legal ramifications might result from the latter status. Even the fact that one does not repeat the evening *amidah* on Rosh Hodesh if he has forgotten *ya'aleh ve-yavo* (the special Rosh Hodesh insertion) does not disprove this conclusion, for that exemption from the requirement to repeat the *amidah* is contingent not on the voluntary nature of its recitation, but on a specific factor concerning Rosh Hodesh which makes the repetition unwarranted.[50]

The thesis of the *Halakhot Gedolot* was utilized in the late twelfth or early thirteenth century by Rabbi Eliezer ben Joel Ha-levi (Ravia) in the following passage:[51]

In the second chapter of the tractate *Shabbat*[52] the question is raised whether or not mention of Hannukah must be made in the grace after meals. It is resolved to the effect that it need not be mentioned, but that if one wishes to mention it he may. The implication is that it is voluntary. Nonetheless, since *nehigei alma* [it is the widespread custom] to mention it, and one who is reciting the grace is therefore doing so with the intention of mentioning it, he accepts it as an obligation and must repeat. And my proof is from the *Halakhot Gedolot*, who decided that even according to the view which affirms that the evening *amidah* is voluntary, once one has begun to pray, he must repeat the prayer if he forgot to mention Rosh Hodesh,[53] since he has accepted it upon himself as obligatory. This case seems no different. That is my opinion.

The Ravia does here what *posekim* have always done. He applies the principle espoused by the *Halakhot Gedolot* to a case which he deems to be similar to the specific case stipulated in the earlier source. On that basis he makes his final judgment that the widespread custom of reciting *al ha-nissim* during *birkat ha-mazon* elevates its recitation from voluntary to obligatory, with whatever legal ramifications may result from that changed status.

Though one can offer no absolute proof that the *Magen Avraham* was aware of these precedents, it is at least plausible. But whether or not he was aware of them, moderns are. Thus, it is logical to posit that his claim vis-à-vis the widespread custom of women to count the Omer is no more than one further extension of the precedent already set up by both the *Halakhot Gedolot* and the Ravia. The widespread observance of the *mitzvah*, which, legally speaking, is voluntary, can effect a change in its legal status, elevating it to the level of obligation. For the *Halakhot Gedolot* and the Ravia this elevation of status had legal significance, dictating behaviors which would seem to be applicable only to matters which are halakhically obligatory.[54] Nor should the matter be taken lightly, for the re-recitation of either the *amidah* or *birkat ha-mazon* might entail recitation of blessings which, from a strict legal sense, were valid when recited the first time, and hence their re-recitation results in the "taking of God's name in vain."

Rabbi Shimshon bar Zadok, a student of Rabbi Meir of Rothenburg (ca. 1215–1293) also speaks of a type of obligation for *mitzvot* which are, in fact, voluntary. He wrote:[55]

> Women are exempt from both *tefillin* and *tzitzit*, for they are both positive time-bound commandments. . . . Nonetheless, they should not be prevented from wearing *tzitzit* and reciting the blessing, for they are allowed to obligate themselves as is demonstrated in *Kiddushin*.[56] However, they should not put on *tefillin*, since they do not know how to keep themselves in purity.[57]

In the late sixteenth century, Isaac Di Molina (d.ca. 1580) wrote:[58]

> Women are exempt from the *musaf* prayer. For this service serves as a commemoration of the obligation to bring sacrifices, in which women did not participate, nor had they part in communal sacrifices. But they are already accustomed to pray everything, and "they have obligated themselves" for all *mitzvot*.[59]

At the barest minimum, the statement of the *Magen Avraham*, and its historical antecedents in the *Halakhot Gedolot* and the Ravia, the Tashbetz and Di Molina, demonstrate two things: (1) The amazement of the *Minhat Hinukh* is not warranted.[60] (2) The term "obligation" is not totally inapplicable to self-imposed observance of *mitzvot*.[61]

Since it is certain that the laws of *aninut* ("mourning before burial") will be raised as potential counter-examples to the point which has been made, a slight digression to indicate the grounds for rejecting *aninut* as a counter-example is in order.

The primary source from which the counter-example might be derived can be found in the *baraita* quoted in the *gemara*[62] which stipulates that an *onen* should eat in as private a manner as his circumstances allow. One gets the distinct impression that if it were but feasible the *baraita* would urge that he not eat at all. In any case, the *baraita* concludes:

> He need not recite *ha-motzi,* nor need he recite *birkat ha-mazon,* nor need others recite *ha-motzi* for him, nor can he be counted among the three required for *zimmun.*

This translation reflects the explanation of Rashi, ad locum. As the Tosafot note,[63] Rashi's explanation exempts the *onen* from these requirements, but does not prohibit him from observing them. Only the last category marks an exception to this principle, for Rashi implies that he cannot be counted toward a *zimmun* even, apparently, if he wished to be counted. That, seemingly, implies that even if he wished to obligate himself, he may not do so in a way which might be publicly understood as implying obligation. To strengthen the point even further, the Tosafot continue:

> Nonetheless, the Yerushalmi states [64] that even if he wants to be strict with himself, we pay him no heed. Therefore, it seems plausible to explain that he may not recite *ha-motzi.* And the Yerushalmi explains why he may not do so "because of the honor due to the dead" or, alternatively, because "there is no one who will carry his burden."

The very stringency which the Yerushalmi applies negates the possibility that the *onen* case could be a counter-example to our thesis. The *onen* is forbidden even voluntary acceptance of an obligation because there are other factors involved which make that inappropriate, not because people who are exempt cannot voluntarily accept obligation. The case of the *onen* is comparable to the claim of the *Halakhot Gedolot* regarding failure to mention Rosh Hodesh in the evening *amidah.*[65] Note, too, Maimonides' statement:[66] "Anyone who is exempt from reciting the Shema may be strict upon himself and recite it, so long as his mind is free enough to concentrate on it." If his mind is at ease, he may voluntarily accept the obligation.

Some *posekim* have extended the implication of the prohibition of counting an *onen* for a *zimmun* to include a prohibition on counting him in a *minyan,* even if he is present and praying. The Hida (1724–1806) responds to that claim. He wrote:[67]

> *Aharonim* have written about an *onen* that he may not be counted in a *minyan.* And the *Peri Hadash* brought proof of that fact from Siman #199, which prohibits his being counted in the *zimmun.* But, if those are the grounds, they can certainly be denied. For the *zimmun* case is very different. For any Jew who does not eat cannot be counted in the *zimmun,* and, therefore, the legal status of an *onen* is to be considered as one who has not eaten. But vis-à-vis being counted in a *minyan* one could claim that since he is still a full-fledged Jew . . . and is even now obligated to comply with all of the negative commandments, the verse "I shall be sanctified in the midst of the Children of Israel"[68] can be applied to him.

The Hida reaffirms the contention that special circumstances warrant the prohibition of counting an *onen* for *zimmun,* but for *minyan* he can surely be counted since those special circumstances are not applicable. Yet, it is clear, the *onen* is exempt from prayer. Thus, it must follow that some degree of obligation applies to him if he chooses to obligate himself voluntarily.

Let me then conclude this digression with the reaffirmation of the contention that the term "obligation" is applicable to self-imposed observance of *mitzvot* from which one is legally exempt. We must now proceed to analyze whether or not the status of obligation voluntarily accepted can be considered the same as that of one who is *metzuvveh ve-oseh,* one who is "commanded and performs."

It must be stressed that the question of the status of self-imposed obligation as compared to other-imposed obligation is of both theological and legal significance. As we shall see, the two aspects of the question cannot always be separated from each other. For the purposes of this paper, the primary concern is with the legal significance of the status, though a few comments on the theological question will be unavoidable.

Theologically, the question involves the following: One

whose obligation is other-imposed (that is, who is "commanded") and does not fulfill his obligation is a sinner. Can the same be true of one whose obligation stems from voluntary self-imposition? Theologically, therefore, the question applies to all commandments. The nature of the specific *mitzvah* is not relevant to the theological issue. Vis-à-vis the woman the question would apply equally to any positive time-bound commandment which she accepted upon herself voluntarily. If a woman accepts upon herself the obligation to wear *tefillin*, is her failure to do so on any given day a sin, or is it a reversion to nonobligatory status?

Legally, on the other hand, the question of the status of self-imposed obligation is of very limited significance. Whether or not the failure of a woman to wear *tefillin* is a sin, sufficient precedent has already been adduced that she may wear them if she wishes. In point of fact, it seems that there are only two areas in which the status of self-imposed obligation is legally significant. The first area involves the question of agency. In a number of instances the *halakhah* permits one who is himself obligated to perform a given *mitzvah* to appoint another individual who is *equally obligated* to act as his agent. The *shatz*—the *sheliah tzibbur*—is "the agent of the congregation" to lead in prayer and to act as its agent in fulfilling the obligation to pray. The halakhic question that thus arises is whether one whose obligation to observe a *mitzvah* is self-imposed may serve as the agent through whom one whose obligation to observe the same *mitzvah* is other-imposed fulfills his obligation? To be specific, can a woman who has accepted upon herself the obligation to pray three times each day, at the appointed hours, serve as a *shatz* for a group which contains people whose obligation to pray is other-imposed?[69] Since one cannot observe the *mitzvah* of *tefillin* through an agent, the question of the status of voluntary versus other-imposed obligation in relation to *tefillin* is irrelevant.

The second area, connected with the first, involves the eligibility of one whose obligation to observe a *mitzvah* is self-imposed to be counted toward a quorum which might be required for the proper observance of the *mitzvah*.[70]

There is one primary source which seems to indicate a negative answer to the question posed above. The Mishnah reads:[71] "This is the general rule: Anyone *she-eino mehuyyav* [on whom an obligation is not incumbent] cannot fulfill that obligation on behalf of the many." If one assumes that the Mishnah in using the term *mehuyyav* ("obligated") intends thereby to refer only to "one whose obligation is other-imposed," it would, of course, follow that women could not serve as agents for others in the fulfillment of positive time-bound commandments. It seems, though, that the meaning of the principle is not quite that clear. In the first place, the word used is *mehuyyav* ("obligated"), a term which has already been demonstrated to be applicable to the voluntary acceptance of *mitzvot*. Secondly, the principle is prefaced by the following clause: "A deaf-mute, imbecile, or minor may not serve as the agent through whom the many fulfill their obligation." Two things stand out immediately when the principle is considered together with its preface. Women are not specifically mentioned in the preface. That alone would not be sufficient to indicate that they were intended to be excluded from the principle. But the omission of women gains increased significance when one notes that the three categories which are specifically mentioned are such that even voluntary acceptance of the observance of *mitzvot* by them would not have any element of obligation attached to it, on the grounds that those three classes are mentally, and, therefore, legally, incompetent. Surely, the same cannot be said of women. Had the principle read *metzuvveh* ("commanded") instead of *mehuyyav* ("obligated"), or had the examples of the preface included women, the answer to the questions posed above would have been clear and unambiguous. Given, however, that neither is the case, the clarity of the answer is open to significant doubt.

Furthermore, one could not claim that women are included in the principle on the grounds that their voluntary fulfillment of *mitzvot* is limited in some way. We have already shown that women may observe *mitzvot* exactly as men do,[72] even if the observance of one *mitzvah* involves the violation of another. If there were any limitations whatsoever on the voluntary observance of *mitzvot*, it would surely be reflected in such instances.

It is most probable that any definitive answer to the question must be contingent upon the meaning of the statement of Rabbi Hanina: "Greater is one who is commanded and performs than one who is not commanded and performs."[73] Thus, attention must now be directed to the meaning of that dictum.

Casual reference to that dictum has already been made in other contexts,[74] indicating that it deals, in essence, with "reward" and not with obligation. There is no inherent logic which would dictate that different degrees of "reward" entail different degrees of obligation.

The classical commentators have offered a variety of explanations of Rabbi Hanina's dictum. Three explanations will be quoted first, and dealt with together. The Tosafot offer two explanations. First, they claim:[75]

It appears that the reasoning behind the dictum "that one who is commanded and fulfills" is preferable [*adif*] is that he worries and is concerned lest he transgress much more than one who is not commanded and fulfills. For the latter has *pat besalo* [an "ace in the hole"] that if he wishes he may forgo observance.

In another place they wrote:[76]

For he is continually concerned to overcome his inclination in order to fulfill the command of his Creator.

Finally, a comment attributed to Ri ha-zaken (d.ca. 1185) reads:[77]

One who is commanded and fulfills has a great reward because he is commanded and accepts the authority of the *mitzvot* upon himself.

Though worded differently from each other, the thrust of the three explanations is the same. Failure to comply with the *mitzvah* is not a viable alternative for one who is commanded. Thus, his efforts must be constantly directed toward avoiding that possibility. Why is nonobservance unthinkable? Since the authority of the *mitzvot* and their divine origin make failure to comply a sin, the commanded does not have any viable alternative. The noncommanded, however, can renounce his own voluntary acceptance of the *mitzvot* without either guilt or remorse. It is he who imposed the obligation upon himself, and it is he who can renounce the obligation.

There would be some reasonableness to Rabbi Hanina's contention, according to these explanations, if he were addressing himself to a distinction between Jews and non-Jews. Since non-Jews are not accustomed to thinking in categories of "commandedness," their observance of *mitzvot* is ultimately self-serving, and they could "take it or leave it." Jewish women, on the other hand, are bound by many commandments and approach observance of non-time-bound commandments with the same lack of viable options vis-à-vis those commandments as do men vis-à-vis all commandments. The mind-set of "commandedness" already exists in Jewish women. Is it therefore unreasonable to assume that they would apply that preexistent mind-set to *mitzvot* which they chose to observe voluntarily? Indeed, historical experience validates the opinion that women observe voluntary *mitzvot* at least as meticulously as do men who are obligated to observe them. If anyone had told our mothers or grandmothers that they could "take it or leave it" as far as reciting the blessing over the *lulav*, or hearing the blowing of the *shofar*, or counting the *omer*, or reciting the *yizkor*, or hearing *birkat ha-hodesh* were concerned, they would have been astounded. They "knew" that they were "commanded." Indeed, one of the oft-used arguments against the decision of the Committee on Jewish Law and Standards of the Rabbinical Assembly to count women in the *minyan* was the contention that women are so much more punctilious in their observance of *mitzvot* that counting them in the *minyan* would result in a radical decrease in the number of men who would attend.[78] Without passing judgment on the claim itself, it must be noted that it denies the contention that women take a self-imposed obligation lightly.

Above all, however, Rabbi Hanina's dictum cannot be the source on the basis of which to distinguish legally between self- and other-imposed obligations, either because it never applied to Jewish women, or because, even if it did, we must all admit that *nishtannu ha-zemannim* ("times have changed"). Jewish women who accept a legal obligation to observe voluntarily do not do so on a "take it or leave it" basis. Since only a "take it or leave it" attitude could possibly justify a distinction between a self- and an other-imposed obligation, it follows that a woman who voluntarily accepts the obligation of daily prayer at the appointed times, and who understands that noncompliance with the obligation is a sin, may be counted in a *minyan* and serve as a *shatz*.[79]

The *minyan* requirement for a wedding *birkat hatanim* is based in the Talmud on two different biblical verses.[80] (1) Rav Nahman derives it from the verse "And he [Boaz] took ten men from the elders of the city" (Ruth 4:2). That derivation would apparently exclude women. (2) Rabbi Abahu deduces the requirement from the verse *Be-makhelot* ("In assemblies bless God, the Lord") *mi-mekor Yisrael* ("from the fountain of Israel") (Psalm 68:27). Rashi, ad locum, thus explains the Midrash: "For the benediction referred to by 'from the fountain' [i.e., the wedding benedictions][81] a *kahal* [assembly] is required." Rashi proceeds to define *kahal* as equal to *edah* and *edah* as equal to ten, based on "How much longer shall that wicked *edah* [community] keep muttering against Thee?" (Numbers 14:27).[82] That verse, in turn, is the Bavli's source for the prayer quorum.[83] According to Rashi's interpretation of Rabbi Abahu's statement, therefore, anyone who may be counted for a prayer quorum may also be counted for a *minyan* for the wedding benedictions.[84] Since the disagreement between Rav Nahman and Rabbi Abahu remains unresolved by the Talmud, there is no greater reason to accept the view of Rav Nahman than to accept the view of Rabbi Abahu.[85] And since we have previously indicated that women who accept the obligation of daily prayer may be counted for a *minyan* for a prayer service, we now further conclude that such women may also be counted for a *minyan* at a wedding service.

Finally, the previous analysis was based on the assumption that Rabbi Hanina's dictum that "one who is commanded and performs is greater than one who is not commanded and performs" was universally affirmed. And indeed it is, in the Bavli, which has long-standing systemic primacy over the Yerushalmi. Nevertheless, a further significant dimension is added to our previous analysis by an opinion expressed in the Yerushalmi which implies the assumption that "one who is not commanded and performs is greater than one who is commanded and performs." It reads:[86]

> Rabbi Elazar said: [Those who returned from Babylonia] voluntarily accepted upon themselves the obligation for tithes [Nehemiah 10:38].[87] What is the source for this claim? [It is the passage:][88] "To all of the following we make a written pledge, attested to by our leaders, Levites, and priests" [Nehemiah 10:1].[89] What does Rabbi Elazar do with "And the first-born of our herds and flocks" [Nehemiah 10:37]?[90] Since they accepted upon themselves things for which they were not obligated, even those things for which they were obligated are considered as though they had accepted them voluntarily.

The passage is obviously complimentary in tone. The Returners are praised for accepting as obligatory those things from which they were actually exempt. So praiseworthy is that act that they are credited by Scripture with the voluntary acceptance of things which were, in actuality, not voluntarily accepted, but obligatory. Surely the passage implies that their acceptance of the voluntary obligations was not on a "take it or leave it" basis, and, even more important, that acceptance of those voluntary obligations was more praiseworthy than their expressed intention to comply with obligatory norms, thus implying that "Greater is one who is not commanded and performs than one who is commanded and performs."

We conclude Section One by noting that it is possible to assume that there could be four potential categories of women:

1. Those who would reaffirm the traditional exemption from positive time-bound commandments and generally refrain from observing those *mitzvot* from which women are legally exempt.
2. Those who would reaffirm the traditional exemption from positive time-bound *mitzvot*, but choose sporadically to observe some of them or all of them without viewing their own observance as obligatory in any way.
3. Those who would reaffirm their exemption from *mitzvot*, but voluntarily accept certain *mitzvot* upon themselves as obligatory, with failure to comply with those *mitzvot* considered as sin. Were a woman to adopt such practice, but without the proviso that failure to observe is sinful, she would be a member of category 2.
4. Those who, though recognizing themselves to be legally exempt, would accept upon themselves as obligatory the observance of all *mitzvot* from which women are legally exempt, with failure to comply with any of those *mitzvot* to be considered as sin. Should a woman choose to do so, but reject the notion of sin as the consequence of noncompliance, she, too, would stand legally in category 2.

We have, we hope, made it abundantly clear that the obligatory status of voluntary observance must be taken very seriously if it is to have the legal status of obligation. That seriousness is reflected in the recognition that, for that woman, there is no viable option to compliance with the norms. That, in traditional terms, means the recognition of sin as the consequence of noncompliance.

SECTION TWO

The issues involved in the question of the right of women to serve as witnesses are at once far simpler and far more complex than the issues involved in the question of their right to observe positive time-bound commandments.

The halakhic sources are unequivocal in prohibiting women from serving as witnesses. Furthermore, though the specific manner of the derivation of the prohibition may vary from source to source, all sources assume that the prohibition is *de-oraita* ("biblical").

Sifrei Devarim[91] derives the prohibition by having recourse to the principle of *gezerah shava.* [92] It reads:

> Might a woman, too, be fit to serve as a witness? Scripture here [Deuteronomy 19:17] uses the word *shenei* [two],[93] and there [ibid., v. 15] it uses the word *shenei* [two.][94] Just as in the case of verse 17, the reference is clearly to men, and not women; so too, in verse 15, the reference is to men and not to women.

According to this source, the word *anashim*, which occurs in verse 17, is to be understood as referring to men alone, and is not to be understood as a generic term meaning "persons"— i.e., both men and women. Furthermore, *midrash halakhah* ("legal hermeneutics") views as irrelevant whether the word *anashim* ("men") in verse 17 refers to witnesses, judges, or litigants. It is the appearance of the word *shenei* in both contexts that allows the deduction that since it clearly refers to men in one context, it also does so in the second context. Thus biblical status is clearly attributed to the prohibition of having women act as witness.

The *gemara* quotes three *baraitot*, each of which seeks to demonstrate that the phrase *shenei ha-anashim* ("two men")[95] of verse 17 itself refers to the witnesses, despite the literal sense of the verse, which speaks of "the parties to the dispute." In each *baraita* that assertion is followed by a counter-claim that perhaps the phrase refers to the litigants, not to the witnesses. In

each *baraita* the counter-claim is refuted. Yet each *baraita* concludes with the assertion that, "if you prefer," the proof that
shenei ha-anashim ("the two men") refers to the witnesses can be
deduced by *gezerah shavah*. Taken at face value, the *baraitot*
assert that by the internal logic of the verse it can be demonstrated that the *shenei ha-anashim* refers to witnesses and that
that logic can be supported by a *gezerah shavah*. The Talmud,
though, interjects an objection into each *baraita* indicating that
one could question the supposed "internal logic" of the verse
and could "prove" that *shenei ha-anashim* does not refer to
witnesses. Hence the need for the *gezerah shavah* to serve as an
alternative source from which to derive the prohibition.

Quoting one of the *baraitot* with its Talmudic amplification
will suffice to demonstrate the nature of the entire passage.
Commenting on the statement of the Mishnah that the witnesses' oath applies only to men and not to women,[96] the
Talmud asks:

> What is the source of the opinion? As our rabbis have taught:
> The phrase *ve-amdu shenei ha-anashim* ["And the two men shall
> stand"] [with which verse 17 opens] refers to witnesses. Are you
> certain that it refers to witnesses? Perhaps it refers to the
> litigants! [No!] Since the verse [later] contains the phrase *asher
> lahem ha-riv* ["the parties to the dispute"], the litigants are here
> specifically mentioned. To whom then does the opening phrase
> of the verse, *ve-amdu shenei ha-anashim* ["and the two men shall
> stand"] refer? It refers to the witnesses. If you prefer [i.e., if the
> foregoing does not satisfy you, then note that] the Torah in this
> verse [17] employs the term *shenei* as well as in verse 15. Just as
> verse 15 refers to witnesses, so, too, does verse 17 refer to
> witnesses. What, then, is the purpose of [the alternative] "If you
> prefer, etc."? You might argue that since the verse does *not* read
> *va asher lahem ha-riv* ["*And* the parties to the dispute"], the entire
> verse refers to the litigants.[97] The *gezerah shavah* therefore comes
> to indicate that *shenei ha-anashim* ["the two men"] refers to
> witnesses.

In any case, the Bavli asserts that women may not serve as
witnesses, and that the prohibition is *de-oraita* ("biblical"). It

may be based solely on the logic of the verse, on the logic of the verse buttressed by a *gezerah shavah,* or on the *gezerah shavah* alone.

Maimonides codifies the law as follows:[98]

Women are disqualified as witnesses from the Torah, as it says: "By the testimony of *shenei edim*—[two witnesses]" [Deuteronomy 17:6], masculine and not feminine.

According to him, too, the prohibition is unequivocal and clearly *de-oraita* ("biblical").[99]

For some, no further comment or analysis is necessary. The prohibition is clear, and its biblical status is universally recognized. Hence to them any attempt to try to explain why the sages saw fit to interpret the Torah so as to exclude females from testifying would be pure guess work, subject to human error, and, therefore, legally irrelevant. According to those who deduce the prohibition from the *gezerah shavah,* no search for reason would be appropriate, since every *gezerah shava* is ultimately Sinaitic (divinely ordained).

Others feel compelled to pursue the subject further. The sources cited above intimate no exceptions to the prohibition. Indeed, if the prohibition were classified as a *gezerat ha-katuv* (an inherently inexplicable biblical injunction), one would not expect to find any exceptions at all, unless the exceptions themselves were spelled out in Scripture. Yet, it is well known that there are exceptions to the prohibition. Certain types of testimony are even referred to as *edut she-ha-isha ke-sherah lah* ("testimony that a woman may legally give").[100] Exceptions to a blanket prohibition beg for some explanation on the underlying reason for the prohibition. Since it is not the purpose of this paper to be a definitive analysis of the exceptions to the prohibition, we shall refer to the exceptions only as needed to support the plausibility of the proposed explanation of the underlying reasons for the prohibition.

The disqualification of a class as witnesses is explicable only if one could assert that the class possesses some characteristic which renders it unreliable. Imbeciles cannot serve as witnesses because the level of their mental competence makes them unreliable. Relatives of a defendant cannot serve as witnesses because their very closeness to the defendant makes them suspect to lie in his favor. Sinners, the nature of whose sin indicates a penchant for illicit gain, are disqualified because they are suspect to take bribes for testifying falsely. However, the disqualification of the entire class of relatives, for example, does not exclude the possibility that there might be some relatives whose sense of justice and right would impel them to tell the truth, even if that truth were detrimental to the case of their relative. It asserts, rather, that, as a class, there is sufficient suspicion to warrant disqualification of the entire class *qua* class. An individual imbecile might give an accurate and truthful account of what he saw, but there is sufficient suspicion that, as a class, the imbeciles' perception of the world makes a truthful and accurate description of an event unlikely. Similarly, if one could demonstrate a stereotypical image of women in general, sufficient to warrant the exclusion of the entire class as unreliable for testimony, it would not assert that every woman always conforms to each of the elements of the stereotype. However, the fact that some women varied from the stereotype would not disprove that the sages might have deemed the stereotype sufficiently widespread as to warrant the disqualification of the entire class because of the suspicion of unreliability.

It is well known that there are many highly commendatory statements in rabbinic literature about women as a class. Their stabilizing familial influence,[101] their devotion to God and *mitzvot*,[102] and their sensitivity[103] are all reflected in the literature. But, however commendatory these statements may be, they do not negate the rabbinic perception of the nature of women in general. Both the positive and the negative characteristics coexist in the rabbinic perception of the nature of the class of women.

Thus, the rabbis found support for their view that the role of the ideal woman is not in the world of the court, or commerce, or academics, but is basically restricted to the home, in the verse, "All glorious is the king's daughter within the palace" (Psalm 45:14).[104] That does not mean that the Rabbis knew of no women who were conversant with "the world." It means only that, generally speaking, they were not.

It cannot be denied that the rabbis perceived that there were significant characterological differences between women, as a class, and men, as a class. "Women," said the rabbis, *"da'atan kalaht aleihen"* ("are unreliable," fickle-minded).[105] Women are talkative, and talkativeness leads to embellishment. "Ten measures of talk were given to the world. Women appropriated nine of those measures, and one was left for the rest of the world."[106]

The following passage leaves little doubt that the rabbis were of the opinion that women possess sufficient characterological traits which warrant their exclusion from testifying.

> The sages say that four traits apply to women: They are greedy, eavesdroppers, lazy, and jealous. . . . Rabbi Yehoshua bar Nahmani adds: querulous and garrulous. Rabbi Levi adds: thieves and gadabouts.[107]

The class of women, as all other disqualified classes, was thus disqualified for what was assumed to be the general nature of women which made them nonconversant with the world of the courtroom, and unreliable as witnesses.

Minors are also disqualified as a class, yet the *mishnah*[108] lists a variety of areas in which their testimony[109] is considered reliable. Why are these exceptions to their general disqualification acceptable? Obviously, because they come from arenas which make a lasting impression upon youngsters, and their reporting of which can be assumed to be generally reliable.[110] If one could show one or two instances in which the same could be said about the testimony of women, it would buttress the contention that their disqualification was for cause, and not because of *gezerat ha-katuv*.

Given the reality that being an unmarried woman was considered a sorry state, and given the empathy which women have for others in that sorry state, and given particularly the fact that even the most incorrigible embellisher would not lie if she thought she would be caught in the lie, the rabbinic abrogation of the prohibition against women's testifying to permit a woman to testify about the death of another woman's husband and, on the basis of that testimony, to allow the widow to remarry, makes perfect sense.[111] The characteristics which generally disqualify the class of women are not salient in this type of case. Given that, the sages waived the prohibition.[112] More interesting yet, and further proof of the thesis, is the exception to the rule. Five categories of women[113] are so suspect to both hate and be jealous of another woman that even their innate feminine empathy for the plight of an unmarried woman, and even the possibility of being caught in a lie, cannot overcome their "jealous" nature, and they are not permitted to testify about a husband's death.

One more example will suffice. As with minors, there are areas which fall within the "world" of women, at least partially because of the "nosy" nature of women in general, like noticing clothing, jewelry, etc. As with minors, women, too, are acceptable as witnesses concerning such areas, because they may be relied upon in such matters.[114]

Admittedly, there is no primary source which directly attributes to their nature the disqualification of the class of women from testifying. But, given the fact that all other disqualified classes can be rationally understood, and given the fact that if the disqualification of women were a *gezerat ha-katuv* (an inherently inexplicable biblical injunction) it would be difficult to justify any exceptions, and given the fact that exceptions do exist, and given the fact that the sources reveal a general stereotype of women which would justify their exclusion as a class, and given the fact that the exceptions to the prohibition are easily comprehensible if the general stereotype is the cause of the class disqualification, the questionable nature of the explanation we have for the exclusion of women from testifying dwarfs to infinitesimal proportions.

Therefore, it is plausible to assert that there were underlying motivations which either led or compelled the sages to interpret as they did the biblical passages on the basis of which they disqualified women from testifying. Indeed, the passage in *Shevuot*[115] in which the disqualification of women as witnesses is related to a biblical text, itself reflects at least two other possible understandings of the biblical verse which might argue against the thesis that it was intended to exclude women. The first is that the phrase *shenei ha-anashim* ("the two persons") can be understood as referring to the litigants, and not to the witnesses. And the second is that even if it refers to witnesses, it may be generic, and was couched in the masculine not in order to exclude women, but merely as a reflection of the reality of the time. As a matter of fact, all the activities of the overwhelming majority of women were limited to the home, and women rarely participated in any kind of courtroom procedures. However, no one should understand any of the aforesaid to imply that the prohibition against women serving as witnesses is not *de-oraita* ("biblical"). By traditional canons of interpretation, it has biblical status.

Having reached this point, we cannot avoid expressing some judgment concerning the applicability of the rabbinic portrait of women to women in modern societies, even assuming that it did apply to women of their own time. Is the halakhically valid argument of *shinnui ha-ittim* ("times have changed") applicable to the supposed "nature" and legal status of women or not? A variety of responses to the question, and to the implications of the potential answers, are conceivable. We shall indicate the possibilities.

1. The nature of women has not changed, and the rabbinic description of it is still accurate. If that be the case, the conclusion is self-evident. The same characterological traits which underlay the original prohibition are still applicable, and the prohibition is reaffirmed in full.

2. The modern woman does not seem to be as described by the sages, but since the sages have so described women, it is moderns who misperceive their nature and it is they who are

mistaken. Such a response will deny the appropriateness of a claim of *shinnui ha-ittim* ("times have changed"). If so, the prohibition will be reaffirmed in full.

3. Modern women are, indeed, not like the image portrayed by the sages and, were that stereotype the sole justification for the prohibition, a claim of "times have changed" would be in order. But the error is the assertion that the stereotype is the sole justification for the prohibition. There are sufficient other reasons to disqualify women from testimony. One such reason might be the claim of long-standing precedent. Another, the claim that an assertion of "the times have changed" would be rejected by large segments of the world Jewish community, resulting in potential schism within the Jewish people, with potential baneful ramifications affecting areas such as family law. The net result of this kind of argument would leave the prohibition untouched on grounds such as *halakhah ke-divreihem ve-lo mi-taamam* ("the law is as they say, but not for their reason").

4. The biblical status of the prohibition leaves us no option other than the reaffirmation of the prohibition in its totality, even if it entails positing that the image of women which underlies it must now be considered a legal fiction, that is, applicable legally, regardless of its actual factualness.

5. The image of women has changed, but the change is not desirable. It is not true today that "all glorious is the king's daughter within the palace," but would that it were. The claim of "times have changed" may be halakhically valid, but in this instance should not be invoked because it would serve only to further a process which ought to be reversed! Hence, the existent norms should be reaffirmed.

6. The original justification for prohibiting women to act as witnesses is the only conceivable justification. But that justification is no longer valid not only because the status of women has changed, but also because the conception of the so-called nature of women has changed. That change is not only irrevocable, it is also desirable. Hence, failure to attempt some halakhically justifiable remedy to an untenable situation re-

flects a lack of seriousness about *halakhah* rather than a commitment to it. Those who affirm this position, and I am among them, and who consider themselves to be committed to the *halakhah*, are therefore in duty bound to spell out what they consider to be halakhically justifiable remedies. They must deal particularly with the objection that the prohibition is "biblical" and with the effect that this position may have upon the problem of maintaining the unity of *kelal Yisrael* ("the whole Jewish people").

I shall spend no time justifying my opinion that the rabbinic image of women is the sole justification for observance of the present halakhic norms regarding testimony by women, nor defending my view that the modern image of woman does not justify the norms, nor proving that the change in that image is desirable. The preceding analysis regarding the justification for prohibiting women from acting as witnesses, I believe, validates my opinion that it is the rabbinic image of the nature of women which is the sole justification for the prohibition. I consider the opinion that the modern image of women does not justify the prohibition, and that this change from the rabbinic image of women is desirable, to be self-evident. I proceed, therefore, to deal with the problem raised by the *de-oraita* (the "biblical" status of the prohibition).

There are three possible approaches to the problem, each with its strengths and weaknesses, and they will be treated in ascending order of systemic difficulty. That is, the second approach requires greater halakhic daring than the first, and the third requires greater halakhic daring than the second.

1. Leave the prohibition theoretically intact, continuing to affirm that women may not serve as witnesses. Since, however, there are already long-standing exceptions to the prohibition, the sages of today will do nothing but add two additional categories of testimony to the list of exceptions, namely, witnessing a *ketubbah* (marriage contract) or a *get* (the document recording a divorce). These are the major areas in which witnessing according to Jewish law is still widely relevant. The justification for these two additional exceptions would be the

same as that given for the previous exceptions, namely, that women may now be considered reliable in such matters because they are *"milleta de-atya le-igaloyei"* (i.e., "matters that are most likely to become generally known," since governmental offices record all marriages and divorces). The obvious advantage of such an approach would be that the basic norm remains untouched. Women would still be forbidden *de-oraita* ("biblically") to serve as witnesses, for example, in capital cases. No change in long-standing legal principles would be necessary.

That, though, is also a disadvantage. It leaves intact the premise that women, by their nature, are generally unreliable as a class. Adding two further exceptions does not deny the premise, and it is the failure of that premise to reflect present realities which motivated the search for a remedy in the first place. To devise a remedy which leaves the premise intact is a strange resolution to the problem. But, in addition, this approach cannot be applied to witnessing a betrothal.

Witnesses can be of two different types. If two people transact a deal in the presence of witnesses, the function of the witnesses is to serve as verification that the deal was transacted. They serve as legal protection for both parties. But if two people transact a deal without witnesses present, and both admit in court that the deal has been transacted, the absence of witnesses will not prevent the court from compelling compliance with the deal. In this sense, the witnesses are no more than verifiers of a valid and binding act. In the second type of witnessing, the witnesses are not simply verifiers of an act which is valid anyway, but are also the validators of the act itself. That is, the act cannot be considered legally valid, even by the admission of the parties, without witnesses. In such a case, the claim of *milleta de-atya le-igaloyei* is inapplicable, since no act could be independently verified as a legal act when the legality of the act itself was contingent upon the presence of witnesses. Thus, if the witness were an invalid witness, the entire act is invalid, even if the parties admit to it. An invalid act cannot be independently verified.

Witnessing a betrothal is of the second type. Based upon the *gemara*,[116] both Rambam and the *Shulhan Arukh* so codify the law:[117]

> The betrothal of one who betrothes without witnesses, or even with one witness, is invalid, even if both admit that it took place.

Hence, the attempted expansion of the list of exceptions to the disqualification of women as witnesses would not work for one of the few areas in which witnessing is still widely relevant.[118]

2. The second approach is very different, and utilizes a statement of Maimonides as its basis. Maimonides wrote:[119]

> If the High Court offered an exegesis of a verse on the basis of one of the acceptable exegetical principles[120] as appeared appropriate to them, and some later court[121] saw some reason to overturn that exegesis, the later court may do so, and may explain as it sees fit.

On the basis of this passage of the Rambam one may posit that the talmudic sages interpreted Deuteronomy 19:17 to exclude women from testifying by invoking a recognized exegetical principle as they saw fit. Since what they "saw fit" was predicated on the general accuracy of an image of women which they espoused, and since that image is no longer considered to be generally accurate, the "court" of today sees "some valid reason" to overturn that exegesis. That valid reason is *shinnui ha-ittim* ("the change that time" has brought to our conception of the character of women). The "court" of today may therefore interpret that verse in a manner that does not prohibit women from acting as witnesses.

This approach is alluring, and has distinct advantages: (1) It invokes the rabbinic right to substitute for the *de-oraita* ("biblically rooted") norm which disqualified women from acting as witnesses by another "biblically rooted" norm which permits them so to act. The status of each norm, in its time, is *de-oraita* ("biblical"). (2) It eliminates the problems stemming from the different types of witnesses. (3) The ground for overturning the earlier interpretation is the recognition of the total inapplicability of the sages' view of women to the women of our time and place.

The second approach, however, has its disadvantages as well: (1) Its basis is a statement of the Rambam which does not seem to have wide support among *posekim*. It is, in other words, a *daat yahid* ("one man's opinion"). (2) The right implied by the Rambam has never been consciously invoked by anyone. (3) Invoking it would work well only according to either the surface meaning of the Bavli[122] or according to the opinion of Rambam himself.[123] According to the former, we would interpret the phrase *shenei ha-anashim* ("the two persons") as referring to the litigants, and not to the witnesses. In regard to Rambam's opinion, we would understand *edim* ("witnesses") as being a generic term, rather than as referring exclusively to males. But, many could argue that according to the *Sifrei* or according to the Bavli's explanation of the *baraitot*,[124] even the position of the Rambam is inapplicable. Since a *gezerah shavah* is ultimately Sinaitic, the prohibition against having women act as witnesses is not based upon a rabbinical exegesis, but on Divine exegesis which the sages merely conveyed, but did not originate. (4) Some would argue that if a "court" of today invoked such a right, it would open a floodgate resulting in the reckless use of this power to the ultimate detriment of the *halakhah*.

3. The third approach bears similarities to the second, though it is different from it in significant respects. This approach would base its claim on the principle that *yesh ko'ah bi-dei hakhamim la'akor davar min ha-torah be-kum ve-aseh*[125] ("the sages may knowingly abrogate a norm which is *de-oraita* [biblical]). Though the general precedent allows rabbinic abrogation of norms only passively, that is, *be-shev ve-al ta'aseh* ("by refraining from doing what is commanded"), there is widespread agreement among *posekim* that "active" abrogation, i.e., permitting an act which is contrary to the Torah, is permissible when deemed warranted by the proper authorities. One such passage will suffice.

The Tosafot record:[126] "Even though generally the sages do not have the right to abrogate a matter from the Torah actively [i.e., by permitting the performance of a forbidden act,] but *be-makom she-yesh panim ve-taam ba-davar* ['when there is good cause and sufficient reason for it'], all agree that they have that right." Interestingly, the final proof of the Tosafot is connected with the very subject under discussion. The right of a woman to testify about the death of her husband[127] is universally recognized. That right is itself an active abrogation of a biblical norm which disqualifies women from *all* testimony. The proponents of this approach would assert that the changed status of women in our society generally and the radical change in our conception of the nature of women is "good cause and sufficient reason" to warrant abrogation of the norm. They reinforce their position by stressing their conviction that adherence to a norm, the sole rationale for which is no longer applicable, does not strengthen *halakhah*, but makes a mockery of it.

This approach has all of the advantages of the second approach, without some of the disadvantages of that approach. It is based on a principle formulated by the *gemara* and reaffirmed by many *posekim*. It is not a *daat yahid* ("one man's opinion"). Not only has it received theoretical affirmation, it has actually been invoked. Furthermore, the right to abrogate the norm rather than to attempt to reinterpret the verse which was the basis of the norm, applies even to norms which are conceived as being *halakhah le Moshe mi-Sinai* ("revealed to Moses at Sinai").

This third approach is not without its disadvantages. Obviously, the floodgate syndrome problem applies to it. Furthermore, some may claim that today's students of the *halakhah* no longer possess the right of active abrogation of a biblical norm, even if sages of the past did. This claim is supported by the fact that this right "to abrogate" has not been invoked for a long time. Finally, some may assert that the change that has taken place in the status of women generally and in our conception of their "nature" is not "good cause and sufficient reason" to invoke the ultimate systemic right, even if it still exists.

In the final analysis, none of the three possible approaches is simple, and all involve great concern for the impact that any one of them may have upon *Klal Yisrael*, the ideal of the unity of the people of Israel, for undoubtedly any action whatsoever would evoke vigorous opposition in certain circles.

SECTION THREE

The number of sources which bear directly on the question of the ordination of women is small. Obviously, to the extent that the absence of actual instances of ordination of women constitutes a legal precedent, the weight of precedent surely does not favor their ordination.

There is, as is well known, one source which seems explicitly to deny the women the right of ordination, or of any other type of appointment. Maimonides, paraphrasing the *Sifrei Devarim*,[128] wrote:[129]

> No woman may reign as a sovereign. . . . And, similarly, nobody but a man may be appointed to any *mesimot* [public office] among Jews.

It seems, therefore, that according to the Rambam the ordination of women would be biblically forbidden. It should be noted, however, that the latter half of Maimonides' statement appears to be his own extrapolation from the *Sifrei*, which restricts its prohibition to the appointment of a woman as queen. Maimonides' contention is not affirmed by other *posekim*, and is not recorded in the other codes. Furthermore, to the extent that Maimonides might have been motivated to expand the *Sifrei*'s prohibition by his own view of the mental competencies of women, the claim of *shinnui ha-ittim* ("times have changed") is not only warranted, it is absolutely necessary. The Rambam asserts[130] that women should not be taught Torah because they would turn the words of Torah into *divrei havai* ("trivialities") and because of *aniyut da'atan* ("their inferior intelligence"). Even if this were true of women of the Rambam's time, no well-informed person could seriously continue to affirm its truth today. It is clearly and overwhelmingly contradicted both by experience and by all scientific evidence. Even if there could or might be disagreement among moderns about the characterological traits of women which might disqualify them from testimony, it is difficult to conceive of anyone asserting that women are intellectually inferior to men. Given that the Rambam's expansion of the *Sifrei* has no presently known source in rabbinic literature, it is most likely that it was his own perception of the intellectual capacities of women which motivated his words. Hence, women could not and should not be disqualified from ordination even on the basis of *safek de-oraita*—that "it might possibly be a violation of a biblical norm." The biblical prohibition is restricted to the exercise of sovereign power by women. That subject, while itself worthy of halakhic analysis, is so theoretical at the present time that it need not be dealt with in this inquiry.

There is one further source which might be understood to proscribe the ordination of women. The Midrash comments on the words of Manoah:[131]

> "And Manoah said [to the angel]: 'Now let your words come.' Manoah said to him: "Until now I have heard from a woman, and women are not *benot hora'ah* ['qualified to give decisions'], *ve-ein lismokh al divreihen* ['and their words are not to be relied on']. But, let your words come—"I want to hear from your mouth."

If Manoah's statement about women is taken out of context, and the words (particularly the word *hora'ah*) are understood in their usual legal sense, his statement should be translated: "Women are not competent to render decisions, and their words [therefore] are not to be relied upon." In context, though, that understanding of the passage is impossible. What kind of decision had the woman rendered? She had done naught but report to her husband what the angel had said to her in his absence. But, bearing in mind that Manoah had requested the appearance of the angel with the words "let him come again to us *ve-yorenu* [and instruct us] how the child to be born should be handled," the meaning of Manoah's statement in the Midrash becomes clear. Neither the angel nor the woman was rendering decisions of any kind. Both were conveying instructions. Thus, Manoah claimed: "Women *einan benot hora'ah* [do not know how to take instructions], and their words cannot be relied upon." Since women do not know how to take instructions, the angel was asked to come again and tell Manoah directly how the child should be handled.

The biblical record of the angel's response puts Manoah in his place. The angel twice repeats: "Do as I told the woman." He never repeats the manner in which the child is to be raised. He repeats only the precautions the wife should take during her pregnancy.

Beyond these two sources, there seem to be no others which, no matter how loosely one would apply any of the rabbinic hermeneutical principles, could possibly be interpreted as stating explicitly that women may not be ordained.

Of the functions which a modern rabbi serves qua rabbi, only two may be halakhically open to any question, and only one seriously so. One involves the right of women to teach Torah, and the other the right to serve as a judge. We shall deal primarily with the latter, in the course of which the former will also be addressed.

The question is based on a *mishnah* which states: "Whoever is fit to judge is also fit to testify, though some are fit to testify even though they are not fit to judge."[132] If the first clause of the *mishnah* means: "Only those who are fit to be witnesses could ever be fit to judge," women are obviously excluded, since they are not fit to be witnesses, and could not, therefore, ever be fit to judge.[133] Indeed, that understanding of the clause is the *prima facie* meaning which the *rishonim* attribute to it. But they were challenged by the fact that the Bible records that Deborah, who was a prophetess, "judged Israel at that time . . . and the Israelites would come to her for decisions" (Judges 4:4–5). The Tosafot offer three resolutions to the problem. These resolutions are relevant to our subject.

First, they suggest that Deborah did not actually judge, but served only as the teacher of the law to others so that they could judge.[134] This answer affirms the prohibition of a woman serving as a judge. In the process, however, it posits as virtually uncontestable the fact that a woman can teach the law, even if she cannot judge. Thus, the minor question which had to be addressed is resolved.

Secondly, they suggest that the clause in the *mishnah* may not mean what we have claimed it to mean. Rather, the *mishnah* may be positing the contingency of judging and witnessing only for those for whom witnessing is a real possibility. For those for whom it is not a real possibility no contingency exists. Thus, the clause in the *mishnah* should be understood: "Those and only those *men* who are fit to be witnesses could ever be fit to judge." Women, though, might judge even though they could never be fit to be witnesses. According to this response, then, there is no prohibition at all on the right of women to serve as judges.

Finally, they suggest that the people may have accepted her as a judge, even though she was technically disqualified.[135] As is clear from the *mishnah*,[136] litigants are entitled to accept as a judge even one who is otherwise disqualified. Thus, Deborah had the right to judge because the Israelites accepted her as such.

In the final analysis, then, there is no legal objection to the technical granting of the title "rabbi" to a woman. The only rabbinic function which might be questionable is that of judging. Regarding judging there is support for the idea that women are not disqualified. Even if that is rejected, a woman rabbi serving a community would be acceptable as a judge on the grounds that they have accepted her, since rabbis today are selected by the communities which they serve.

It should be noted that the area of judging is connected with the area of testifying. Thus, the resolution of the issue of testifying, which was the subject of the previous section of this paper, takes on significance vis-à-vis this issue as well. If any of the potentially viable approaches discussed there were adopted, the question of the right of women to judge would become a non-issue.

SECTION FOUR

The exemption of women from positive time-bound commandments has been variously rationalized. Some have affirmed that the exemption is intended to emphasize the centrality of the woman's role in relation to her husband, the home, and the family. That function is so central that the observance of *mitzvot* which might conflict with it is suspended because of it. Others contend that women have been exempted from such *mitzvot* because they have an innate religious sensitivity which makes their observance unnecessary. Whether either of these rationalizations is correct is of little moment to our present inquiry. Suffice it to say, that whatever the reason for the traditional exemption of women, the exemption itself has had the long-standing weight of precedent to support it. To solve the halakhic difficulties that these exemptions present in relation to the question of the rabbinic ordination of women, I posited at the end of Section One the existence of four categories into which women might be classified.[137] I urge the Faculty to go on record as accepting all four of those categories as defensible and viable options for women to adopt.

I am opposed to two alternatives which are often proposed. The first alternative recommends the adoption of a *takkanah* obligating all women to observe all *mitzvot* from which they are exempt. The second alternative recommends a pronouncement affirming that women should refrain from the observance of those *mitzvot* from which they are exempt, even if they may have the legal right to observe them. I am opposed to the issuance of a *takkanah* because the imposition of legal obligation by *takkanah* would make noncompliance with the dictates of that *takkanah* sinful. That would result in the creation of a large class of sinners where none now exists. I dread the thought that the Faculty of the Seminary, or any other segment of the Conservative Movement, should seek to impose a set of obligations not already recognized by the tradition upon any woman who is satisfied with the status quo.

On the other hand, there is an ever increasing number of Jewish women who see their roles differently, if not for their entire lives, then at least for significant segments of their lives. If such women view the traditional exemption as based upon the claim of the mother's familial centrality, they may yearn greatly to be more active participants in Jewish religious life during the years that they are not actively "mothering." Indeed, many may find it possible to remain equally religiously active even during peak periods of "mothering." If women are capable of holding full-time and responsible jobs without serious encroachment on their familial responsibilities, there is no reason to believe that the "onus" of the observance of positive time-bound commandments would become the "straw that broke the camel's back." If such women see the traditional exemption as based upon the innate female religious sensitivity, they may choose to abide by the traditional patterns. But many women do not perceive themselves as more sensitive religiously than their male counterparts. In the final analysis, it is their own perception of their need for *mitzvot* which is most important.

Women who wish to observe *mitzvot* should be given every encouragement to do so, since there is sufficient legal precedent for allowing them to do so. At present, regrettably, such women are subjected to the most virulent type of vilification by two very different groups. Observant men have looked so askance at women who have adopted the observance of *mitzvot* from which they are exempt, that they give the impression that their behavior must be forbidden. The very people to whom such women turn for assurance that their behavior falls within legal parameters, for that is a great concern of many of them, give the opposite impression by merely tolerating their behavior, even if they do not actively attempt to discourage it.

These women, too, are often castigated by women who accept their traditional exemption from *mitzvot*. They are told either that they are trying to be like men or that they are allowing men to dictate what women should be. To the best of my knowledge and observation, these women are motivated, by and large, by purely religious motives. That does not imply that they were not at all affected by the spirit that animates the various women's or feminist movements.

Women must be allowed to increase their patterns of religious observance without hindrance from men or other women. Indeed, since their observance of *mitzvot* is permissible, there is no reason why they should not be encouraged in their quest, if that is the path they have chosen.

To be sure, it must be made absolutely clear to all women who adopt the observance of *mitzvot* that there is often more involved than observance alone. That is particularly true either where a *minyan* is needed or where the issue of agency is involved. They must understand that only obligated individuals constitute a quorum and only one who is obligated can serve as the agent for others. Just because a woman comes to services, or dons *tallit* and *tefillin*, or receives an *aliyah* does not mean she has the right to be counted toward a *minyan* or to act as agent in behalf of one who is obligated to perform a *mitzvah*.

Women may be counted in a *minyan* or serve as *shatz* only when they have accepted upon themselves the voluntary obligation to pray as required by the law, and at the times required by law, and only when they recognize and affirm that failure to comply with the obligation is sin. Then they may be counted in the quorum and serve as the agents for others. This is the position which I would recommend to the Faculty for adoption.

I anticipate that objections of various sorts will be raised against this recommendation, and would like to respond in advance to those objections which I foresee.

How can I require women to accept a voluntary obligation and recognize the consequence of noncompliance as sin when the concepts of "obligation" and "sin" are rarely mentioned by men? How can I count men in a *minyan* if they show up at services sporadically, never praying otherwise, and surely not viewing their regular failure to pray as sin in any way, yet refuse to count toward a *minyan* any woman who comes every day in order to say *kaddish*, or even without saying *kaddish*, but refuses to recognize the sinful nature of her noncompliance if she ever fails to pray?

I answer that I am fully aware of these realities, but my concern is for the halakhic status of behaviors, not for the common misconceptions of the halakhic status of those behaviors. If we have failed to educate our constituents that, from our perspective, obedience to Jewish law is obligatory and not voluntary, that does not deny that it is, in fact, obligatory. A man is obligated to pray whether or not he recognizes that obligation. Any time he does pray he complies with the obligation and can be counted toward the quorum. When he does not pray at the required times he sins whether or not he recognizes that failure as sin.

The halakhic status of a woman's prayer is very different. She can be considered obligated, and count toward the *minyan*, only when she accepts the status of obligation upon herself. Her obligation is self-imposed, and not other-imposed. It requires *recognition* of the obligatory state, and that, in turn, demands conscious recognition of the consequences of failure to comply with the obligation. The consequences are called sin. Only when those elements are present can she be considered legally obligated. If a woman prays without considering herself obligated, she exercises a right of hers, but does not fulfill an obligation. A prayer quorum requires people who are obligated, not people who are exercising a right. Whenever men pray they are fulfilling an obligation; women, though, may pray as the exercise of a right, as opposed to the fulfillment of an obligation. Thus, men always count toward a *minyan*, but women may not.

Some, I suspect, will object to the distinction between obligated and nonobligated women on practical grounds, even if they admit the distinction on halakhic grounds. The objection may be couched in theoretical terms such as *hakhamim lo natenu et divreihem le-shi'urin* ("the sages formulated their norms to be applicable without distinction"), but the objection will really be quite practical. How could one possibly count some women and not others, as a practical matter? I do not find the objection at all compelling. In a vast majority of cases, when ten men are present, the question will be entirely academic. The issue will be actual only when the ten persons present include both men and women, and it must be ascertained whether or not there is a *minyan*. Even then, the distinction between categories of women will not be as complex as it might seem. If the women are in their home communities they are likely to be known as "obligated" or "nonobligated" women, in much the same way that youngsters in their home communities are known as "bar mitzvah" or "non–bar mitzvah." The issue becomes troublesome only in the rare instance when a woman in a strange community is necessary to complete the quorum. Is it any more unworkable in those circumstances to ask her if she considers herself obligated than it is to ask a youngster, under similar circumstances, if he is a bar mitzvah? I think not.

It would be worthwhile to create a religious ceremony celebrating a woman's acceptance of *mitzvot* as obligatory. Such a ceremony would have multiple functions. It would mark the occasion as religious. It would be important psychologically for both the woman and her community. It would be a practical guide for the determination of the woman's status.

In Section Two, I stated my conviction that failure to attempt some rectification of the testimonial status of women reflects a lack of seriousness about *halakhah* rather than a commitment to it.[137] Obviously one could attempt to resolve the problem and fail. It is only failure to attempt which reflects a lack of seriousness, not failure to succeed. Both because of its universally accepted *de-oraita* ("biblical") status and because of its implications for unity of the Jewish people, the matter of women and testimony is extremely difficult.

Before offering a specific proposal for consideration, I would like to emphasize as strongly as I can that the issue of male-female equality plays no part in my thinking on the subject. I find no ethical objection to discrimination against an entire class, when the discrimination is justified and defensible. I have made it quite clear, I hope, that I would be opposed to any argument for women's ritual rights which was predicated on an *a priori* claim that men and women *must* be equal. Testimonial equality between men and women may be the *result* of grappling with the issue of women and testifying, but it is not its underlying motivation. I reiterate that for me the underlying motivation for the difficult struggle is the firm conviction that the grounds for the disqualification of women as witnesses, which grounds are, in my opinion, the only possible continuing justification of the proscriptive norm, are no longer applicable. It is simply inconceivable to me that anyone could cogently argue that modern women are generally unreliable as witnesses, that the entire class of women should be disqualified. If ever a claim of *shinnui ha-ittim* ("times have changed") is appropriate, surely it is so regarding the rabbinic perception of the character of women.

I recommend, therefore, the exercise by the faculty of the ultimate systemic right of the learned who are committed to the *halakhah* to openly and knowingly abrogate the prohibition against women serving as witnesses. This is the ultimate *halakhically warranted* act. It is not a *non-halakhic act.*

We have demonstrated in Section Three of this paper that there are no insurmountable halakhic objections to the granting of ordination per se to women. Sections One and Two were intended to apply to all women, a vast majority of whom would never seek ordination as rabbis. What remains to be discussed is the relationship of Sections One and Two to the ordination question.

The Minority Opinion of the Commission's report has cogently demonstrated that ordination should not be considered as a narrow question, but as a broad one.[139] To be sure, the issues addressed in the first two sections of this paper "flow from it [the ordination question] almost inexorably."[140] If one can say about issues that some flow more inexorably and others flow less inexorably, the issues of women in the *minyan* and as *shatz* belong to the first category and the issue of women as witnesses belongs in the second category.

The Minority Opinion restricts its concern to the issues of *minyan, aliyyot,* and *shatz.* My concern reaches beyond these issues. I would expect that a rabbi should serve his community as an example par excellence of commitment to the study of Torah and the observance of *mitzvot.* That should be no less true of female rabbis than of male rabbis. I recommend, therefore, that the Seminary admit women as candidates for ordination, on condition that they accept the observance of all *mitzvot* as an obligation. Should a woman rabbi renounce her obligatory status, she would be required to cease functioning as a rabbi.

If my recommendation concerning women in general and the problem of witnessing were accepted, that would obviously apply no less to women rabbis than to other women. The question which remains, however, is whether the rejection of that proposal would be sufficient reason for denying women ordination as rabbis. Since a woman acting as a rabbi would be greatly tempted to act as a witness to a *ketubbah* or a *get,* and would be hard put to explain to her congregants why she may not do so, would we by ordaining women *be mesayye'in li-dvar averah* ("accomplices to a transgression")? The frequently heard negative answer to this question is based on the fact that the Seminary does not refrain from ordaining *kohanim* as rabbis even though the functions of the rabbinate include officiating at funerals and burials, and the *kohen*-rabbi might find himself in a "compromised" position. I find that answer, as it is generally understood, to be inadequate. If a *kohen*-rabbi officiates at a funeral, he sins. But, the funeral is completely valid. Nobody claims that the deceased has not been "legally" eulogized or buried. But if one disqualified from serving as a witness were to witness a betrothal, the betrothed couple would not be legally betrothed.

I am nevertheless of the opinion that even if the proposal concerning *edut* is rejected, women should not be denied ordination. Though the case of the woman-rabbi is not an exact analogy to that of the *kohen*-rabbi, there is one aspect in which the two cases are alike. We function on the presumption that every graduate of the Rabbinical School is committed to the observance of the *halakhah*. Individual rabbis violate one or another of the *halakhot*. They do so for different reasons. Often, though rarely verbalized as such, the "violation" stems from the conviction that the *halakhah* being "violated" ought not to be the law. Many a *kohen*-rabbi who officiates at funerals does so because of the strong conviction that many or even all of the laws dealing with the priest should no longer be considered as valid. I disagree with them. Yet, I am unwilling to claim that such rabbis have no commitment to *halakhah*. If the faculty of the Seminary, acting as a synod, affirmed that a woman even though ordained may not serve as a witness, the number of Seminary students and graduates who would ignore the expressed halakhic judgment of the faculty would be negligible.

Moreover, it is the widespread practice among Seminary students and Rabbinical Assembly members to consider the interests of those whom they serve and not merely their own personal convictions. Thus, couples contemplating *aliyyah* are usually urged by Conservative rabbis to use a *ketubbah* recognized by the Israeli rabbinate, or to have a *get* written by a rabbi recognized by them, in order to forestall any possible complications when they actually go on *aliyyah*. No matter how "liberal-minded" a Seminary student or graduate may be, he does not exercise his "liberal-mindedness" at the expense of those who might be adversely affected by it.

One of my most revered teachers has recommended to me in private discussion that women should be encouraged to adopt the observance of *mitzvot* and that the question of ordination be put off for a generation, until such behavior by women becomes common.[141] I must respectfully disagree with that recommendation. I have already stated my view that only women who have accepted the obligation to observe all the *mitzvot* should be considered candidates for ordination. If this position is affirmed, then the Committee on Admissions would seek evidence that the women who apply have complied with that requirement. In that case, the earliest group of women applicants would undoubtedly be those whose observance of *mitz-*

vot already reflects voluntary acceptance of all of the *mitzvot*. They will be the women who have had the fortitude to be trailblazers on previously unmarked paths. I cannot see why the forerunners should be denied the right which their very behavior will have bequeathed to those who follow them.

NOTES

1. Mishnah Kiddushin 1:7.

2. For example, eating of *matzah* at the Seder. Kiddushin 34a.

3. For example, the study of Torah. Kiddushin 29b and 34a.

4. Kiddushin 34a.

5. See analysis of Louis Ginzberg, *A Commentary on the Palestinian Talmud*, vol. II, pp. 158–164. Note particularly his comment at the bottom of p. 162.

6. On these two questions see David Feldman, "Woman's Role and Jewish Law," *Conservative Judaism*, vol. 26, no. 4, pp. 29–39, reprinted in Seymour Siegel, *Conservative Judaism and Jewish Law* (New York: Rabbinical Assembly, 1977), pp. 294–305. See specifically pp. 297–300.

7. Commentary to Sifra, par. 2, Weiss edition, 4c.

8. Lev. 1:4.

9. On the basis of Erubin 96b.

10. 4:8.

11. I.e., practicing blowing the *shofar* even on Shabbat. Sounding the *shofar* on Shabbat comes under the category of *shevut* and ought to be prohibited.

12. Male children are permitted to practice blowing the *shofar* even on the Sabbath because even though they, as minors, are not yet obligated to observe the *mitzvah* of blowing the *shofar*, they may do so voluntarily. Their practicing is therefore antecedent to their voluntary observance of the *mitzvah* and is permitted because they may observe the *mitzvah* voluntarily. The fact, therefore, that the *mishnah* excludes women, whom the *halakhah* exempts from the *mitzvah*, from the permission to practice blowing the *shofar* on the Sabbath implies the view that they cannot observe it even voluntarily. That, then, applies to all *mitzvot* from whose observance they are now exempted by the *halakhah*.

13. 96b.

14. 3:15.

15. Sukkah 42a.

16. In the printed *gemara: Ho'il ve-ishah lav bat hiyyuva he, eima lo tekabbel*. But see Rashi's explanation ad loc.

17. Hilkhot Tzitzit 3:9. Cf. comment of *Hagahot Maimoniyot*, ibid., letter *mem*.

18. It does not seem plausible that Maimonides understands the benediction to be an additional *mitzvah*. Were that the case, a man who performed a *mitzvah* without reciting the blessing would have fulfilled his obligation. Hilkhot Lulav 7:6, for example, clearly implies the opposite.

19. The recitation of a benediction over a *mitzvah* which one is not

obligated to perform involves the "taking of God's name in vain." It is *berakhah le-vattalah*—a purposeless benediction. However, if women were allowed to observe *mitzvot* qua *mitzvot*, it is difficult to fathom why it would be a "purposeless" benediction. See above, note 18, and below, pp. 131 f. Maimonides seems to allow women to perform the *mitzvah* without reciting the benediction in order to give them the opportunity to experience spiritual satisfaction *(nahat ruah le-nashim)*.

20. *Or Zarua*, Sukkah and Lulav, 314:2, 68d.

21. Ibid., 266, 62a.

22. The view of Rabbenu Tam receives regular mention, though we will not quote it directly. It can be found in Tosafot Eruvin 96a, s.v. *dilma* and parallels listed there in *Masoret Ha-shas*.

23. I.e., she could handle it for the *mitzvah* itself, but not take it unnecessarily from her son or husband to replace it in water on Shabbat.

24. And, as such, she may handle it even for nonritualistic or otherwise noncompelling reasons, such as putting it in water.

25. *Teshuvot Rashi*, #68, Elfenbein edition, pp. 80 f., and parallels.

26. Even his statement in Rosh Ha-shanah 33a, s.v. *Ha*, does not necessarily demonstrate his own position. Though that statement clearly implies that a woman who sounds the *shofar* would violate the commandment "not to add" (Deuteronomy 13:1) and, therefore, that the recitation of the blessing would be a purposeless benediction. Rashi's comment is no more than his explanation of the prima facie inference of the *gemara* that women are prohibited from practicing the sounding of the *shofar* on Shabbat. There is no greater reason to suppose that this statement reflects Rashi's own view than to suppose that his statement, s.v. *somekhot reshut*, reflects his own view. The latter statement asserts that there is no prohibition whatsoever on a woman's observance of positive time-bound commandments.

27. Kiddushin 1:7, 29a.

28. Kiddushin 31a. The statement here made that "those who observe because they are commanded are greater than those who observe without having been commanded" would be meaningless unless the *halakhah* recognized the existence of such a class. This implies that voluntary observance of non-commanded *mitzvot* is not only not forbidden, but that it is included within the halakhic framework. Legally speaking, women could surely not be excluded from that class. They must, therefore, be permitted to observe voluntarily.

29. The final sentence of the responsum reads as follows: "Proof: For we claim [Megillah 23a] that 'all count to the seven called to the Torah, even a woman,' who can go up to the Torah and recite the blessing, without it being considered a purposeless blessing, even though she is exempt from the *mitzvah* of *Talmud Torah*." From this "proof" it would appear that Rabbi Yitzhak Ha-levi assumed that this *baraita* allowed a woman to be called to the Torah even first or last, as well as among the intermediate *aliyyot*, since only the first and the last one recited the blessing. The matter is one of significant disagreement among *posekim*, but analysis of this question per se is irrelevant to this paper.

30. *Shulhan Arukh, Orah Hayyim* 589:6.

31. *Responsa of Rashba*, vol. I, #123.

32. Eruvin 96a.

33. Tel Aviv, 5717, #1.

34. See above, note 22.

35. Kiddushin 31a.

36. *Hiddushei Ha-Ran* to Rosh Ha-shanah 33a, s.v. *ve-ein*, end.

37. *Hiddushei Ha-Ritba* to Kiddushin 31a, s.v., *ve-yesh dohin*.

38. Kiddushin 1:7, 61c and Pesahim 8:1, 35d. Cf. Bavli Pesahim 91b. It is irrelevant whether the statement refers to the First Pesah or to the Second Pesah (see Numbers 9:4–12), for if it refers only to the Second Pesah, it is because women are obligated to observe the First Pesah.

39. The P'nei Moshe (d. 1780) accepts this reading both in Kiddushin and in Pesahim. The Korban Ha-Edah (1704–1762) emends the reading to "obligatory." The latter was obviously motivated to "correct" Rabbi Elazar's statement because of the question of the Bavli (Pes. 91b), *"I reshut amai doheh et Ha-Shabbat"* ("If it is a voluntary [rather than obligatory] act, why may one violate the Shabbat [in order to perform it]?"). But the statement of Rabbi Elazar himself seems to indicate that precisely that is his *hiddush* ("innovation").

40. Sifra, par. #2. See above p. 129.

41. The laying on of the hands on an animal during the Shabbat or a Festival is ordinarily prohibited, because in leaning heavily upon the animal, he is "making use" of the animal (Hagigah, 16b). This prohibition is categorized as a *shevut*. Since, however, men are obligated to bring certain sacrifices during a Festival, the *halakhah* permits them to violate this *shevut*. The question therefore arises, whether a woman who voluntarily brings a sacrifice on a Festival may also violate this *shevut*.

42. I.e., *tzitzit* containing a mixture of wool and flax.

43. See *Shulhan Arukh, Orah Hayyim* 17:2 in Rema, and the explanation of the *Arukh Ha-shulhan*, ad loc. Note that Isserles (1525–1572) prefaces his contention of *yohara* with the statement that if women wish to wear *tzitzit* and recite the blessing, they may do so. I shall comment but briefly on the question of the right of women to wear *tallit* and *tefillin:* (1) It is difficult to accept "arrogance" as properly applying to an act totally independent of either numbers or intention. If many women wore a *tallit* it would seem less, if at all, "arrogant." (2) To define the act as "arrogant" seems to imply that its intention must be understood to be "to appear manlike." I shall address that subject in the final section of this paper. Regarding *tefillin* the Rema (O.H. 38:3) is more strict, adding to Caro's statement that they are not obligated, the claim that women should be prevented from wearing *tefillin*. The *Mishnah Berurah* (ibid.), quoting the *Taz* and the *Magen Avraham*, explains the reason for this stringency on the grounds that *tefillin* require a *guf naki* ("a clean body") and that women are not inclined to be careful. The contention that *tefillin* require a *guf naki* applies no less to men than to women. See Shabbat 49a, and is, according to *Orah Hayyim* 37:2, the reason that *tefillin* are no longer worn all day by men. Abayee and Rava define *guf naki* as refraining from expelling intestinal gas and refraining from sleeping while wearing them. The *Shulhan Arukh* lists Abayee's definition explicitly, and adds that

"one may not permit his attention to wander from them." According to Tosafot (Shabbat 49a, s.v. *she-lo*), that may be what Rava means. In any case, experience contradicts the contention that women are any less careful or capable of being careful about these prohibitions than men. In traditional terms it seems absolutely appropriate to claim that *nishtannu ha-zemannim* ("times have changed") vis-à-vis this issue. That is particularly so considering the relatively brief time span during each day when *tefillin* are actually worn. Thus, in the absence of any cogent reason to retain the Rema's stringency regarding women's right to wear *tefillin*, we are systematically entitled to revert to his own general premise that women may observe *mitzvot* from which they are exempt, and apply it even to this, a specific case in which he varies from his general premise.

44. *Shulhan Arukh, Orah Hayyim* 489, *Magen Avraham*, par. 1.

45. *Minhat Hinukh* (New York: Shulsinger Bros., 1952), Mitzvah 306, vol. I, p. 241.

46. See below, note 60.

47. Hilkhot Tefillah, Ezriel Hildesheimer edition, p. 29. Cf. *Siddur Rashi*, #130.

48. Berakhot 30b.

49. Ibid., 27b.

50. One point is unclear in the *Halakhot Gedolot*, and I wish to spell out specifically what I am unwilling to deduce from it. One could conceivably deduce from his words that the option to recite the evening prayer or not to recite it applies each night, and that its legal status should be considered obligatory on any night that it is recited, even if one does not usually recite it nightly. The potential implications of this view for "women's issues" are vast and important. Therefore, I wish to state clearly that I reject any such interpretation. Since the primary purpose of the passage in *Halakhot Gedolot* was to deal with the repetition of the *amidah* when one has forgotten a special addition to it, it would be overstretching his words to make so far-reaching a deduction. Furthermore, it is unlikely that the author ever considered that possibility as potentially actual, since Jews had by then customarily recited the evening *amidah* every night.

51. *Sefer Ha-ravia*, pt. II, #563, Aptowitzer edition, p. 284, quoted in *Hagahot Maimoniyot*, Hilkhot Berakhot, chap. 2, letter *het*.

52. 24a.

53. The *Halakhot Gedolot* specifically excluded Rosh Hodesh, as we have seen. Nevertheless, this apparent error in the Ravia has no bearing upon the focal point of the present discussion.

54. See Tosafot Arakhin 3a *la-toyei* regarding the reading *be-mishna megillah* instead of *be-mikra megillah*.

55. *Sefer Tashbetz*, #270 (New York, 5730), p. 20a.

56. It is not clear exactly to what he refers. Page 31 is listed in parentheses. It may be that he refers to the principle that "one who is commanded and performs is greater than one who is not commanded and performs." We shall address ourselves to this principle shortly. In any case, his actual proof from the *gemara* surely does not include the words *yekholot le-hayyev atzman* ("they can obligate themselves"). That is clearly *his* statement. Note, too, the

difference between this statement and that of Rashi, above, p. 132, *le-havi atzman be-ol ha-mitzvot* ("to place themselves under the yoke of the commandments").

57. See above, note 43.

58. *Responsa Besamim Rosh*, #89.

59. Di Molina clearly cannot mean that literally. He may mean that they have obligated themselves to all of the "prayer" *mitzvot*, like *lulav, shofar, sefirah, musaf*. But whatever the last clause means, he speaks, too, of women obligating themselves. Since the primary reason for quoting Di Molina is to demonstrate the use of the term *hiyyevu et atzman* ("they have obligated themselves"), it is not particularly relevant who the actual author of the responsum is. Even if Rabbi Saul Berlin forged the responsum (see *EJ* entry on Saul Berlin, 4:663), he would not have used terms and ideas which legalists would have immediately dismissed as outlandish.

60. The clause eliminated on p. 136 immediately following "anywhere" . . . includes the claim that Gumbiner's contention about *sefirah* is not comparable to *tefillat Maariv*. Babad, however, does not explain why they are not comparable. He may well have known the view of the *Halakhot Gedolot* through its quotation by the Tosafot, Yoma 87b, s.v. *ve-ha'amar*, for example. If he knew it from such a context, it is plausible to hypothesize that he considered the two cases non-comparable because the *reshut* status of *ma'ariv* is different from the *reshut* status of *sefirah* on several grounds: (1) not everyone agrees that *ma'ariv* is *reshut*; (2) even if it is *reshut*, it is not "completely" voluntary—see the view of Ri at the beginning of the aforementioned Tosafot; (3) even if *ma'ariv* is "completely" voluntary, nobody denies the right of a man to recite it if he wishes; whereas there are some who categorically deny to women the right to perform positive time-bound commandments.

Given such factors, all unmentioned by the *Halakhot Gedolot*, Babad asserts that even the right of women to count the Omer could not be deduced from a comparison to *ma'ariv*, and surely not the claim of "obligation." These factors force him to minimize (or ignore entirely) the obvious fact that both the *Halakhot Gedolot* and Gumbiner utilize identical language—*shavyei aleia hovah* ("he accepted it as an obligation"). Surely it is reasonable to assert that the *Magen Avraham* employed the language he did precisely because he wished to affirm that women may perform positive time-bound commandments, rendering their performance of them directly comparable to the *ma'ariv amidah* for men and even vis-à-vis the claim of "obligation."

61. Five passages have been quoted to demonstrate the applicability of the term *hiyyuv* ("obligation") to self-imposed observance: Gumbiner, *Halakhot Gedolot*, Ravia, Tashbetz, and Di Molina. These five can be divided into two categories. Gumbiner, Ravia, and Di Molina constitute one category. In these three passages the "acceptance of obligation" seems to be contingent upon widespread and long-standing acceptance of obligation by the nonobligated class. If the circumstances for the acceptance of voluntary obligation were deduced from these three alone, one would be inclined to postulate both the "widespread nature" and the "long-standing behavior" as necessary condi-

tions for "acceptance of obligation." Were that the case it would follow that recent and/or individual acceptance of voluntary obligation would not qualify. The passages from the Tashbetz and the *Halakhot Gedolot* demonstrate that such a conclusion would be misleading. No greater proof of that could be sought than the statement of the Tashbetz. He applies the term *le-hayyev atzman* ("to obligate themselves") to the wearing of *tzitzit* by women. Not only does he fail to mention either the "widespread nature" or the "long-standing behavior" characteristics, but the example of *tzitzit* for women was surely never widespread nor long-standing.

It is true that one might say of the passage in the *Halakhot Gedolot* that his failure to mention either of the characteristics is explicable on the grounds that the recitation of the *ma'ariv amidah* was both widespread and long-standing. But since the thrust of his argument is couched in terms like, "if one has already made the effort and prayed" and "once reciting it, he accepts it upon himself as obligatory," it is highly unlikely that he considered "widespread" or "long-standing" as necessary conditions for obligatory status. Indeed, the tone of the *Halakhot Gedolot* implies *individual* acceptance of obligation. The terms he uses and the tone of the passage render his failure to mention either the "widespread" or "long-standing" characteristics most likely to be both conscious and purposeful.

62. Berakhot 17b.

63. *Ibid.*, s.v. *ve-eino*.

64. Berakhot 3:1, 5d.

65. See above, p. 136.

66. Hilkhot Keri'at Shema 4:7.

67. *Birkei Yosef, Orah Hayyim* 55:5.

68. Lev. 22:32, used by the Yerushalmi, Berakhot 7:3, 10c, as a source for the quorum of ten. Cf. Bavli, Berakhot 21b.

69. Some wish to resolve the question by denying that a *shatz* today serves as an agent. Rather, they claim, he is more of a prayer leader who helps the congregation keep its place. I would oppose such a resolution to the problem for the following reasons: (1) It begs the question rather than answering it. It ignores the basic question of whether a woman could serve in this capacity without changing the definition of a *shatz* in a way that is certain to be deemed unacceptable by most. (2) Allowing women to serve on the basis of a changed definition would create the odd anomaly of allowing a woman who could not be counted in the *minyan* to serve as prayer leader for those (men and women) who do count toward a *minyan*. Our discussion of women in the *minyan* follows shortly. (3) It is not accurate to describe the *shatz* as merely a prayer leader rather than an agent even when everyone has a *siddur* to pray from, because there are elements of the service in which the *shatz* remains an agent, even under those circumstances. I refer primarily to the *devarim she-bi-kedusha, barekhu,* and *kaddish*. In these, the congregation is a respondent to the doxology offered by its agent on their behalf. No greater proof of this is needed for the communal nature of these prayers than the fact that they cannot be recited with less than a *minyan*. (4) The issue of the nature of a *shatz*, even in a congregation where all can pray, has already been widely

discussed in the literature. *Orah Hayyim* 124:3 stipulates that even in a congregation where all are expert, the *shatz* must repeat the *amidah*, in order to maintain the *takkanat hakhamim*. The commentators understand this to imply that since, at times, the *shatz* does serve as an agent for those who cannot recite the *amidah* properly (an all-too-frequent occurrence in our own congregations), he must repeat the *amidah* as a communal agent even when he is, in fact, not serving as an agent for any specific individual. The Abudraham (14th century) (Wertheimer edition, p. 117 [Jerusalem, 5723]), quoting a responsum of Maimonides, goes even further. He asserts that the blessings recited by the *shatz* in the repetition of the *amidah* in a fully expert community are not to be considered *berakhot le-vattalah*. The *takkanat hakhamim* requiring a repetition was made in order to remedy a possible situation, but its fulfillment is not contingent upon the actual existence of that situation. It is similar to the recitation of *kiddush* in the synagogue, which was instituted for the benefit of guests, but is recited even when guests are not present; or to the recitation of *berakhah ahat me-ein sheva*, which was instituted for the benefit of latecomers, but is recited even if there are none.

Only if one were to claim that there are no congregants anywhere who remain inexpert in the recitation of the *amidah* would it be defensible to claim that the *shatz* no longer serves as an agent. (And even then it would apply only to the repetition of the *amidah*, but not to *devarim she-bi-kedushah*.) Surely this is not true of our communities, regrettably. In the final analysis, it seems to me far preferable to retain the definition of a *shatz* as it has always been, and to restrict women who are not obligated from serving in that capacity.

70. The Committee on Jewish Law and Standards of the Rabbinical Assembly has dealt with the issue of women in the *minyan* in a variety of ways. A letter from the Committee Chairman to all members of the Rabbinical Assembly, dated October 5, 1973, is accompanied by a "Digest of discussion at the CJLS meeting of August 29, 1972" and by excerpts from papers prepared for the Committee. Two responsa permitting the counting of women were discussed. A version of the responsum by Rabbi Phillip Sigal appears in Seymour Siegel, *Conservative Judaism and Jewish Law* (New York: Rabbinical Assembly, 1977) pp. 282–292. Rabbi David Feldman responded to those responsa in a paper which is also excerpted in the aforementioned "Digest". I concur completely with Feldman's rebuttal of the two responsa. See, as well, Feldman's article, referred to above in note 6, particularly, pp. 300–302. The final vote of the CJLS "was not a vote of acceptance of a *teshuvah* but rather a vote of *takkanah* that men and women may be counted equally for a minyan" (quoted from p. 3 of "The Role of Women in Jewish Ritual," a summary of decisions of the CJLS, sent to all members of the Rabbinical Assembly by the Committee Chairman with a cover letter dated Jan. 6, 1975). The wording of the *takkanah* appears in the Committee Chairman's letter of Oct. 5, 1973. It reads: "Men and women should be counted equally for a minyan."

I find the *takkanah* inadequate. Its final wording ignores the question of obligation. Even if it had imposed obligation on women equal to that of men, I would be opposed to the *takkanah* for reasons which are discussed below, pp. 166–67.

71. Rosh ha-Shanah 3:8, 29a (Danby's Translation).
72. Above, p. 135.
73. Kiddushin 31a and parallels.
74. Above, p. 132 and p. 134.
75. Kiddushin, loc. cit., s.v. *gadol*.
76. Avodah Zarah, 3a, s.v. *gadol*.
77. Kiddushin, loc. cit.
78. See the Committee Chairman's letter of October 5, 1973, paragraph 4.
79. Careful distinction must be drawn between possible categories of obligation. There are two categories of other-imposed obligation, namely, obligation *de-oraita*, deriving from the Bible, and obligation *de-rabbanan*, deriving from rabbinic legislation. These two categories are not generally considered to be legally equal. Thus, one whose obligation derives from the rabbis cannot be the agent through whom one whose obligation derives from the Bible fulfills his religious obligation. The classical statement of this premise is reflected in the question of the *gemara*, "*attei de-rabbanan u-mapik de-oraita?*" ("Can one who is rabbinically obligated act in behalf of one who is biblically obligated?") (Berakhot 20b).

Even granting this premise, it would be erroneous to equate the voluntary acceptance of *hovah* ("obligation") by one whose observance is *reshut* ("voluntary") with *hiyyuv de-rabbanan* (a rabbinically imposed obligation). The former is self-imposed, not other-imposed. Obligations which for some are other-imposed and for others are self-imposed have the same halakhic status. In other words, the voluntarily accepted obligation to fufill a biblical *mitzvah* has the same legal status as the other-imposed obligation to fulfill a biblical *mitzvah*, and the voluntarily accepted obligation to fulfill a rabbinic *mitzvah* has the same legal status as the other-imposed obligation to fulfill a rabbinic *mitzvah*. Thus, a woman who accepts the obligation to recite Shema could serve as the agent for men (assuming that that obligation is biblical for men; though see Berakhot 21a and Tos. Baba Kamma 87a, s.v. *Ve-khen*, end).

There is ample evidence for this thesis, as unusual as it may appear on the surface. (1) The view of Rabbi Elazar (above p. 134) is explicable only by this thesis. Were he to equate the voluntary sacrifice of women with a rabbinically imposed obligation, he would be allowing a positive rabbinic injunction to take precedence over a biblically enjoined prohibition. Indeed, his view is very liberal, for it allows a woman's voluntary performance to have the legal status of a biblical obligation even without her "accepting the obligation." (Admittedly, though, the strength of this proof is weakened by the Bavli's reinterpretation of his statement, and by the emendation of his statement by the Korban Ha-Edah. See above, note 39). (2) The view quoted by the Ravad (above, p. 135) is equally strong. If our thesis were not implied by it, that view, too, would allow a purely voluntary act (even without "accepting the obligation") to take precedence over a biblically enjoined prohibition. (3) The claim of Rav Yosef, who had become blind (Baba Kamma 87a, Kiddushin 31a), that until he had heard Rabbi Hanina's dictum that "greater is he who is commanded, etc.," he would have rejoiced if the law were in accordance with Rabbi Yehudah (that a blind person is exempt from all of the *mitzvot*) has been widely used by the *rishonim*. It is generally quoted (see Tos. Rosh ha-Shanah

33a, s.v. *ha* and *Eruvin* 96a, s.v. *dilma*) in reference to the right of one who is exempt from reciting blessings to recite them. The thesis is that Rav Yosef could not possibly have meant to change his life-style one iota by virtue of having been exempted from obligation. Quite the contrary, he would have rejoiced because continued observance of his previous life-style would have been even more praiseworthy because he was "not commanded." Following the very reasoning of the Tosafot one could ask: Would Rav Yosef have rejoiced if he had thought that exemption from obligation would have denied him the right to be *shatz* in his own school? Would not the loss of that right have upset him as much as the loss of the right to recite blessings? Even the assertion that the blind are "rabbinically obligated" would not be sufficient to account for Rav Yosef's joy. His feeling could be explained only on the assumption that as one who was no longer "commanded" he could still have done everything he had always done, including serving as the agent for others. His status as "non-commanded" would have in his opinion resulted in greater "reward," and would not have caused any curtailment of his rights as one who is obligated. He would still have been "obligated" on the basis of self-imposed voluntary obligation. (4) The *gemara* (Berakhot 33a) states quite clearly that the unnecessary recitation of a benediction is biblically prohibited. The Rambam accepts this statement (see Hilkhot Berakhot 1:15 and *Teshuvot Rambam*, Blau edition, #124). Most other *rishonim*, following the lead of the Tosafot (Rosh Hashanah 33a, s.v. *ha*) interpret that statement as merely an *asmakhta*. Consistent with his own view, the Rambam forbids women from reciting blessings (see above, p. 130). The Tosafot assert that the scriptural verse is an *asmakhta* in order to "justify" the *hava amina* of Rav Yosef. Though such a "justification" would "defend" Rav Yosef on the grounds that "rabbinic prohibitions" are less severe than "biblical prohibitions," it is not at all clear that the defense is unassailable. The end of the *sugya* in Pesahim 116b, in discussing the behavior of Rav Yosef and Rav Sheshet, both of whom were blind, regarding the recitation of the Hagaddah, rejects the leniency of "rabbinic prohibitions" as the justification for their behavior on the grounds that *kol de-tikkun rabbanan ke-ein de-oraita tikkun* ("rabbinic legislation is governed by rules that are the same as those that govern biblical legislation"). The same objection could be raised to the "justification" of the *hava amina* of Rav Yosef. Would he not perhaps have thought that the recitation of blessings might be forbidden to him, even if he were "rabbinically obligated," because of the dictum that rabbinic legislation is governed by rules that are the same as those that govern biblical legislation? Would it not have made perfectly good sense to claim that the prohibition of reciting "a needless benediction" is biblical but that it was inapplicable to Rav Yosef (and also to women) on the ground that voluntary observance is not to be equated with "rabbincally imposed obligation," but rather that voluntary observance has the same legal status as other-imposed observance of the same *mitzvah*. If the other-imposed obligation is biblical, the self-imposed obligation has the legal status of the biblically imposed obligation. If the other-imposed observance is rabbinic, the self-imposed observance has the legal status of the rabbinically imposed observance.

There is an apparent logical paradox which should be noted. Assume, for example, that the recitation of Shema were voluntary for women and biblically enjoined for men until year X. During that time, the recitation of the Shema by a woman who voluntarily assumed the obligation would have the same legal status as the recitation of the Shema by those who were biblically obligated. Now assume that after the year X the rabbis had imposed upon women the obligation to recite the Shema. Thenceforth the women would be "rabbinically obligated." It would follow from this thesis that prior to year X, women who accepted the recitation of Shema as a voluntary obligation would have been entitled to serve as the agents through whom men fulfilled their obligation, but those same women could not serve as the agents of men following year X because their observance would be rabbinically enjoined, and one who is rabbinically enjoined to fulfill a *mitzvah* cannot act as the agent to fulfill that *mitzvah* for one who is biblically enjoined to observe it. That would imply that the self-same act would have a higher legal status when it is self-imposed than it does when it becomes other-imposed; a halakhically inconceivable situation.

The premise which underlies the paradox is the "given" that one rabbinically enjoined cannot act as the agent for one biblically enjoined to perform a given *mitzvah*. Without that premise there would be no paradox. Indeed, there is inherent logic to the premise that rabbinically imposed obligations should have the same legal status as obligations biblically imposed on the grounds that both are other-imposed. The two subcategories of other-imposed obligations would be distinguished from each other primarily by the source of the *mitzvah*; biblically imposed obligations finding their source in God Himself and rabbinically imposed obligations finding their source in the sages. If voluntarily assumed obligations have the same legal status as the same observances have for those for whom they are other-imposed, and if the legal status of the "biblical" and the "rabbinic" obligations could be considered legally equal, there would be no paradox. A woman whose obligation to recite Shema became rabbinically other-imposed after year X, could continue to serve as the agent for men.

There are indications that the sages recognized that rabbinically imposed obligations share some equivalence with obligations biblically imposed. The classical statement of this thesis is found in Shabbat 23a, oft quoted by *rishonim*, in the justification of the right to say *ve-tzivvanu* ("and He commanded us") for rabbinically imposed *mitzvot*. According to the *hava amina*, the word *ve-tzivvanu* seemed inapplicable to such *mitzvot*, since God did not command them. The *gemara's* resolution posits that *ve-tzivvanu* is applicable because God empowered the sages to act. Thus, *ve-tzivvanu* is applicable because rabbinically imposed *mitzvot* are equal, in that sense, to biblically imposed *mitzvot*. Both are other-commanded. Only the direct source of the commands differs. The Tosafot (Rosh Hashanah 33a, s.v. *ha*, and Eruvin 96a, s.v. *dilma*) expand the principle to include the right of recitation of blessings (including the word *ve-tzivvanu*) to the blind. Surely they might have distinguished between biblically rooted *mitzvot* imposed upon the blind by the Rabbis and the *mitzvah* of Hanukkah which is rabbinically rooted and imposed on all. But they do not.

Even the claim of Berakhot (20b) that one "rabbinically enjoined" cannot act as the agent for one "biblically enjoined" is not as clearly uncontested as it appears. The *sugya* in Berakhot 48a apparently allows one "rabbinically obligated" to serve as the agent for "one biblically obligated." Rashi himself (ibid., s.v. *ad*) recognizes that as the *p'shat* ("patent meaning") of the *gemara*. Furthermore, Rashi is certainly correct to reject the statement of the *Halakhot Gedolot* as a viable explanation of the *sugya*.

To the extent that the paradox referred to above exists, it is predicated on an uncertain assumption. The logical paradox is not inherent to the claim that voluntary observance has the same legal status as other-imposed observance of the same *mitzvah*.

80. Ketubbot 7b.

81. Understood by the Geonim to refer to "entering under the canopy." See *Otzar Hageonim*, Ketubbot, pt. II, p. 7, par. 8.

82. The *edah* ("community") referred to consisted of the ten spies who brought evil reports from the Promised Land.

83. Berakhot 21b, completed according to Megillah 23b.

84. The *sugya* in Berakhot 50a does not necessarily affect the tenability of Rabbi Abahu's position. There, Rabbi Akiva utilizes the *be-makhelot* ("in assemblies") of Psalm 68:27 as the source of Rabbi Meir's claim that even unborn fetuses sang at the Red Sea, thereby negating the possibility that the verse could be used to distinguish between 100, 1,000, and 10,000 for the formula of *birkat ha-zimmun* ("calling upon the assembled to recite the grace after meals"). Rabbi Yose HaGelili retorts that *be-makhelot* alone is sufficient to distinguish between 100, 1,000, and 10,000, while the word *mi-mekor* ("from the fountain") could serve as the basis for Rabbi Meir's comment. In the *sugya* in Ketubbot (7b), Rabbi Abahu (ostensibly) rejects the use of *mi-mekor* as the source of Rabbi Meir's view on the grounds that if it were intended as his source it would have read *mi-beten* ("from the belly"). The *sugya* in Berakhot would bear directly on the *sugya* in Ketubbot only if one posits that Rava's statement in Berakhot (that the law is according to Rabbi Akiva) refers both to Rabbi Akiva's conclusion *and* to this utilization of the verse as the grounds for Rabbi Meir's statement. Since the latter claim is not attributed to anyone in particular, i.e., it is *stam*, it is highly unlikely that Rava was even aware of it. Rava himself provides no reason whatsoever for his rejection of Rabbi Yose's view concerning the formula for *birkat ha-zimmun*.

Rava's statements are used to link the two *sugyot*. That linkage is far from necessary, as the following will demonstrate. Rava rejects Rabbi Yose ha-Gelili's view on the formula for *birkat ha-zimmun* because the verse on which it is predicated must be utilized as the source for a *minyan* for the wedding benedictions, as Rabbi Abahu does. He rejects, as well, the possibility that it could be the source for Rabbi Meir's opinion on the ground that it would have to read *mi-beten*.

85. In Rabbi David Feldman's rebuttal paper, referred to above in note 70, he quotes the statement of the *Shita Mekubbetzet* to Ketubot 7b (New York: Feldheim, 5713, 39c), which excludes women from being counted for the wedding benedictions. Feldman, however, cojoins the statement with the view of Rav Nahman, as though it were clearly the source for the prohibition. That is an error. The comment of the *Shita Mekubbetzet* is made in a discussion

of the requirement of *panim hadashot* (guests not previously present). It is not made in the context of a discussion of the dispute between Rav Nahman and Rabbi Abahu. It is totally independent of that dispute. Women who could not be counted to a prayer quorum could also not be counted for the wedding benedictions in the opinion of either Rav Nahman or Rabbi Abahu. For Rav Nahman, though, even women who could be counted toward a prayer quorum could not be counted for the wedding benedictions. For Rabbi Abahu, they could be.

86. Yerushalmi Sheviit 6:1, 36b.

87. That is, they were at the time under no legal obligation for performing the *mitzvot* that were associated specifically with the land of Israel, such as the bringing of tithes.

88. The chapter lists both the obligations to be voluntarily assumed by the people and the signatories to the document.

89. Verse 1 states that these are voluntary obligations, and verse 38 lists tithes. Thus, the obligation to give tithes, as implied by the words "we make a written pledge," was voluntary.

90. This refers to biblically ordained *mitzvot* in no way associated with the land and, therefore, should not have been included in a list of voluntarily accepted obligations.

91. Piska 190, Finkelstein edition, p. 230.

92. One of the hermeneutical principles whereby the Rabbis interpret the biblical text. "Literally: similar injunction or regulation. 'Inference by analogy' by virtue of which, because in two pentateuchal passages, words occur which are similar or have the identical connotation, both laws, however different they may be in themselves are subject to the same regulations and applications" (Herman L. Strack, *Introduction to the Talmud and Midrash*, p. 94).

93. "The two men who are parties to the dispute shall appear, etc."

94. "A case can be valid only on the testimony of two witnesses or more."

95. Shevuot 30a.

96. Shevuot 4:1, 30a.

97. That is, the addition of the *vav* ("and") to the *asher* would indicate that the phrase "the parties to the dispute" refers to individuals different from the *shenei ha-anashim* ("the two men") spoken of in the opening phrase of the verse. Without the *vav* ("and"), the phrase "the parties to the dispute" could be understood as explanatory of *shenei ha-anashim* ("the two men") with which the verse opens.

98. Edut 9:2.

99. The *Kesef Mishnah*, ad loc., wonders why the Rambam ignored the proof of the *gemara*, viz., the *gezerah shavah*. Indeed, Maimonides' proof is not nearly as conclusive, since "the Torah usually uses the masculine form to include both men and women."

Perhaps, though, Maimonides was basing himself on the Yerushalmi, Shevuot 4:1, 35b, where Rabbi Yose ben Bun deduces that women may not serve as witnesses by *gezerah shavah* of Deut. 19:17 (*shenei ha-anashim*) and *al pi shenayim edim* (ibid. 17:6). His deduction seems to be claiming that *ha-anashim* cannot be generic because *edim* is not generic, but masculine. In essence, then, *edim* alone proves that only men can testify and is used by Maimonides as clarification of the meaning of *anashim* as nongeneric.

100. See Mishnah Rosh ha-Shanah 1:8.

101. See, Berakhot 17a.

102. See Sotah 11b and *Sifre Numbers*, Piska 133, Horovitz edition, p. 177, lines 13–15.

103. See Megillah 14b and Baba Metzia 59a.

104. See Shevuot 30a. The New Jewish Publication Society translation reads: "the royal princess, her dress embroidered with golden mountings is led to the king," and notes that "meaning of the Hebrew is uncertain."

105. Shabbat 33b, Kiddushin 80b.

106. Kiddushin 49b.

107. *Bereshit Rabbah* 45:5, Theodor Albeck edition, pp. 452 f.

108. Ketubbot 2:10.

109. The fact that they must have attained majority in order to be believed does not disprove the point. That requirement exists only to ensure that they recognize the importance of their testimony, which, as youngsters, they would not. In the final analysis though, their testimony is about matters which they witnessed as *minors*.

110. It is irrelevant whether the exceptions in the case of minors are instances of rabbinically required testimony or biblically required testimony, since the exceptions in the case of women are clearly instances of biblically required testimony (see below). Though the Bavli (Ketubbot 28a & b) explains the exceptions in the case of minors as instances of rabinically required testimony, the Yerushalmi (Ketubbot 2:10, 26d) obviously understands the Mishnah to refer, as well, to biblically required testimony. See David Halivni, *Mekorot U'mesorot*, Nashim, p. 116, note 4.

111. Cf. Maimonides' statement (Gerushin 13:29): "Let it not seem difficult in your eyes that on the basis of a woman's testimony, the sages allowed even strict matters of possible forbidden relations [For if the testimony were false and the assumed widow would remarry, the consequences for her when her supposedly dead husband would be found to be alive, would be dire indeed]. For the Torah is not insistent either upon the two-witness requirement or the other rules of testimony . . . in a case in which the witness could not escape detection if the testimony were not true. [In that case] it is highly unlikely that a witness would testify falsely."

112. Mishnah Yebamot 16:7.

113. Mishnah Yebamot 15:4.

114. For a partial listing, see Rema in *Hoshen Mishpat* 35:14.

115. 30a.

116. Kiddushin 65a.

117. Rambam, *Ishut* 4:6; *Shulhan Arukh, Even ha-Ezer* 42:2. The quotation in the paper is from the latter.

118. It probably could work, with difficulty, for divorce. See, carefully, Rambam, Gerushin 12:2, 3, 5, for intimations that if two parties admit that a divorce between them took place, the divorce is valid.

It must be stressed that I have been addressing myself to the possibility of categorizing betrothal and divorce as instances of *milleta de-atya le-igaloyei.*

Obviously, it would be easier *after the fact* to recognize the validity of a marriage witnessed by an ineligible witness. The betrothal could be validated by the assumption that the husband *ba'al le-shem ishut*, "had had relations with his bride with the intention of thus making her his wife." There would be no comparable leniency for *after the fact* recognition of an invalidly witnessed divorce.

119. Mamrim 2:1.

120. See Herman L. Strack, *Introduction to the Talmud and Midrash*, chap. 11.

121. Evidently implying that the latter need not be *gadol be-hokhmah u-ve-minyan* ("superior in wisdom and numbers"). See Jose Faur, *"De-oraita', de-rabbanan ve-dinim muflaim be-mishnato shel ha-Rambam," Sinai,* vol 67, no. 1 (Nissan 5730), p. 35.

122. Above, pp. 150–51.

123. Ibid.

124. Ibid.

125. See Yevamot 89b–90b for the *locus classicus* of the principle. The subject is very complex, and I apologize for referring to a volume which I have written which is not yet published. The volume is entitled *The Halachic Process: A Systemic Analysis.* The entire seventh chapter is devoted to an analysis of rabbinic rights vis-à-vis matters that are *de-oraita* ("biblical"). The book, which is scheduled for early publication, will provide analysis of far more sources than I present in this paper. (This volume is now available.)

126. Nazir 43b, s.v. *ve-hai.*

127. Yebamot 15:1.

128. #157, to Deut. 17:15, Finkelstein edition, p. 208.

129. Melakhim 1:5.

130. Talmud Torah 1:13.

131. *Bamidbar Rabbah* 10:5, based on Judges 13:12.

132. Niddah 6:4, 49b.

133. The Yerushalmi (Shevuot 4:1, 35b) deduces the disqualification of women as judges from "and *shenei anashim* ['two men,' i.e., Eldad and Medad] had remained in camp" (Numbers 11:26). The reference here is clearly to men, Eldad and Medad, and clearly to judging. The Yerushalmi then applies the exclusive masculinity of this *shenei anashim* to *shenei ha-anashim* ("the two persons") of Deuteronomy 19:17, deducing that women may also not serve as witnesses.

134. Tosafot Niddah, 50a, s. v. *ha-kol.* Cf. Tos. Shevu'ot, 29b., s. v. *shevu'at* and Tos. Yevamot, 45b, s. v. *mi.*

135. Tosafot Shevu'ot 29b, s. v. *shevu'at.*

136. Sanhedrin 3:2.

137. Above, p. 148.

138. Above, p. 161.

139. See p. 29.

140. Ibid.

141. See note 61.

הנדון: קבלת בנות כתלמידות מן המנין בבית המדרש לרבנים באמריקה והכתרתן בתואר "רב, מורה ודרשן"

הרב שלמה בן משה גרינברג

(המאמר הזה הוגש לחברי הסנאט של בית המדרש לרבנים כמה שבועות לפני ישיבתו ביום ל' כסלו תש"מ, בעשרים לחודש דצמבר 1979)

מעין הקדמה

הכנס השנתי של כנסת הרבנים (כנה"ר) בחודש מאי 1977 הגיש עצומה לנגיד בית המדרש לרבנים (בהמל"ר), שבה הביע את בקשתו, שהנגיד ימנה ועדה שחבריה יהיו אנשי שם ומומחים במקצועות שונים, ותשקף את רבגוניותה הרעיונית של התנועה השמרנית, ושתפקידה יהיה לחקור ולדרוש את מקומה של האשה כמנהיגה רוחנית בתנועה. ושומה תהא עליה להגיש את מסקנותיה לכנס כנה"ר בשנת 1979.

הכל ידעו כי המשימה היחידה שהוטלה על הועדה היתה לתת תשובה ברורה לשאלת הכתרת בנות ע"י בהמל"ר בתואר "רב, מורה ודרשן". באותו כנס הודיע הנגיד כי אכן ימנה ועדה כזו והוא יתמוך בהצעותיה. הועדה מלאה את תפקידה והגישה לכנס כנה"ר בשנת 1979 דו"ח על פעולותיה השונות והשיקולים ששכנעו אחד־עשר מחבריה והנגיד ביניהם, להמליץ בעד הסמכת בנות. שלושה חברים התנגדו. הנגיד, שהיה גם יושב ראש הועדה, הגיש את הדו"ח לפני הכנס ובהרצאתו באותה שעה תמך במסקנות רוב הועדה.

היות וההחלטה הסופית בשאלה זו היא בידי חברי הסנאט של בהמל"ר וכדי לא להפעיל לחץ על חבריו, החליט הכנס לא להביע דעה בנוגע לתוכן הדו"ח ולמסקנותיו, אלא רק לקבלו בהבעת תודה. בישיבה בחודש פברואר 1979 הוגש הדו"ח לפני הסנאט. כמה מחבריו ביקשו לדחות את ההחלטה הסופית בנידון זה עד אחרי הקיץ כדי שיוכלו להעמיק חקר בכל פני הבעיה, להבהיר את דעותיהם ולנסחן בכתב. הנגיד נענה לבקשתם וקבע כי ישיבת הסנאט, שתחליט סופית בנידון זה, תתקיים בחודש ינואר 1980. חברי הסנאט נתבקשו להעלות את תגובותיהם ומסקנותיהם על הנייר.

קראתי ועיינתי עיון היטב בדו"ח הסופי של הועדה ובחומר שצברה במשך ישיבותיה ופגישותיה עם מנהיגי וחברי קהילות השייכות לתנועה השמרנית. בחנתי

אם לא את כל המקורות ההלכתיים המתייחסים לנידון — שהלא הם מים שאין להם
סוף — לפחות אותו חלק ממנו שיש לו חשיבות חיונית לענייננו. אני תפילה שלא
ימצאוני חברי בחינת מגלה פנים בתורה שלא כהלכה.

רבים הם פני השאלה הנידונה. את דברי אערוך לפי הכותרות כדלקמן:

1. הפן ההלכתי.
2. הפן הפסיכולוגי והסוציולוגי.
3. הפן התנועתי.

חלק א׳ — הפן ההלכתי

קבלת עול ההלכה היא בין עיקרי היסוד של התנועה השמרנית. לכן קבעה
הועדה בראשית דרכה שלא לקבל החלטה ולא להסיק מסקנה המנוגדת להלכה. היות
ובין מקבלי עול ההלכה היו תמיד, ונמצאים גם היום, לא רק הבדלים קלים אלא גם
חמורים בנוגע לפירושה ולהחלטה של ההלכה, הודיעה הועדה כי היא תיחשב גם
בפסקי הדין של The Committee on Law and Standards של כנה״ר, ועם
המנהגים המקובלים על רוב בתי הכנסת המשתייכים לתנועה או על חלק סביר מהם.
בין חברי הועדה היו תלמידי חכמים שבקיאותם בספרות ההלכתית היא למעלה מכל
ספק. הם חקרו ודרשו את המקורות והביאו את ממצאיהם לפני מליאת הועדה. דו״ח
הועדה מפנה את תשומת לבנו לעובדה **שכל חבריה**, כולל השלושה שלא קבלו את
דעת הרוב, הסכימו כי הכתרת בנות אינה מתנגדת להלכה, היות שההכתרה כשהיא
לעצמה אינה מטילה על המוכתרות חובות שההלכה אוסרת עליהן. הפורשים מדעת
הרוב ביססו את התנגדותם לא על שיקולים הלכתיים אלא על השערותיהם בנוגע
לתוצאותיה המזיקות של הסמכת בנות, תוצאות שהן, לפי דעתם, בבחינת "פסיק
רישיה ולא ימות". לדעתם עשויה זאת:

א. להשפיע לרעה על נאמנותם של חברי התנועה השמרנית להלכה בכלל,
נאמנות שהיא כבר היום רפה מדי.

ב. לתרום להרס יציבותה של המשפחה היהודית המסורתית שהיא יסוד היסודות
של העם ההולכת ומתרופפת.

ג. לטשטש את ייחודה הרעיוני של התנועה השמרנית המתיימרת בנאמנותה
להלכה.

ד. לסכן את אחדותה ההסתדרותית של התנועה ותגרום ח״ו להתפוררותה או
להתנוונותה.

כנראה שכל הנחוץ להאמר בנוגע לפן ההלכתי של הנידון כבר נאמר בדו״ח של
הועדה והמקום היחידי שהועדה הניחה לנו להתגדר בו הוא תחום ההשערות על

תוצאותיה של קבלת המלצתה. בכל זאת נדמה לי כי להבנה מקיפה יותר של הנדון צריכים לדון לא רק בהלכות המשתייכות במישרים לנידון, כפי שהן מנוסחות בספרות ההלכה. הלא התנועה שלנו הופיעה על שמי חיי עמנו כאסכולה היסטורית שהתעניינה לא רק בפשט ההלכה כפי שנוסחה בספרי ההלכה אלא גם בהבנת האווירה התרבותית שבה נוסחה. לכן שומה עלינו לחפש ולחשוף את היסודות התרבותיים והרעיוניים של ההלכות הנוגעות לנידון. את דברי אלה אני מגיש כתרומה צנועה לדיוננו בפן זה של השאלה העומדת לפנינו.

ההלכות הקובעות את מעמדה של האשה בחברה היהודית והמתייחסות במישרין לנידון שייכות לסוג הלכות "הפורחות באיר", ול"הררים התלוין בשערה"[1] שהן מקרא מועט והלכות מרובות. הן מבוססות בראש וראשונה לא על המקרא אלא על כללים ופתגמים המתארים את טיבה של האשה, את כוחותיה הנפשיים והרוחניים, ואת תפקידה בחברה שעד לפני כמאתים שנה היו מקובלים **על כל העמים בלי יוצא מן הכלל**. וכמדומני שניעזר בהבנת הבעיה העומדת לפנינו אם נשים לב לכללים ולפתגמים אלה ולהלכות שבהן הם מומחשים. חז"ל המחישו את הכללים המקובלים האלה בהלכות פסוקות ומצאו להם אסמכתאות במקרא על ידי דרשות שלפעמים נראים בעינינו דחוקות למדי.[2]

חלק ב׳ — הפן הפסיכולוגי והסוציולוגי

א. נשים דעתן קלה.[3]

איך הומחשה הדעה הזו בהלכה ובחברה.

1. **בהלכות שחיטה:** המשנה אומרת בפירוש: "הכל שוחטים,"[4] "השחיטה כשרה בזרים ובנשים . . . ואפילו בקדשי קדשים"[5] אבל היו אלה שהתנגדו להלכה זו. "בגמרא מוכח דנשים שוחטות, אפילו לכתחילה . . . מכאן תשובה למה שכתבו בהלכות א"י דנשים לא ישחטו מפני שדעתן קלה . . ."[6] "והפוסקים הסכימו לדעת התוספות, והאגור כתב שאף על פי שדעת הפוסקים כן ה"מנהג בכל גלות ישראל

---

1. חגיגה משנה פ"א מ"ח — וראה שם ר"ע מברטנורה ועיקר תוי"ט.
2. ראה — המשפט העברי, מנחם אלון, חלק ב׳ פרק תשיעי — בפרט, סעיף ה, "מדרש מקיים" דף 254.
3. שבת ל"ג; קיד׳ פ; וראה גם דף הערה.
4. חולין ב.
5. זבחים ל"א:
6. תוס׳ שם ד"ה שהשחיטה כשרה, וראה גם חולין ב. תוס׳ ד"ה הכל שוחטין.

שלא ישחטו, ומעולם לא ראיתי נוהג לשחוט ולכן אין להניחם לשחוט כי המנהג מבטל
הלכה, מנהג אבותינו תורה היא", עכ"ל. ואני אומר שאם היה אומר שהיו רוצות
לשחוט ולא הניחם היה אפשר לומר שהיא ראיה, אך ראית לא ראינו אינה ראיה,
וכתב הכל בו וה"ר יצחק כתב שהנשים שוחטות לעצמן, משמע שאין שוחטות
לאחרים עכ"ל,[7] ודבר תימה הוא מה חילוק יש בין שוחט לעצמו לשוחט לאחרים
דכמו כן הכשר צריך לזה כמו לזה ומ"ש ר"י לעצמן היינו לומר שהן לבדן וא"צ
שיעמוד אחר על גבן"[8] . . . . והיינו לפי שיטתו (של ב"י) שכתב דעתן קלה פי' שמא
יתעלפו דלענין שמא יתעלפו לא שנא לעצמן או לאחרים במ"ש הב"י אבל לפי מה
שכתבתי שאין הטעם משום שמא יתעלפו אלא משום שדעתן קלות ואינן נזהרין, לכן
אין להאמינן על השחיטה, שפיר יש לחלק, דלעצמן שוחטין דאין לחושדן שיאכלו
נבילות, אבל לאחרים ששם ליכא איסורא אלא לפני עור לא תתן מכשול, בזה אין
הנשים נזהרות הואיל ודעתן קלות לפיכך אין שוחטין לאחרים"[9].

2. **בהלכות צניעות:** מתני'[10]: "לא יתייחד אדם עם שתי נשים (רש"י — מפני
שדעתן קלה ושתיהן נוחות להתפתות ולא תירא זו מחברתה שאף היא תעשה כמותה),
אבל אשה מתייחדת עם שני אנשים" (שהאחד בוש מפני חבירו — רש"י). גמ': מ"ט,
תנא דבי אליהו הואיל ונשים דעתן קלות עליהן (רש"י — ושתיהן נוחות להתפתות)
מנא הני מילי א"ר משום ר' ישמעאל רמז ליחוד מן התורה מנין לנו "כי יסיתך אחיך
בן אמך (דב' י"ג; י"ז) וכי בן אם מסית בן אב אינו מסית אלא לומר לך בן מתייחד
עם אמו ואסור להתייחד עם כל עריות שבתורה",[10] וידוע "מעשה ברוריה — שפעם
אחת לגלגה על שאמרו חכמים נשים דעתן קלות הן עלייהו ואמר לה (בעלה, ר'
מאיר) סופך להודות לדבריהם וצוה לאחד מתלמידיו . . . והפציר בה . . . עד
שנתרצית וכשנודע לה חנקה עצמה וערק ר' מאיר מחמת כסופא"[11].

3. **בהלכות תלמוד תורה:** "ר"א אומר כל המלמד בתו תורה כאילו לימדה
תיפלות" א"ר אבהו מ"ט דר"א דכ' אני חכמה שכנתי ערמה (משלי ח; י"ב) כיון
שנכנסה חכמה באדם נכנסה עמו ערמומית" (רש"י ד"ה כאילו שמתוכה היא מבינה
ערמומית ועושה דברים בהצנע[12] והמהרש"א מוסיף "ולגבי איש הוא תועלת להבין
ערמת הרשעים ולהורים כנגדם. . .אבל נשים דעתן קלות פן יערימו ויבואו לידי

7. האגור א: סב.
8. ב"י — טור יו"ד הלכות שחיטה א:ו
9. דרישה שם בסוף סימן ד'.
10. קידושין פ:
11. ע"ז י"ח. רש"י ד"ה ואיכה דאמרי משום מעשה ברוריה.
12. סוטה כ"א:

עבירה וקילקול", ובעל החינוך הרואה אשה לומדת תורה בעין טובה, שכן הוא אומר "וגם אשה שלמדה תורה שכר יש לה" מוסיף "ואף על פי כן ציוו חכמים שלא ילמד אדם לבתו תורה לפי שדעת הנשים קלה ומוציאין דברי תורה לדברי הבאי בעניות דעתן."[13]

4. **בהלכות עדות:** מצות עדות "נוהגת בכל מקום ובכל זמן בזכרים אבל לא בנשים, שאין הנשים בתורת עדות לקלות דעתן"[14].

"ויאמר מנוח (שופטים י"ג; י"ב) אמר לו מנוח עד כאן ששמעתי מן האשה והנשים אינם בנות הוראה ואין לסמוך על דבריהם . . . שאיני מאמין בדבריה שמא חלפה בדבריה או פיחתה או הותירה."[15]

5. "אזל הוא (רשב"י) ובריה טשו בית מדרשא, כל יומא הוה מייתי להו דביתהו ריפתא וכוזא דמיא וכרכי, וניתקיף גזירתא א"ל לבריה נשים דעתן קלה עליהן, דילמא מצערי לה ומגליא לן, אזלו טשו במערתא וכו'"[16].

ב. "האשה משועבדת לבעלה"

הדעה שמעמדה של האשה בחברה היהודית מראשית ימיה עד הזמן החדש (אבל לא עד בכלל) עלה על מעמדה בחברות לא יהודיות, יש לה על מה לסמוך[17] ומיותר לצטט עשרות מאמרי חז"ל המדברים בשבח האשה, והמשווים את כבוד האם לכבוד האב ומונים את חובותיו ההלכתיות והמוסריות של האיש כלפי אשתו. בכל זאת הכלל שהאשה משועבדת לבעלה — ש"יפה היה לו לאדה"ר שנטלו ממנו צלע אחת ונתנו לו שפחה לשמשו"[18] לא זז ממקומו. איך הומחש הכלל הזה בהלכה?

1. **בנישואין:** הרמב"ם פוסק: "הדברים שיאמר האיש כשיקדש צריך שיהיה משמעם שהוא קונה האשה ולא שיהא משמע שהקנה עצמו לה. כיצד, הרי שאמר לה או שכתב בשטר שנתנו לה, הריני בעלך, הריני ארוסך, הריני אישך וכל כיוצא בזה אין כאן קידושין כלל, אמר לה או כתב לה הרי את אשתי, הרי את ארוסתי . . . הרי את זקוקה לי ככל היוצא בהן הרי זו מקודשת"[19].

---

13. ספר החינוך סוף מצוה תי"ט.

14. שם מצוה קכ"ב — בנוגע לאסמכתאות שחז"ל מצאו במקרא שהאשה פסולה לעדות ראה להלן דף 200.

15. במ"ר פ"י:ה. באמצע ד"ה וישמע אלקים בקול מנוח.

16. שבת לג:

17. "האשה באספקלריה היהודית" — שלמה אשכנזי — מוסד הרב קוק ירושלים, חלק א'.

18. סנהדרין לט.

19. הלכות אישות פ"ו, מ"ט.

2. **במשפחה:** "האב קדם לאם בכל מקום יכול שכבוד האב עודף על כבוד האם ת"ל איש אמו ואביו תיראו" (ויק', י"ט; ג') מלמד ששניהם שקולים, אבל אמרו חכמים האב קודם לאם בכל מקום מפני שהוא ואמו חייבין בכבוד אביו .... [20] הרמב"ם מסכם את די-ערכיותם של חז"ל בנוגע ליחס של הבעל לאשתו באמרו: "וכן ציוו חכמים שיהא מכבד אדם את אשתו יותר מגופו, ואוהבה כגופו, (סנה' ע') ואם יש לו ממון מרבה בטובתה כפי ממונו ולא יטיל עליה אימה יתירה ויהיה דיבורו עמה בנחת ולא יהיה עצב ולא יהיה רגזן" [21] והוא ממשיך ומוסיף "וכן ציוו על האשה שתהיה מכבדת את בעלה ביותר מדאי ויהיה עליה מורא ממנו ותעשה כל מעשיה על פיו, ויהיה בעיניה כמו שר או מלך מהלכת בתאות לבו ומרחקת כל מה שישנא. וזה דרך בנות ישראל ובני ישראל הקדושים והטהורין בזווגן. ובדרכים אלו יהיו ישובן נאה ומשובח". [22]

3. **בדברים שבינו ובינה:** אף על פי שאמרו "אסור לאדם שיכוף אשתו לדבר מצוה" [23] ואשה שאמרה "מאסתיהו ואיני יכולה להבעל לו מדעתי כופין אותו לשעתו לגרשה לפי שאינה כשבויה שתבעל לשנוא לה" [24] בכל זאת "להרבה מן המפרשים וכל מי שראיתי דבריו כתב שבדין הגמרא אין כופין את האיש להוציא אף באומרת מאוס עלי, ועל זה הרבו בראיות ברורות וקראו תגר על כל הנוטה מדבריהם ... וכבר פשטה הוראה הזאת בכל ארצותינו שלא כדברי רבנו בזה שאין כופין את האיש לגרש, ולא עוד אלא שאפילו היה הדין כדבריו היה ראוי לגדור בזה משום פרוצות ומפני קלקול הדור... כ"ש שהם ז"ל הכריחו והוכיחו שאין כופין אותו מן הדין. ...". [25]

4. **בגיטין:** הסימן המובהק ביותר כי במעמדה של אשה בכלל וביחסה לבעלה בפרט, נשאר אבק או אולי יותר מאבק של עבדות הוא מספר המקומות שבהם ההלכה משווה את האשה לעבד. כגון: בג' דרכים שוו גטי נשים לשחרורי עבדים" [26]. "כל מצוה שהאשה חייבת בה עבד חייב בה, כל מצוה שאין האשה חייבת בה אין העבד חייב בה דגמר לה, לה מהאשה". [27] והעובדה המעציבה שבעניני גטין יד הבעל על העליונות ויש בידי מנוול גמור הכח ההלכתי לעגן אשה חפה מפשע.

20. משנה כריתות פ"ו, מ"ט.
21. הלכות אישות פט"ו; י"ט.
22. שם, כ.
23. עירובין ק:
24. הלכות אישות פי"ד:ח.
25. מגיד משנה שם. וראה גם נדרים כ: ותוס' שם ד"ה התורה התירתך.
26. גיטין ט.
27. חגיגה ד.

5. **במצווה שהזמן גרמא:** חז"ל נסחו את הכלל שנשים פטורות ממצוות עשה שהזמן גרמא וחפשו לו בסיס במקרא. לשאלה הנשאלת "ובמצוות עשה שהזמן גרמא נשים פטורות מנלן" עונה הגמרא "גמר מתפילין, מה תפילין נשים פטורות אף כל מצוות עשה שהזמן גרמא נשים פטורות, ותפילין גמר לה מתלמוד תורה, מה ת"ת נשים פטורות אף תפילין נשים פטורות.[28] מהשקלא וטריא שם בגמרא ובתוספות נראה לעין שחז"ל בעצמם הרגישו כמה רפה הוא הבסיס המקראי. לכן מתעוררת השאלה מה דחף אותם לנסח כלל שיש בו כל כך הרבה יוצאים מן הכלל? (ראה שם) כמובן שאין תשובה וודאית לשאלה כזו, אבל אחד מגדולי הראשונים מֵעז להציע תשובה: "והטעם שנפטרו נשים מהמצוות עשה שהזמן גרמא לפי שהאשה משועבדת לבעלה לעשות צרכיו. ואם היתה מחוייבת במצוות עשה שהזמן גרמא אפשר בשעת עשיית המצוה מצווה אותה הבעל לעשות מצוותו ואם תעשה מצוות הבורא ותניח מצוותו אוי לה מבעלה ואם תעשה מצוותו ותניח מצוות הבורא אוי לה מיוצרה, לפיכך פטרה הבורא ממצוותיו כדי להיות לה שלום עם בעלה, וגדולה מזאת מצאנו שהשם הגדול הנכתב בקדושה וטהרה נמחה על פי המים כדי להטיל שלום בין איש לאשתו" (שבת קט"ז.).[29] אינני יודע אם אבודרהם צודק או לא, אבל המעניין אותי הוא כי לא נימק את הכלל הזה על ידי התחייבויותיה של האשה כעקרת הבית כמו שבני דורנו רגילים לעשות[30] אלא על ידי השתעבדותה לבעלה.

6. **בהלכות ת"ת:** כידוע אמרו חז"ל "ולמדתם אותם את בניכם, בניכם ולא בנותיכם"[31] אבל נראה לעין שאף על פי שהדרש הזה מתקבל על הדעת אין ההגיון ודרכי הדרש מכריחים אותו. הלא אפשר היה לומר שהמושג בנים כולל בנות, שהלא נאמר "בנים אתם לד' אלוקיכם" (דברים י"ד;א) וזה לא נאמר בנוגע לחצי העם בלבד. ועוד: הלכה פוסקת "עמוני ומואבי אסורין (לבוא בקהל) ואיסורין איסור עולם,

28. קידושין לד. "ואולם בירושלמי לא לבד לא נמצא בו אפילו רמז קל שנשים פטורות מק"ש משום שהיא מ"ע שהזמן גרמא, אלא בפרוש דרשו את בניכם וכו'/למעט נשים מק"ש, ופירוש דרשה זו הוא שק"ש ות"ת הן דבר אחד, אלא שק"ש הוא השעור היותר פחות של ת"ת שאין אדם יכול להפטר ממנו (ראה בבלי מנחות צ"ט:)" (פירושים וחידושים בירושלמי לוי גינצבורג — חלק ב — דף 133) ואין הכל מודים בכלל שנשים פטורות מכל מ"ע שהזמן גרמא (שם דף 134).

29. אבודרהם השלום — הוצאת אושא — ירושלים, תשי"ט, דף כ"ה.

30. "ובעקבות יעודה העיקרי כעקרת הבית נפטרה אשה ממצוות עשה שהזמן גרמן — אליקים ג' אלינסון — בין האשה ליוצרה — האשה והמצוות ספר ראשון — ההסתדרות הציונית העולמית המחלקה לחינוך ולתרבות תורניים בגולה. דף 11.

31. קידושין כ"ט:

אבל נקבותיהם מותרות מיד"[32] והגמרא ממשיכה "תנינא עמוני ולא עמונית מואבי
ולא מואבית, אלא מעתה ממזר ולא ממזרת . . . מצרי ולא מצרית"[33] והמהרש"א
מהדורה בתרא מבאר "ושפיר איכה למימר נמי מצרי ואדומי ולא מצרית ואדומית
אלא דלא דייק ליה עמוני ומואבי למעט הנקבות **דכל התורה בלשון זכר נאמר**" ולכן
לא ההגיון ולא כלל שלפיו נדרשת התורה מכריחים את הדרש "בניכם ולא בנותיכם".
אלא נדמה לי שביודעין או בלא יודעין מקושרת ההלכה שהאשה פטורה מתלמוד
תורה בעובדה שבכל העולם כולו לא ראו שום צורך לספק חינוך מסודר לבנות או
מפני שדעתן קלה או מפני שהן נחשבו כמשועבדות או לאביהן או לבעליהן. וע"י
דרשה זו של "בניכם ולא בנותיכם" מצאו חז"ל אסמכתא במקרא למנהג של העולם
כולו בלי יוצא מן הכלל. ותשובתו של אבדרהם לשאלה למה "נפטרו נשים מהמצוות
שהזמן גרמא" חלה ביתר שאת על היותן פטורות מת"ת כי הלא בנוגע לת"ת כתוב
"והגית בו יומם ולילה" (יהושע א'; ח) ואם מצוות ת"ת תחול באותה מידה על
הנשים כעל הגברים יש לאשה אמתלה הגונה מוכנה תמיד לא לעשות מה שהבעל
מצווה עליה.

ג. האשה "כולה ערוה"[34]

אחת העבירות שלפי רב "אין אדם ניצול מהן בכל יום"היא הירהורי עבירה,[35]
רבא (רבה) אמר "גמירי (מסורת היא מרבותי, רש"י) שאין יצר הרע שולט אלא במה
שעיניו רואות"[36] וחז"ל הבדילו בין גזל לעריות ששניהם "נפשו מחמדתן ומתאווה
להם", באמרם כי בנוגע לגזל "בפניו נפיש יצריה, שלא בפניו לא נפיש יצריה", אבל
בנוגע לעריות "בין בפניו בין שלא בפניו נפיש יצריה".[37] וידוע כמה הפליגו חז"ל
בתוארם "נפיש יצריה" של האיש עד שאמרו שהוא (היצר) מתגבר עליו בכל יום
ומבקש להמיתו . . .[38] ואלמלא הקב"ה שעוזר לו אינו יכול לו"[39] "שאפילו בשעת
אנינותו של אדם יצרו מתגבר עליו"[39] ושהוא מתגרה "בתלמידי חכמים יותר מכולם"
ו"כל הגדול מחברו יצרו גדול ממנו"[40] והיות שמחד גיסא דעתן של נשים קלה

32. יבמות ע"ו:
33. שם ס"ט.
34. סוטה ח.
35. בבא בתרא קס"ד:
36. סוטה ח.
37. חגיגה י"א: ראה גם סנהדרין מ"ה. תוס' ד"ה אלא במה וכו'.
38. סוכה נ"ב:
39. קידושין פ:
40. סוכה נ"ב:

ומתפתות על נקלה להפצרת גבר ומאידך גיסא "נפיש יצריה" של האיש אפילו שלא
בפניו, ועל אחת כמה וכמה בפניו, לא נילאו חז"ל מלהזהיר את האיש, שישמר
מלהימצא "בפניו", ז.א. בפני דבר המגרה את יצרו. ו"כיוון שנבראת אשה נברא שטן
עמה"[41] האשה היא הכוח הכביר ביותר המגרה את יצרו של האיש, ושומה עליו
להתרחק ממנה, וכל המרבה להתרחק הרי זה משובח.

בחומש אין אף רמז למצוה האוסרת על נשים ואנשים להמצא בחברותא אחת.
בכל סיפורי התנ"ך מופיעות הנשים יחד עם האנשים. במסופר אודות מעמד הר סיני
לא נאמר כי האנשים היו "ערוכים לבד והנשים לבד"[42] וחז"ל בדרשותיהם מדגישים
כי באותו מעמד חלק הקב"ה כבוד יתר לנשים. אמרו "כה תאמר לבית יעקב אלו
הנשים ותגיד לבני ישראל אלו האנשים" "למה לנשים תחילה, שהן מזדרזות במצוות,
ד"א כדי שיהיו מנהיגות את בניהן לתורה. א"ר תחליפה דקיסרין, אמר הקב"ה
כשבראתי את העולם לא ציויתי אלא לאדם הראשון ואחר כך נצטוית חוה, ועברה
וקילקלה את העולם, עכשיו אם איני קורא לנשים תחילה הן מבטלות את התורה.
לכן נאמר "כה תאמר לבית יעקב."[44] ובמצוות "הקהל את העם האנשים והנשים
והטף" (דב' ל"א, י"ב) אין זכר להפרדתם למחנות מיוחדים. ובספר נחמיה מסופר:
"ויביא עזרא הכהן את התורה לפני הקהל מאיש ועד אשה וכל מבין לשמע . . .
ויקרא בו . . . נגד האנשים והנשים והמבינים. (נחמיה ח: ב-ג). יש מפרשים את
הפסוק "קדמו שרים אחר נוגנים בתוך עלמות תופפות" (תה' ס"ח כ"ו) "שבתהלוכות
החגיגיות בבית המקדש היו השרים והנוגנים מוקפים עלמות מכות בתופים."[45]

ויש המפרשים שהעלמות היו בין השרים וה"נוגנים", ואפשר לומר שהיו מחנות
נפרדים, אבל רק בדוחק יש לומר שמחנה אחד לא היה נראה למחנה השני. רק
במקום אחד בתנ"ך מדובר בפירוש על הפרדת נשים וגברים. "ביום ההוא יגדל
המספד בירושלים . . . וספדה הארץ משפחות לבד, משפחת בית דוד לבד . . . כל
המשפחות הנשארות, משפחות משפחות לבד ונשיהם לבד" (זכריה י"ב, י"א-י"ד)
ועל פסוק זה סמכו חז"ל את "התיקון הגדול" שעשו במקדש במוצאי יום טוב ראשון
של חג. "אמרו ק"ו ומה לעתיד לבוא שעוסקין בהספד ואין יצר הרע שולט בהם

---

41. בראשית רבה יז:ו.

42. לפי דברי ר' פנחס בפד"א פ' מ"ט. מובא בתורה שלמה שמות י"ט סימן מ"ט.

43. מכילתא דרבי שמעון בר יוחאי — דוד צבי האפפמאנן — פראנפורט א. מ.
תרס"ה פרק יט, ג — דף 94.

44. שמות רבה פ' כח: ב. וראה גם מכילתא, הערה 43.

45. פירוש שלמה זלמן אריאל בתנ"ך לחיי צבא הגנה לישראל, הוצאות הרבנות
הראשית, צה"ל.

אמרה תורה אנשים לבד ונשים לבד עכשיו שעוסקין בשמחה ויצה״ר שולט בהם על אחת כמה וכמה״.[46]

יוסי בן יוחנן איש ירושלים הוא הראשון הידוע לנו, שיעץ במפורש לא להרבות שיחה עם האשה[47] ולא ברור אם כיוון לאשה סתם או רק לאשתו. הבאים אחריו הניחו כי כיוון לאשתו ״מדקאמר עם האשה ולא אמר עם אשה למדנו שבאשתו אמרו״.[48]

ואמרו ״ק״ו באשת חברו, מכאן אמרו חכמים כל זמן שאדם מרבה שיחה עם האשה גורם רע לעצמו ובוטל מדברי תורה וסופו יורש גיהינם״.[49] יוסי בן יוחנן הזהיר רק לא להרבות שיחה ואלה שבאו אחריו הוסיפו ואמרו שאין משתמשים באשה כלל בין גדולה בין קטנה (רש״י, שלא ילמדנה להיות רגילה בין האנשים) ולא לשאול בשלום אשה (רש״י, אם אשאל בשלומה תשיבני, וקול באשה ערוה)[50] ולא ע״י שליח ״הרי אמר שמואל אין שואלים בשלום אשה כלל״ (רש״י, שמא מתוך שאילת שלום יהיו רגילים זה עם זה ע״י שלוחים ויבואו לידי חיבה)[51] ולא נחה דעתם עד שאמרו שאסור להסתכל אפילו בבגדי צבע של אשה[52] ובאצבע קטנה של אשה ״וכל גוף האשה ערוה לפיכך לא יסתכל בגוף האשה כשהוא קורא ואפילו אשתו ואם היה מגולה טפח מגופה לא יקרא כנגדה״,[54] ז.א. אפילו אינו מסתכל בה!

בבית שני היו ״חמש עשרה מעלות יורדות מעזרת ישראל לעזרת נשים״ אבל כנראה שההפרדה הזאת לא הספיקה כדי למנוע קלות ראש בעת שמחת בית השואבה. ״בראשונה היו נשים מבפנים (רש״י בעזרת נשים) ואנשים מבחוץ (רש״י — ברחבה של הר הבית בחוץ) והיו באים לידי קלות ראש. התקינו שיהיו נשים יושבות מבחוץ ואנשים מבפנים ועדיין היו באין לידי קלות ראש. התקינו שיהיו נשים יושבות מלמעלה ואנשים מלמטה״.[55] והתוספתא מוסיפה: וכשראו בית הדין שהן באין לידי קלות ראש עשו שלוש שלוש גזוזטראות בעזרה כנגד שלוש רוחות, ששם נשים יושבות

46. סוכה נב.

47. אבות, א:ח.

48. ר״ע מברטנורה וראה יתר דבריו שם.

49. שם.

50. קידושין ע

51. שם ע: וראה גם ב״מ פז: תוס׳ ד״ה ע״י בעלה.

52. עבודה זרה כ.

53. ברכות כד.

54. הלכות קריאת שמע פ״ג: ט״ז.

55. סוכה נ״א:

ורואות בשמחת בית השואבה, ולא היו מעורבין, חסידים ואנשי מעשה היו מרקדין
לפניהן. . .[56] לפי פשט הדברים היו "אנשי מעשה" מרקדים לפני הנשים, שהלא כל
התיקון נעשה כדי שהנשים תוכלנה לראות את השמחה. כנראה שהרעיון שחסידים
ואנשי מעשה ירקדו לפני נשים לא מצא חן בעיני האחרונים ובפסקי הרי"ד נאמר
ש"היו מרקדים לפני הלויים שהיו עומדים במעלות, והם היו למטה בעזרה."[57] המנהג
להפריד בין גברים ונשים היה נפוץ בכל העולם כולו בעבר. נשים לא השתתפו לא
בחיים הפוליטיים של היונים והרומאים ולא בתחרויות אולימפיות ולא במסיבות
חברותיות.[58] וזהו בעצם המצב הנוכחי בחברות האסלם, המזרח הרחוק ובחברות של
האורתודוקסיה היהודית העקבית. נשים אינן באות עם בעליהן לחצר הרבי לחוג את
החגים, אינן משתתפות באספות של רבנים או אדמו"רים, נשים וגברים אינם מסובים
על אותו שולחן בחתונה, ועל אחת כמה וכמה שאינם מרקדים יחד, וכו'. "הצדיק"
לא יתקע כף עם אשה, לא ישוחח אתה וישתדל אפילו לא להביט בפניה. וההפרדה
מתחילה בגן הילדים, והיות שאין לך מקום ואין לך זמן שבהם צריכה דעתו של אדם
להיות נקיה מהרהורי עבירה כבית הכנסת ובעת התפילה נתקבל המנהג להפריד בין
אנשים לנשים בבית הכנסת בכל תפוצות ישראל. ועד התחלת התנועה הרפורמית
בראשית המאה התשע עשרה, לא היה יוצא מן הכלל. מקומה של עזרת-נשים בבית
הכנסת היה או בעליה גבוהה גבוהה מעל ראשם של הגברים או מאחורי סבכה או
וילון כדי שלא יוכלו הגברים לשמוע קולן של המתפללות ולא להסתכל בהן. התנועה
הריפורמית הנהיגה הנהיגה שנשים וגברים ישבו זה על יד זה בבית הכנסת בשעת התפילה.
מורינו הרב שניאור זלמן שכטר ז"ל הנהיג שבבית הכנסת של בית המדרש לרבנים
באמריקה תישבנה נשים לחוד וגברים לחוד אבל באותו חדר ובאותה קומה ורק חציה

56. תוספתא סוכה פ"ד; א־ב.

57. מובא בתוספת כפשוטה — שם.

"Our ancestors thought it not proper that woman should 58.
perform any, even private business without a director, but that they
should be ever under the control of parents, brothers or husbands.
"If Romans, every individual among us had made it a rule to maintain
the prerogative and authority of a husband with respect to his own
wife, we should have less trouble with the whole sex." Cato, the Elder
(234-149 B.C.E.) Livy 34:2

עד כמה שידוע לי לא היה אף אחד בין חברי הועדה שחברה את התחוקה האמריקאית שעלה
על דעתו שגם אשה תוכל להיות אזרחית מלאה ולהיות בין הבוחרים והנבחרים.

מפרידה ביניהם. ובבית המדרש של בית המדרש לרבנים שבו מתפללים כל יום מפריד קיר שגבהו כמטר בין שני המחנות. אבל בכל שמונה מאות וחמשים הקהילות המשתייכות לתנועה השמרנית יושבים גברים ונשים יחד בבית הכנסת בזמן התפילה, ואפילו באותן הקהילות האורתודוכסיות המודרניות בארצות המערב שבהן נשים וגברים יושבים נפרדים, הנשים אינן נמצאות לא בעליה ולא מאחרי סבכה או וילון, אלא במקום שהן נראות ונשמעות, ורואות ושומעות כל מה שנעשה במשך התפילה.

ד. "כל כבודה בת מלך פנימה" (תה' מ"ה: י"ד)

למרות שהאשה היתה משועבדת או לאביה, או לאחיה או לבעלה, היא אינה מתוארת בתנ"ך כמנותקת מהחיים התוססים סביבה. היא מעורבת בהם בכל רמ"ח אבריה. האשה יוצאת לבדה לעבוד בשדה, כגון אשת מנוח (שופטים, י"ג;ט). נשים רועות צאן ומתאספות עם הרועים מסביב לבאר (בראשית, כ"ט; ו, שמות ב, ט"ז-י"ז). דבורה "שפטה את ישראל" ויוצאת עם הצבא למלחמה (שופטים, ד: ד, ח-ט) בכמה תקופות משבר בחיי המשפחה של האבות ובחיי העם מעשיהן של נשים מכריעים את הכף לטובתו של העם.[59] "אשת חיל" המתוארת במשלי פרק ל"א עוסקת במשא ומתן, במסחר ובחקלאות וגם בפלך. היא "כאניות סוחר ממרחק תביא לחמה" (שם י"ד) "זממה שדה ותקחהו, מפרי כפיה נטע כרם" (שם ט"ז) "ידיה שלחה בכישור וכפיה תמכו בפלך" (שם כ) והיא מתגאה שבעלה היה "נודע בשערים בשבתו עם זקני ארץ" (שם כ"ב). רבות היו הנשים במשך הדורות אשר עשו כמוה, שעבדו או ניהלו חנויות כדי לפרנס את המשפחה ולאפשר לבעל לעסוק יומם ולילה בתורה.

בהשקפת חז"ל האשה המופתית כולה מסורה ומשועבדת לביתה, לבעלה ולמשפחתה, ומנותקת כמעט לגמרי מחיי החברה והקהילה, ממסחר וממשא ומתן של השוק. היא כלילת הצניעות עד כדי כך שאפילו קירות ביתה אינם רואים את שערה.[60] האסמכתא לדמותה זו של האשה מצאו חז"ל בדברי המשורר "כל כבודה בת מלך פנימה". הרמב"ם מסכם את השקפת חז"ל על מקומה של האשה בחברה בכתבו "אבל גנאי היא לאשה שתהיה תמיד יוצאת פעם בחוץ פעם ברחובות ויש לבעל למנוע אשתו מזה, ולא יניחנה לצאת אלא כמו פעם אחת בחודש או כמה פעמים

---

59. שרה ויצחק (בראשית כא: ט-יב) רבקה ויעקב (שם כז: ה -י"ג) דבורה (שופטים ד: ד-כג) יעל (שם ח-כא) אבימלך שם ט: נב-נג) אשת מנוח (שם יג:ב-ז). חנה ושמואל (שמואל פרק א'.), האשה התקועית והמלך דוד (ש"ב, יד:ד) אשה חכמה ויואב (שם כ: ט"ז-כב) חלדה (מל"ב; כב:יד).

60. יומא מז:

בחודש לפי הצורך, שאין יופי לאשה אלא לישב בזוית ביתה שכך כתוב כל כבודה
וגו׳[61] ועל פסוק זה סמכו חז״ל כמה וכמה הלכות.

אשה לעדות: הכלל הוא שאשה פסולה לעדות[62] עדותה מתקבלת רק באותם
מצבים שגם עדותם של עבד וקטן מתקבלת[63] אסמכתא לפיסולה מצאו חז״ל בדרשם
כי ״ועמדו שני האנשים״ (דב׳ י״ט: יז) ״מדבר בעדים״,[64] המתבונן בסוגיא שם יראה
על נקלה עד כמה דחוק הוא הדרש הזה,[65] וכנראה הכירו החכמים את חולשתו, ומצאו
לנחוץ לאששו בפסוק ״כל כבודה״ וגו׳. וכדאי לצטט את דברי הגמרא שם ופירוש של
התוספות. ״תניא, ואידך ״ועמדו שני האנשים״, בעדים הכתוב מדבר, אתה אומר
בעדים או אינו אלא בבעלי הדין אמרת וכי אנשים באין לדין נשים אין באין לדין״
(זאת אומרת אם נאמר שהכתוב מדבר רק בבעלי הדין ולא בעדים, והיות שהפסוק
אומר במפורש ״אנשים״ נצטרך להסיק שרק גברים יכולים להיות בעלי דין וזה אי
אפשר להניח) ״ואם נפשך לומר נאמר כאן שני ונאמר להלן (שם פסוק ט״ו) שני מה
להלן בעדים אף כאן בעדים, מאי אם נפשך לומר, וכי תימא אשה לאו אורחה משום
״כל כבודה בת מלך פנימה״ נאמר כאן שני ונאמר להלן ״שני״, מה להלן בעדים אף
כאן בעדים״. והתוספות שמה, ד״ה ״כל כבודה״ מבאר: ״וא״ת השתא נמי דאיירי
בעדים מנא ליה למעוטי נשים, דלמא הא דנקט קרא אנשים משום ״כל כבודה בת
מלך פנימה״, ויש לומר דגבי עדים ע״כ צריכין לבא (לבית הדין) דאין עד מפי עד
כשר, אבל לדין יכולה למסור טענותיה ביד אחר״. מכאן בלי הפסוק ״כל כבודה״ וגו׳
לא יכלו להסיק בבטחה שאף על פי שבפסוק כתוב ״אנשים״ ומדבר בעדים שהוא בא
״למעוטי נשים״, ״דכל התורה בלשון זכר נאמר״.[66]

61. הלכות אישות פי״ג: יא.

62. ראה למעלה דף 192 ושבועות ל.

63. ראה אנציקלופדיה תלמודית — כרך שני דף רנ״ב ע׳ אשה ד״ה בנאמנות.

64. שבועות ל.

65. על הדרש הזה מעיר בעל התורה תמימה (דברים יט: סימן נו) ״לכאורה אי משום
דמיון המלות לבד קשה . . . מצינו מלת שני גם בבעלי דינין, שני אנשים ניצים, עד האלקים
יבוא דבר שניהם, שני אנשים היו בעיר אחת (ש״ב: יד) וכדומה, וגם מה טעם ללמד משווי
המלות, אבל באמת נראה הכוונה דכיון הפסוק הקודם דכתיב בו שני בודאי בעדים איירי
כדכתיב שם עפ״י שני עדים ועליו סמוך וסובב הפ׳ הזה. ועמדו שני האנשים א״כ בודאי גם
הוא מוסב על העדים, ואעפ״י דהכרח גם בבע״ד איירי כדכתיב אשר להם הריב, אך משוי
הלשונות ש״מ תרתי, דקאי גם על בע״ד גם על עדים, ודריש אשר להם הריב כמו ואשר להם
הריב, כלומר ועמדו העדים וגם אלה אשר להם הריב, ודו״ק״.

66. ראה למעלה דף 201 דברי המהרש״א.

2. **עמוני ולא עמונית, מואבי ולא מואבית:** מסופר [67] כי בבית דינו של שמואל דרשו את הפסוק "לא יבא עמוני ומואבי בקהל ד'" (דברים כ"ג;ד) "עמוני ולא עמונית. מואבי ולא מואבית". אצטט את סיפור המעשה כמו שהוא נמצא במדרש רות רבה [68] . . . "כיון שראה שאול את ראש הפלישתי בידו התחיל שואל עליו (על דוד) אם מפרץ הוא, מלך הוא, אם מזרח הוא שופט הוא, והיה שם דואג האדומי באותה השעה ואמר לו אפילו מפרץ הוא לא פסול הוא? לא פסול משפחה הוא? לא מרות המואביה הוא? א"ל אבנר ולא כבר נתחדשה הלכה עמוני ולא עמונית. א"ל (דואג לאבנר) אם כן אדומי ולא אדומית, מצרי ולא מצרית. (א"ל אבנר לדואג) אנשים למה נתרחקו לא על דבר אשר לא קדמו אתכם בלחם ובמים? (דב' כג:ה) אמר לו דואג לאבנר היה להם לנשים להוציא לקראת נשים.[69] נתעלמה הלכה מאבנר לשעה. אמר לו שאול הלכה שנתעלמה מעיניך צא ושאל לשמואל ובית דינו. כיון שבא אצל שמואל בבית דינו אמר לו הדא מנין אית לך, לא מן דואג? דואג מיני הוא (ואינו מאמין בדברי חז"ל הדורשים מן הקבלה עמוני ולא עמונית"[70] — ואינו יוצא בשלום מן העולם. להוציאך חלק אי אפשר דכ' כל כבודה וגו'. לאשה שלא להוציא ולאיש להוציא [71] — ואשר שכר עליך (דב' כ"ג;ה) לאיש ליתן שכר ולא לאשה"[72] והמהרש"א מבאר: "בתוס' ד"ה כתנאי, מוסיף "ושפיר איכא למימר נמי מצרי ואדומי ולא מצרית ואדומית אלא דלא דייק ליה עמוני ומואבי מצרי ואדומי למעט הנקבות דכל התורה בלשון זכר נאמר".[73] הרי שבלי הפסוק "כל כבודה" אי אפשר לקיים את הדרש של עמוני ולא עמונית וכו'.

3. **שכר תלמוד תורה לבנות:** "המדיר הנאה מחברו. . . מלמד הוא את בניו ואת

<hr />

67. יבמות ע"ו: — עז"י.

68 רות רבה פ"ד: ט ד"ה ויאמר בועז לנערו.

69. בדברים כג: ח-ט כתוב "לא תתעב אדמי. . . לא תתעב מצרי . . . דור שלישי יבא להם בקהל ה' ואת הפסוק הזה לא דרשו חז"ל אדומי ולא אדומית וכו', אלא גם הנשים המצריות אסורות עד דור שלישי — והתשובה היא כי בנוגע לעמונים ומואבים התורה מבארת כי הזכרים נתרחקו "על דבר אשר לא קדמו אתכם בלחם ובמים" (שם כג:ה) והנשים לא היו מחויבות לקדם אותם. ולזה הושיב דואג האדומי "והלא הנשים מחויבות היו "להוציא לקראת נשים", ולזה לא היתה תשובה לאבנר.

70. מתנת כהונה שם.

71. ועל זה הושיבו לאבנר בבית מדרשו של שמואל, כי האשה אינה מחויבת "להוציא" על סמך הפסוק של כבודה וגו'.

72. האיש יוצא ושוכר ולא האישה.

73. מהדורה בתרא — יבמות ע"ז.

בנותיו מקרא . . . [74] מפני שהוא חייב ללמדם מקרא בחנם.[75] "רב אמר שכר שימור
(רש"י — מה טעמא התירו למשקל שכר מן המקרא מפני שאין נוטלין שכר אלא על
שכר שימור שמשמרין התינוקות שאין מניחין אותן לצאת ולעסוק בדברים בטלים
. . . וקטנים דצריכין שימור למדין מקרא . . . ולהכי לא ילמדנו מקרא לקטנים בחנם
דהואיל ושרי למשקל עלייהו שכר וכו'). ורבי יוחנן אמר שכר פיסוק טעמים (רש"י
— שקיל מנייהו שמלמדם ניקוד וטעמים וההוא שכר מצי למישקל ופיסוק טעמים
אינו אלא במקרא ולהכי לא ילמדנו מקרא) "ולמאן דאמר שכר פיסוק טעמים מ"[76]ט
לא אמר שכר שימור? קסבר בנות בעיין שימור? (רש"י — בנות שמלמדין
אותן תורה מי בעיין שימור, אינהו לא אורחייהו למיפק אבראי דכתיב כל כבודה וכו'
וליכא לאוקמא בה שכר שימור).

4. **אשה שגלתה לעיר מקלט**: ומעניין לשים לב שבמקום שהשמוש בפסוק "כל
כבודה" לא היה לטובתו של האיש לא השתמשו בו. אשה שגלתה לעיר מקלט, בעלה
חייב במזונותיה אע"ג דאמר לה צאי מעשה ידיך במזונותיך. בראשונה אמרו "הכא
במאי עסקינן . . . בדלא ספקה" (רש"י — לזון במעשה ידיה וצריך להוסיף משלו)
"והא מדקתני סיפא ואם אמר לה צאי מעשה ידיך במזונותיך רשאי . . . ה"ק ואם
מספקת ואמר לה צאי וכו' רשאי והגמרא שואלת "מספקת מאי למימרא" (תוס' שם
ד"ה מספקת — מאי למימרא דזה אינו שום חידוש) והגמרא משיבה "מהו דתימא
"כל כבודה בת מלך (רש"י — כל ישראל בני מלכים) פנימה" (רש"י — צנועה ואין
דרכה לצאת לסבב בעיר שאינה משם ואין מכירים אותה להביא לה מלאכה בביתה
אלא אם כן מסבבת בעיר למצוא מלאכה להשתכר) קמ"ל", דבכל זאת רשאי הבעל
לאמר לה, צאי מעשה ידיך במזונותיך!

5. **אשה שהדירה את בנה וכו'**: "תני המדיר את בנו לתלמוד תורה מותר למלאת
לו חבית של (יין) (מים) ולהדליק לו את הנר, ר' יעקב בר איידי בשם ר' יונתן אף
לוקח לו חפציו מן השוק (ופליגין) מה פליגי כאן באיש כאן באשה, אם היה אדם
מסויים עשו אותו כאשה.[78] פני משה מפרש: "שואל הש"ס אם פליגי, וקאמר דלא
פליגי, אלא כאן באיש כאן באשה, שהאשה היא צריכה אף לחפצים להתקשט בהן
כדי שיקפצו עליה לישא אותה — אם היה אדם מסויים וחשוב עשאו אותו כאשה
לחפצי הצריכים לו". גליונות הש"ס שם מוסיף: ". . . פי' דר' יעקב איירי באשה

74. משנה נדרים פ"ד מ"ג, מ"ד.
75. נדרים ל"ז.
76. שם לז:
77. גיטין יב:
78. ירושלמי סוף מסכת בכורים.

המדרת את בנה לת"ת שאין דרכה לצאת לשוק ליקח לה חפצים דכל כבודה דבת מלך
פנימה ולכן הבן לוקח לה חפצים מן השוק, והת"ק איירי באיש המדיר דיכול לצאת
בעצמו וליקח ולכן אסור לבן ליקח וכו' ואם היה האב המדיר דאין דרכו מסויים וחשוב
שגם כן אין דרכו ליקח חפצים מן השוק (והא דאמר ר' יעקב כו' אף לוקח לו חפציו
כו' אף דבאשה איירי והלו"ל אף לוקח לה חפצי' כו' אין קושיא דאיידי דאמר ת"ק
המדיר כו' ל' זכר אמר איהו נמי ל' זכר אף דבכוונתו אאשה ... ובל' מקרא נמי
מצינו תיבת איש על אישה ע' ירושלמי סוטה פ"א ה"ה אם יחטא איש לאיש וכו'
ריב"ל פתר קריי באשה כו' ע"ש) ואז מצטט עוד כמה מקומות בבבלי ומסיים "וכך
בירושלמי כאן איידי דאמר תחילה המדיר וכו' מותר למלאת לו כו' אמר נמי ר' יעקב
כו' לוקח לו בלשון זכר אף דכוונתו אאשה וז"ה.

ה. כל משימות שבישראל אין ממנים אלא איש"[79]

1. **מלך ולא מלכה:** הפסוק "שום תשים עליך מלך" (דברים י"ז: ט"ו) נדרש
בספרי[80] מלך ולא מלכה, "לא תוכל לתת עליך איש נכרי" (דב' שם) המלים "איש
נכרי" נדרשות "מכאן אמרו האיש ממנים פרנס על הציבור ואין ממנים האשה
פרנסת על הציבור". (ספרי שם) והרמב"ם מרחיב את תחום החלתה של ההלכה ...
"וכן כל משימות שבישראל אין ממנים בהם אלא איש".[79]

2. אשה כשופטת: ההלכה פוסקת[81] "כל ישראל כשרין למהדרין לדון אפילו
ממזר. אשה פסולה לדון ... מפני שכל הכשר לדון כשר להעיד". (נידה מ"ט:).
ואשה פסולה לעדות. אבל אין העניין פשוט כל כך:

א. הלא נאמר במפורש בנוגע לדבורה ש"היא שופטה את ישראל" (שופטים ד:
ד) ועל זה משיבים "ואל יקשה עליך מה שכתוב דבורה הנביאה היא "שפטה את
ישראל" שאפשר לנו לתרץ שלא היה הדין נחתך על פיה אבל היתה אשה חכמה
ונביאה והיו נושאים עמה אפילו דברים של איסור והיתר ודינין גם כן ... או נאמר
שקיבלוה עליהם ראשי ישראל ואחריהם כל אדם לדון על פיה, דבקבלה ודאי הכל
כשרים, דכל תנאי שבממון — קים, ומכל מקום כל זה שאמרנו שאינן דנות, הוא
כדעת קצת המפרשים וכדעת ירושלמי (בסנה' פ"ג: ה"ט) לכן נמצאים שם מפורש
אבל לדעת קצת מן המפרשים, כשרות הן לדון, ואמרו כי מקרא מלא הוא שנאמר
"היא שפטה" ומה שאמרו בסנהדרין (ל"ד:) דכל שאינו כשר להעיד אינו כשר לדון,

79. הלכות מלכים פ"א: ה"ה.
80. ספרי פיסקא קנ"ז — וראה שם הערה ג'.
81. טור חו"מ ז:א.

ונשים ודאי אינן כשרות להעיד כדמוכח שם, אפשר שיאמרו לפי דעתם זה, לפי שאין
למדין מן הכללות".[82]

ב. דברי החינוך "אבל לדעת קצת המפרשים כשרות הן לדון" שהבאתי למעלה
מבוססים כנראה, על דברי התוספות[83] "...". וכן יש בירושלמי מעתה שאין האשה
מעידה שאינה דנה מיהו תימה דספ"ק דב"ק (ט"ו.) ובקידושין (ל"ה.). דרשינן
"מאשר תשים לפניהם" (שמות כ"א:א) דהשוה הכתוב אשה לאיש לכל הדינים, ואי
אשה פסולה לדון הא לא מיירי לפניהם אלא בכשרים לדון כדדריש פרק המגרש
(גיטין פ"ח:) לפניהם ולא לפני עובדי כוכבים, לפניהם ולא לפני הדיוטות, וי"ל דקרא
אמרי בתרוייהו בדיינים ובנידונים, וממעט עובדי כוכבים והדיוטות משום דלפניהם
קאי אאלהים דמשמע מומחין וקאי נמי אנידונין וקאי ישראל האנשים והנשים בכלל
זה".

ג.   **אשה כמלכה:** כידוע מלכה שלומציון כתשע שנים אחרי מות בעלה ינאי
המלך. אחיה היה הפרושי שמעון בן שטח[84] והיא תמכה בידי הפרושים, וכנראה קבלו
הפרושים ברצון את מרותה כי הלא אין אף רמז בספרות חז"ל שמישהו מחה נגדה.

ו. כבוד הצבור

"תנו רבנן הכל עולין למנין שבעה ואפילו קטן ואפילו אשה.[85], אבל אמרו
חכמים אשה לא תקרא בתורה מפני כבוד הציבור[86] והיות שטעמם של חז"ל הוא
"כבוד הציבור" נראה בעליל כי דעתם כי שמדובר בציבור של אנשים. בנוגע
לפירוש המלים "עולין למנין שבעה" אין הסכמה כללית בין המפרשים.[87] ההבדלים
ביניהם אינם מעניינו פה, המעניין אותי הוא דבריו האחרונים של הב"י שם: "והר"ן
כתב הכל עולין למנין ז' ואפילו קטן פי' עולים להשלים קאמר ולא שיהיו כולם
קטנים ולא נשים דכיון דלאו בני חיובא נינהו לא מפקי לגמרי, ולפום עיקר דינא נמי
שאינו מברך אלא הפותח והחותם אשה וקטן אין קורין ראשון ואחרון משום ברכה,
משום דא"א לקורין האחרים שיצאו ברכתן ומיהו השתא שתקין רבנן שיברכו כולם
אשה וקטן קורין אפילו ראשון ואחרון וכיון דקורין ודאי מברכין מידי דהוה אקטן

82. ספר החינוך מצוה ע"ז, בסוף.

83. שבועות כ"ט: ד"ה שבועת העדות.

84. ברכות מ"ח.

85. תוספתא מגילה פ"ג:מי"א.

86. מגילת פ"ב:ג.

87. ראה מגילה תוספתא כפשוטה דף 1176, וטור או"ח רפ"ב ובפרט הב"י והפרישה
שם.

דמפטיר בנביא ומברך ברכת הפטרה עכ"ל". והנה באו החכמים ואסרו מה שהיה מותר וטעמם הוא, לא ש"קול באשה ערוה" ולא "כבודה בת מלך פנימה" ואין לאשה להראות ולהיות מעורבת בציבור של אנשים אלא הטעם הוא "כבוד הציבור". בנוגע לקטן נשאר הטעם של "כבוד הציבור" בתקפו עד היום רק בזה שהוא אינו עולה למנין שבעה, אבל מתירים לו לקרוא מן התורה ואת ההפטרה וברכותיה, אבל בנוגע לאשה הטעם של "כבוד הציבור" דחה לגמרי את ההלכה המפורשת של "הכל עולין".

הוא הדין לגבי קריאת המגילה, שנאמר במפורש "הכל כשרין לקרות את המגילה (ר"ע מברטנורה: הכל לרבות נשים) חוץ מחרש, שוטה וקטן. ר' יהודה מכשיר בקטן"[88] והלא גם בעניין זה אין להניח שהמשנה מכוונת להגיד לנו שאשה מותרת לקרוא את המגילה לפני ציבור של נשים, ומעניין שבנוגע לקטן יש ויכוח ארוך גם בגמרא[89] וגם בתוספות[90] "והנהיגו שיהו קטנים קורין אותה לרבים, נראה דקטן שהגיע לחינוך מיירי"[91] אבל בנוגע לאשה אין אף מילה.

בהלכות ברכת המזון נמצא גם כן אותה אי-בהירות בנוגע להתחייבויותיהם או לזכויותיהם של האשה והקטן,[92] בתוספתא[93] נאמר: ועבדים וקטנים פטורין (מבהמ"ז) ואין מוציאין את הרבים ידי חובתן" והגר"ש ליברמן בפירוש הקצר מבאר המלה "פטורין" צריכה מחיקה וצ"ל אין וכו', כג' כי"ע כי"ע והראשונים, ונשים אין מוציאות את הרבים בברהמ"ז מפני כבוד הציבור", והתוספתא שם ממשיכה "באמת אמרו אשה מברכת לבעלה בן מברך לאביו עבד מברך לרבו" ובפירוש הקצר של הגר"ש ליברמן נאמר: "לבעלה, כלומר ומוציאה אותו בברהמ"ז, ולאו דוקא בעלה אלא שדברו חכמים בהוה שאין דרכה של אשה לאכול עם אחר ביחידות". ו"מעדני יום טוב"[94] מדגיש "אשה מברכת לבעלה אבל לאחר לא, שאין חברתן נאה כדלקמן פרק שלושה שאכלו". התוספתא מובאת בגמרא בקצת שינוי נוסח ובהוספה חשובה: "באמת אמרו בן מברך לאביו ועבד מברך לרבו ואשה מברכת לבעלה אבל אמרו חכמים תבא מארה לאדם שאשתו ובניו מברכין לו". ורש"י כנראה מבאר למה תבא מארה עליו באמרו "בן קטן מברך ברכת המזון לאביו אם אין אביו יודע לברך" ולכן פה מדובר

---

88. משנה מגילה, פ"ב מ"ד.

89. מגילה י"ט:

90. שם ד"ה ורבי יהודה מכשיר, וראה גם ברכות ט"ו.

91. הגה"ה רבינו אשר שם.

92. תוס' ברכות כ': ד"ה נשים בברכת המזון.

93. ברכות פ"ה מי"ז.

94. מעדני יום טוב, סימן "ש" על ברכות כ.

באיש שאינו יודע לברך. ולכן הקהל הסומך על אשה להוציא את חבריו ידי חובתם
מעיד על עצמו שאין ביניהם היודע לקיים אותה מצווה, וכמובן שזה עלבון לו.

כמדומני שכולנו נסכים כי הקשר בין רב ההלכות הקובעות את מעמדה של
האשה בחברה היהודית ובין הדעות שהיו מקובלות בכל העולם כולו בדורות שקדמונו
על אודות אופיה האינטלקטואלי והפסיכולוגי של האשה, הרבה יותר הדוק מזה של
הקשר בינן ובין המקרא. הבנתנו את היחס בין עובדה זו ותקפתן של ההלכות האלה
בימינו ובמקומנו היא המפרידה בינינו. ישנם הטוענים כי אין שום קשר בין יחסן של
הלכות מסויימות לתנאים סוציולוגיים, היסטוריים, פסיכולוגיים מסויימים וכו' ובין
תקפן. דעה זו מבוססת על הלאו ד"לא תסור" (דברים י"ז, י"א) הלאו ד"לא תשיג
גבול רעך אשר גבלו ראשונים" (שם י"ט,י"ד) ועל העצה של "שאל אביך ויגדך זקניך
ויאמרו לך (שם ל"ב, ד') וגם על שיקולים הגיוניים. "נמנעו מלחלוק על בעלי הקבלה
עליהם השלום ומלשנות את דבריהם ולצאת ממצוותם בכל ענייני התורה. ועל זה
נאמר "לא תסור מהדבר אשר יגידו לך ימין ושמאל" (דברים י"ז;י"א) . . . משרשי
המצוה, לפי שדעות בני אדם חלוקין זה מזה . . . שאלו תהיה כוונת כתובי התורה
מסורה בידי כל אחד ואחד . . . וירבה המחלוקת בישראל במשמעות המצווה ותעשה
התורה   כמה תורות . . . ועל דרך אחת והשבח הגדול בזאת המצוה אמרו זכרונם
לברכה "לא תסור וגו'" אפילו יאמרו על ימין שהוא שמאל . . . וטוב לסבול טעות
אחת ויהיו הכל מסורים תחת דעתם הטובה תמיד ולא שיעשה כל אחד ואחד כפי
דעתו, שבזה יהיה חורבן הדת וחלוק לב העם והפסד האומה לגמרי".[97] ובנוגע לנידון
דנן הלא ההלכות הקובעות את מעמדה של האשה בחברה היו מקודשות בעיני העם
כולו זה אלפי שנים. הועדה שמינה הנגיד התחשבה בעובדה זו, לכן הפנתה את
תשומת ליבנו לפרצות הרבות שכבר נפרצו ע"י כל חלקי העם בחומת ההלכה
שהקימו חז"ל סביב לאשה היהודית. ולהלן אני עוד אחזור לפן זה של הנדון. פה אני
אציג בקצרה את הבנתי של הגישה השמרנית (קונסרבטיבית) לשאלת הנאמנות
להלכה.[98]

95. ברכות כ:
96. ברכות י"ט:
97. ספר החינוך מצווה תצ"ו.
98. עסקתי בשאלה זו באריכות ב-Greenberg, S., *The Ethical in the Jewish*
and American Heritage. Chapter III. *Foundations of a Faith* pp. 45–69,
90–112, 156–174. *A Jewish Philosophy and Pattern of Life.* pp.
449–464.

מהי נאמנות להלכה

הגישה השמרנית קובעת, בין היתר, כי שורשי ההלכה נטועים בשמים אבל
ענפיה ופירותיה גדלו וגדלים בארץ, וצורתם וטעמם נקבעו על ידי דור דור ודורשיו
דור דור וחכמיו ומנהיגיו, "יפתח בדורו כשמואל בדורו"[99] והושפעו על ידי הזמן
והמקום שבהם פעלו. ואף על פי שאנו "עם לבדד ישכון" (במדבר כ"ז;ט') לא היינו,
ואין אנו מחוסנים נגד השפעת הגורמים הפוליטיים, הכלכליים, האינטלקטואליים וכו'
של הסביבה, תהיה התבדלותינו הגיאוגרפית, התרבותית והדתית, אשר תהיה. החרם
של רבנו גרשם לא הוכרז בארצות האיסלאם, ואת המשך קיומה של הקהילה היהודית
בארצות הנצרות אי אפשר היה לתאר בלעדיו. תנועתנו הופיעה כאסכולה היסטורית
וחכמיה תרמו להבנת המסורת התורנית — הלכתית, בין היתר, על ידי חקירות
מעמיקות שחשפו את היחס בין הזמן והמקום ובין המנהג וההלכה. ותנועתנו אינה
שואפת להתבודד מסביבתנו.

הזמן והמקום השפיעו על ההלכה אבל לא קבעו אותה. מובן מאליו שהמסורת
החזיקה מעמד לא מפני שקבלה כל מה שהציעה הסביבה. להיפך, על פי רוב מוכרחה
היתה להתייצב נגד הגורמים המוסריים, הדתיים והתרבותיים בסביבה, אבל לא תמיד.
היו מקרים שהסביבה איפשרה ועודדה את גילויים והתפתחותם של רעיונות וערכים
שהיו טבועים וטמונים במסורת אבל לא הומחשו בכתב ובמעשים.[100] המסורת,
כביכול, עיכלה אותם הגורמים שהתבלטו בסביבה והתאימו לרוחה ודחתה את הזרים
לה. כך התעשרה והתאבנותה נמנעה. השפעת גומלין זו בין המסורת והסביבה ניכרת
בתולדות עמנו מתקופת התנ"ך עד ימינו והיא ידועה לכל המתיימר להיות אדם מן
היישוב.[101] אנחנו נמצאים בזמן ובסביבה שהכללים כי "נשים דעתן קלה" וכו' אינם
מקובלים על הרוב המכריע של האוכלוסיה ואני מניח שאין אף אחד מבין חברי
הסנאט של ביהמ"ר המקבל אותם. התהליך להשוואת זכויותיה של האשה בכל ענפי
החיים לזכויותיו של האיש בחברה הדמוקראטית המערבית, הגיע לשלב שלפי

---

99. ר"ה כ"ה:

100. למשל הדמוקרטיה והסבלנות כמו שהם נוסחו והומחשו בארצות הברית ובחברה
הדמוקרטית המערבית. ראה: S. Greenberg, *Foundations of a Faith*, The
Burning Bush Press, N.Y. City, 1967. Chapter IV — Judaism and the
democratic Ideal. A Jewish Philosophy and Pattern of Life — Jewish
Theological Seminary, N.Y. 198 p. 285–288. Pluralism and Jewish
Education in Religious Education Vol. 81 no. 1. Winter 1986.

101. ראה: הגר"ש ליברמן — יוונית ויוונות בארץ ישראל — מוסד ביאליק 1962.

ידיעותינו אין לו תקדים בכל תולדות האנושות ועלינו להחליט אם המסורת מוכשרה
לעכל תהליך זה, ואם עלינו לעודד, להאט או לדחות את עיכולו. אנו חיים בזמן
ובמקום שהמחיצה בין החיים הרב־גוניים של החברה ובין האשה כמעט שנהרסה
כולה. בראש ובראשונה הלא אנו גדלים בחברה שבה רגילים בנים ובנות, גברים
ונשים להמצא בחברותא מהגיל הרך ביותר ועד זקנה, בגן הילדים, באוניברסיטה,
ברחוב,בעבודה, בחיים הכלכליים והפוליטיים, בתיאטרון, במעונות נופש, במגרשי
ספורט וכו' וכו'. ההיסטוריה אינה מכירה חברה כחברתנו, שבה הנשים לא רק
משתתפות בכל מקצועות החיים אלא לוקחות חלק בהם כשווות בין שווים. במאות
הקהילות השמרניות נשים וגברים יושבים יחד בזמן התפילה ונשים משתתפות גם
בטקס התפילה. אבל התפילה בציבור היא רק אחת הפעולות של קהילה שמרנית או
אורתודוקסית מודרנית. בכל הקהילות האלו ישנן כל מיני פעולות חברתיות
ותרבותיות וחלקן של הנשים בהן רב, הן בתור מנהלות והן בתור משתתפות. נוכחותה
של האשה בכל מיני תנאים ומסיבות, הוא מהדברים השכיחים והמצויים ביותר
בחיינו, ואף על פי שהופעתה בתור רב תהיה רב חידוש לזמן מה חידוש, נוכחותה כאשה בין
גברים לא יהיה בה כל חידוש,[102] אני מניח, כי המסורת מוכשרת לעכל את התהליך
מפני שעקבותיו המובהקים נראים בה מראשיתה, מדברי ה' לאברהם, "כל אשר
תאמר אליך שרה שמע בקולה" (בראשית כ"א;יב), עד ייסודם של בתי ספר

102. אצטט רק כמה קטעים מכתבה שהופיעה בשבועון "כל העיר" בירושלים ביום ו'
כ"ד באב תשל"ט, על אודות ארוע שקרה בגן "פעמון הדרור" בטלביה, אחת השכונות
המפוארות של ירושלים, תחת הכותרת "הרבנית אסתר יונגרייז שומעת קולות". הופעת
הבכורה הארצית של הרבנית יונגרייז היתה . . . שילוב של מסע התעוררות והטפה צעקנית
בליווי צלילי להקה חסידית. המופע התקיים בחסות עירית ירושלים, המחלקה לתרבות והאגף
למפעלים תורניים . . . אסתר יונגרייז עומדת בראש תנועה עולמית הנקראת "הנני". התנועה
שעד עתה פעלה בעיקר בארצות הברית, מטיפה לחזרה לערכי התורה ולהזדהות עם
ישראל וארץ ישראל . . . הרבנית עולה על הבמה בנעלי פלטפורמה לבנות כמו סוליות של
להקת רוק חסידי, איפור עיניים ירקרק, ריסים מאורכים, תסםורת בלונדינית מדוייקת.
תזמורת של "כלי זמרים" מסיימת ניגון "שמע ישראל" והרבנית יונגרייז משתלטת על הערב.
קולה מלא ויבראציות ומשתנה במעברים מהירים מלחישות רגישות, כשהיא קוראת לקהל
"ידידי" לצעקות היסטריות, כשהיא מכריזה עליהם כעל "אומה של טיפשים" וכו' וכו' . . .
הרבנית יונגרייז הינה בעצם אישתו של רב אורתודוקסי בארצות הברית, ולא שמעתי לא בירושלים
ולא בארצות הברית, שמישהו מבין גדולי התורה ירים את קולו בפומבי על "חילול השם"
שבהופעה כזאת בעיה"ק ירושלים.

"שולמית". ואת דברי אלה איני צריך להדגים לקוראים[103]. אני רק אפנה את תשומת
ליבכם למאמר אחד של חז"ל המתייחס לעניננו "אמר ר' יהודה אמרו לפני רבן
גמליאל, הואיל וזכה באשה לא יזכה בנכסים. אמר להן על החדשים אנו בושין אלא
שאתם מגלגלין עלינו את הישנים"[104]. "על החדשים שנפלו לה משנשאת אנו
בושין", מה ראו חכמים לומר אם מכרה ונתנה הבעל מוציא מיד הלקוחות", אלא
שאתם מגלגלין עלינו את הישנים". נכסים שנפלו לה בעודה ארוסה, כלומר שאם
מכרה בטל לפי שזכה בהם הבעל[105]. אני משער שרבן גמליאל היה בוש מפני
שהאמין שכל החוקים והמשפטים של התורה צדיקים הם (דב' ד';ח') ובחוק זה שהוא
מדרבנן, ראה את הפלייתה של האשה לרעה והתבייש. ואני משוכנע כי הרמתה של
קרן ההלכה בזמננו ובמקומנו דורשת, שהתנועה השמרנית דווקא, תצעד בכיוון זה[106].
כי למרות השינויים שחלו בתנועה הריפורמית ביחס לציונות, יחסה להלכה לא
נשתנה ומוסדותיה המרכזיים של התנועה אינם מתחשבים ברצינות עם דרישותיה,
ועד כמה שאפשר לראות עתידות מעשיה של התנועה הריפורמית לא יגרעו ולא
יוסיפו ליוקרתה של ההלכה.

103. "Wives Match Their Husbands in Some Courses *at Yeshiva
University*."
. . . Orthodox Judaism prohibits women from serving as Rabbis and
generally separates the sexes beginning in grammar school. In recent
years, however, many Orthodox women and men have insisted that
women should be able to aspire to professional careers without violating religious laws. Because of the policy of the school, seven wives and
seven husbands are now among the 150 students at the school . . . all
couples agree . . . that studying in the same program has been a positive experience."

New York Times, March 16, 1979.
in second section — Metropolitan
Report.

104. כתובות פ"ח, מ"א.
105. ר"ע מברטנורא, שם.

106. "By choice and by necessity Conservatism remains the
proving ground of American Jewry, reflecting its pattern of change
and its degree of stability."

Ruth R. Wisse — *Commentary* — October 1979 p. 59

ובנוגע ל"אורתודוכסיה" הלוא לא נמצא בה הכוח הרוחני לתקן מצב שאי הצדק שלו משווע עד השמים ושהרבה גדולי תורה הודו בפומבי באי צדקו. אני מתכוון להפלייתה לרעה של האשה בעניני גיטין. ואני משוכנע שלא ירימו אצבע מרצונם הטוב כדי לעשות דבר שיעודד את התהליך לקראת שיוויון בזכויות הדתיות והחברתיות של האשה והאיש.[108] ונדמה לי כי אין אף אחד בין חברי הסנאט המאמין כי מעמדה הנוכחי של האשה בהלכה מוסיף כבוד ויוקרה להלכה. אין אף אחד בין חברי הסנאט שיצביע על ההלכות האלה כהוכחה שאנחנו "גוי גדול אשר לו חוקים ומשפטים צדיקים" (דברים ד';ח') ואינני יכול להתפשר עם הדעה, שמעמדה ההלכתי הנוכחי של האשה מוכרח להשאר כמו שהוא עד שיבוא אליהו מפני שאין מוצא הלכתי ממנו. לא מוחי ולא לבי יכולים לקבל מערכת חוקית שאין מוצא לה מעיוותיה הנראים לעין כל.

הפן התנועתי — התוצאות המשוערות

אין להכחיש, כי ההחלטת בהמל"ר ביחס לבעיה זו תסמן כעין מפנה בתולדות התנועה השמרנית אבל אינני מייחס לה אותה השפעה גורלית שאחרים מייחסים לה. היא לא תביא את הגאולה ולא תגרום ח"ו לכישלון. אינני מסכים עם המנבאים כי אנו עומדים לפני משבר שאין ממנו מנוס ותהיה תשובתנו לבעיה זו מה שתהיה, חיובית או שלילית, היא תסמן את סוף דרכה של התנועה השמרנית כתנועה מסויימת, הנבדלת מן האורתודוקסיה ומן הריפורמה. מנבאים שאם נחליט לסמוך בנות עתידה התנועה השמרנית להתמזג עם הרפורמים, ואם נחליט שלא לסמוך אותן ניהפך לאחד הזרמים האורתודוקסים. לנבואה זו אין יסוד כי הדברים המבדילים בינינו לא יעלמו על ידי החלטה בענין זה. ההבדלים ההלכתיים בין תנועתנו ובין התנועה הריפורמית בנוגע לכשרות, שמירת שבת, גיור וגיטין, תפילין וכו' ובנוגע למרכזיותה של התורה שבעל פה במערכת הלימודים לתואר רב, לא יעלמו. ואותו הדבר בנוגע לדברים המבדילים בינינו לבין האורתודוקסיה. אנחנו לא נוותר על גישתנו ההיסטורית-מדעית

---

108. "אויב גדולים פין פרירדיגען דור האבען גיאסרט אזאך צוליב וועלכע מאטיוועך סע זאל ניט זיין קען קיינער שפעטער ניט ענדערן זייער מיינונג". הרב שמחה עלבערג — אלגעמיינער זשורנאל, אפריל 27, 1979, דף 9) "Her present status (according to my halakhic scholar acquaintance) appears to defy emendation or modification within the Halakhic context."

Cynthia Ozick — "Forum" no. 35 — Spring/ Summer 1979 — World Zionist Organization — Dept. of Information — Jerusalem.

למסורה ואת פתיחותנו הרוחנית והאינטלקטואלית לכל ענפי מסורתנו הדתית
והתרבותית ולכל הנעשה בעולם המחשבה האנושית.

וכדאי שנפנה את תשומת לבנו לכמה מהתוצאות השליליות המשוערות אם
נחליט להכתיר בנות. א. זה ירחיב את הפער בינינו לבין האורתודוקסים וזה יצדיק
עוד יותר בעיניהם ובעיני האחרים את התנכרותם אלינו. האמת היא שהרבה שנים
לפני עלית הבעיה הזאת על הפרק הכריזו בפומבי, שיהודי השומע תקיעת שופר בבית
כנסת שמרני אינו יוצא ידי חובתו, פסלו את הגיור שלנו, אף על פי שנעשה כדת
וכדין והתרבו גם אלה שלא נתנו לנו להשתמש במקוואותיהם וכו'.

הקיצוניים ביניהם דוחים בשתי ידיים כל מי שאינו מתנהג כמוהם בכל פרט
ופרט, ולדאבוננו עמדתם החוקית וכוחם הפוליטי במדינת ישראל מעודדים את
הקיצוניות ההולכת ומתגברת בחברה כולה בישראל ומשפיעה לרעה על היחסים בין
הזרמים השונים בחברה היהודית גם בתפוצות.

הם מתנגדים לנו לא רק מפני שסרנו מכמה הלכות ומנהגים המקובלים עליהם,
אלא גם מפני שסרנו מגישתם הטרום־מדעית־היסטורית אל המסורת כולה. התנגדותם
העוינת לנו לא תשכך עד אשר נשוב לגיטו הרוחני־אינטלקטואלי של המאות
הקדומות שהם בוחרים לגור בהם. ונוסיף ל"האני מאמין" שלנו גם את האמונה כי
כוכב־הלכת שאנו יושבים עליו נברא לפני חמשת־אלפים שבע־מאות וכו' שנה, וכי
באותה שעה שהקב"ה ברא את העולם יצר גם את המאובנים[109]. מה שנעשה ביחס
להסמכת בנות לא ישנה את יחסם אלינו. כמובן אם נחליט לסמוך בנות ישמחו, הם
יראו בזה הצדקה מירבית לטענותיהם נגדנו. אבל אם נחליט שלא לסמוך בנות יפרשו
את מעשינו כמעשה נוסף של אונאת־דעת, כמו שהם מפרשים כיום את שמירתנו את
המצוות. ולכן אל לנו לתת את תשובתנו לשאלת הסמכת הבנות על פי השערתנו מה
יקרב או מה ירחיק מאתנו את העולם האורתודוקסי.

הטענה, שהנשים האורתודוקסיות, שחייהן מוגבלים, שביעות רצון ושמחות יותר
מאלה ש"השתחררו"[110] מזכירתנו את טענותיהם של אדונים ביחס לעבדיהם. ואם יש
לפחד כי הסמכת בנות יכולה לעודד תהליך של פריצות, יש גם לשים לב לאפשרות
שסירובנו כעת לסמוך בנות, יכול לעודד תהליך, שגם עקבותיו כבר נראים בינינו,
להחזיר את האשה ל"מקומה" הקודם. נדמה לי כי העוול העלול להיעשות לאשה אם

109. Rabbi Menachem M. Schneerson (Rabbi of Lubavitch) in "A
Science and Torah Reader" Jewish Youth Monthly — Union of Orthodox Congregation of America — N.Y. 1970 — p. 24.

110. Gregory Jaynes — *Iranian Women*, New York Times Magazine, April 22, 1979.

נסרב לסמוך בנות יותר גדול הוא מהעוול שנוכחותה של אשה על הבמה תגרום לחיים הרוחניים של האיש.

ג. הטענה כי זה יעודד את הריסת המשפחה.[111] אין שום ספק, שהשתתפותה של האשה בכל המקצועות, שקודם היו מיועדים לגברים בלבד, גרם לשינוי יסודי בחיי המשפחה, אבל מה שנעשה בנוגע להסכמת בנות לא ישנה את המצב. מספר הנשים העוסקות במקצועות מחוץ לבית הולך וגדל, הן מפני שהן צריכות לעזור לפרנס את המשפחה והן מפני שהן רוצות להיות עצמאיות ולהתפרנס ממעשי ידיהן והן מפני שהן רוצות לפתח את כשרונותיהן ולהשתמש בהן ולא להיות מוגבלות למטבח או לבית. ונוסף או מעבר לזה העובדה היא שהחברה המודרנית זקוקה לכשרונותיהן. אי אפשר לתאר את חיי החברה המודרנית בתחומי הכלכלה, הפוליטיקה, התרבות וכו' בלי השתתפותה של האשה בהם. אין ספק כי כל זה תרם במידה לא קטנה להדרדרותה של המשפחה כגורם חינוכי ומוסרי בחיי הפרט והכלל, וישנם הטוענים כי שיקומה של מרכזיותה של המשפחה בחיינו תלוי בהחזרת תוקפם של הכללים "כל כבודה בת מלך פנימה" ו"אשה משועבדת לבעלה" מפני שאשה שמתפקדת במקצוע המוציא אותה מן הבית לכמה שעות בכל יום אינה יכולה למלא את תפקידה החשוב ביותר, להיות "אם הבנים" ו"עקרת בית". ואין תפקיד העלול להשפיע לרעה על חיי המשפחה יותר מתפקידו של רב בקהילה שמרנית, כי הלוא אחת הטענות הנשמעות ביותר באסיפות של חברי כנסת הרבנים כיום היא כי אחריותם הרבה מסכנת את חייהם המשפחתיים. ואשה בתפקיד של רב תחת אשר תהיה מופת לבנות בקהילה תעיד על מעמדה המרכזי של המשפחה ועל אחריותה של האשה כאם הבנים, היא תעודד אותן לחפש את סיפוקן בחיים שמחוץ לחוג המשפחתי.

אבל הרי נראה לעין כל, כי הבנות בדורנו, בפרט בחברה המערבית הדמוקרטית אינן זקוקות לעידודם של אחרים כדי ללכת בדרך שרוב בנות דורן הולכות. הנשים של חברי כנסת הרבנים משמשות כיום במקצועות שונים במספר הולך וגדל ואם

"The ethical traditions of Judaism justify the exclusion of .111
women from such political office in order to permit them to better
perform their most significant role as the backbone of the Jewish
family, which is the cornerstone of Jewish life and indeed of civilization itself. No ethical value can possibly supersede the need for
assuring the continuity of the Jewish family."
Rabbi Samuel A. Turk.
Letter to the New York Times that appeared on the editorial page on
January 14, 1980.

נאסור על אשה להיות רב מפני החשש שתהיה למופת לא הגון לבנות הקהילה, עלינו
לאסור גם על אשת רב מלעסוק במקצוע מחוץ לביתה. כמדומני שאין אף אחד
בחברתנו המניח כי אפשר — אפילו אם נסכים שרצוי — להחזיר את האשה ל"בית
ולמטבח". התגובה למצב הנוכחי היא לא חזרה לתמול שלשום אלא חיפוש דרך
נכונה למחר.

מליוני נשים הוכיחו כי אפשר למלא כראוי תפקידה של עקרת בית ואם הבנים
יחד עם העיסוק במקצוע מחוץ לבית. הן הצליחו לא רק מפני סגולותיהן המיוחדות
אלא גם מפני שינוי ההשקפה על תפקידו של האיש במשפחה, וכדאי לנו לזכור
ולהזכיר, שהשינוי הזה מתאים לא רק לרוחה אלא גם לכתבה של ההלכה. לפי ההלכה
אחריותו של האיש כלפי המשפחה הרבה יותר גדולה משל האשה. הוא ולא היא
מצווה על פריה ורביה[112]. "הוא חייב בבנו למולו, לפדותו וללמדו תורה ולהשיאו
אשה וללמדו אומנות וי"א אף להשיטו במים"[113]. ולא ידועה לי הלכה המפרטת את
התחייבויותיה של האשה כלפי בניה[114] אף על פי שההלכה אמנם מפרטת את
התחייבויותיה כלפי בעלה[115]. במשפחה של היום ושל מחר, חלקו של האב בגידול
הבנים והבנות ובהנהלת כל ענפי המשפחה, יצטרך להיות הרבה יותר גדול ממה שהיה
אתמול.

נשאלת השאלה אם השוויון הגמור בין איש לאשה במשפחה בכלל אפשרי.
השוויון הגמור בין שני שותפים בכל פעולה שהיא, אפשרי אם הם מכבדים איש את
רעהו וכל אחד מאמין ביושרו ובנאמנותו של האחר. בשותפות כזו שניהם מסכימים
כי מטרתם הראשית היא השמירה על המשך קיום השותפות ושניהם מוכנים לפשרות
ולויתורים. כיום שותפות כזו נדירה היא מדי, אבל עתידה של המשפחה תלוי במידה
מרובה בקיומה, ואשה המשרתת כרב ובעלה עסוק במקצוע אחר יכולים לשמש יחד
מופת של שותפות כזאת לזוגות של בעלי מקצועות שונים, שמספרם הולך ורב.
כמובן שקל יותר לקיים "שותפות" כשהאחד מסכים להיות משועבד לשני, ולמרות
השינויים הגדולים שנתהוו ביחסים בין האשה והבעל, האשה ברוב המקרים ממשיכה
להיות משועבדת, ואני נוטה לחשוב, שההתנגדות להסכמת בנות קשורה בידיעין או

112. יבמות פ"ו, מ"ו.
113. קידושין כט:
114. ריש לקיש סבר כי האשה אינה חייבת לחנך את בנה במצות (נזיר כט.) וראה אורח
מישור שם הטוען כי אעפ"י שלא נאמר בהדיא יש לשער שר' יוחנן סבר כי היא כן חייבת
לחנך את בנה במצוות, והלכה כר' יוחנן לגבי ר"ל) וראה חגיגה ב' רש"י ד"ה איזהו קטן.
115. כתובות פ"ה, מ"ה.

בלא יודעין להתנגדות הטבעית לתהליך המשווה את מעמדה של האשה בחברה לשל
האיש.

ישנם הטוענים שהצעירים והצעירות הפונים היום אל הדת, פונים על פי רוב
"ימינה" ולא יבואו אלינו אם נסמוך בנות, כי בעיניהם תהיה זו פניה "לשמאל". אבל
אי אפשר לנו לדעת כמה בחורים לא פנו אלינו במשך השנים האחרונות מפני שהם
חשדו בנו שאנו פונים יותר מדי ימינה ואנו יודעים, שכמה צעירות לא באו אלינו
מפני שסרבנו להכתירן. טענות כאלה נשמעו נגדנו מיום היווסדו של ביהמ"ד לרבנים.
אלה האשימו אותנו באורתודוקסיות יתרה ואלה בריפורמה יתרה. לא מפיהם אנו
חיים. התנועה השמרנית הופיעה לא כמפנה שמאלה ולא כמפנה ימינה אלא כתשובה
לשתי שאלות: א. האם אפשר להיות יהודי מאמין בשם ושומר מצוות בלי לפנות
עורף לתרבות העולמית של זמננו?

ב. המסוגלת המסורה לוותר על אחד או יותר מהמחשותיה של ערכיה הנצחיים
בהלכה ולהעניק להם המחשה חדשה בלי להתפורר ובלי להרגיש שניתקה השושלת?

התשובה של התנועה השמרנית לשתי השאלות האלה היתה חיובית ונראה שהדרך
שהלכנו בה משכה את לבם של "אלפי רבבה" יהודים בארה"ב ובארצות אחרות.
ישנ —י מוסדות המוכנים לשרת את השואפים לחיות היום בתנאים האינטלקטואלים
של ה"שטטל" שהיתה במזרח-אירופה במאה התשע עשרה, וישנם גם די מוסדות
המשרתים את הרוצים ל"הידבק" באלקים בלי מצוותיו. אנו מאמינים כי לא זו ולא
זו הדרך, ושעתידה של היהדות תלוי באלה שילכו בדרכנו. ולמרות כל הפקפוקים
וההיסוסים אני נוטה להאמין כי הכתרת בנות על ידי ביהמ"ד יהיה חידוש המתאים
לערכי המסורה ולהתפתחותה של ההלכה.

ושוב אנו חוזרים לאותה שאלה שאין עליה תשובה ברורה. נניח כי החידוש
מתאים למסורה, האם הציבור מוכן לקבלו? ואני חוזר ועונה כי השינויים שנתהוו
במעמדה של האשה בחברה בכלל ובחיי הקהילה היהודית בארצנו בפרט הכינו את
הרוב המכריע של חברי קהילותינו לקבל בהבנה ובהסכמה את הסמכת בנות. אין זאת
אומרת שחברי הקהילות יעדיפו מחר להזמין אשה במקום איש לשרתם. הלא גם
בחיים הפוליטיים ובמקצועות החפשיים הגברים ממשיכים להיות הרוב המכריע בין
ראשי המדינות וראשי המדברים בכל מקום. אבל כולנו מודים שקבלת הכלל שיש
לאשה הזכות לבחור ולהיבחר, לאיזה תפקיד שהוא במדינה ולהתעסק באיזה מקצוע
שכשרונותיה מאפשרים לה, מצביע על התקדמות מוסרית ואינטלקטואלית בחיי

116. "לא לכל ידוע שעוד לפני קום מדינת ישראל התעוררה השאלה, האם מותר לנשים
לבחור ולהיבחר למוסדות הלאומיים? רוב רבני ארץ ישראל דאז פסקו בצורה קטיגורית

האנושות[116]. אני מאמין כי שורשיה של התקדמות זו נטועים בתורה, ואני מקווה
שהיהדות תימצא בין התומכים והנהנים מהתקדמות זו.
ר"ח כסלו תש"מ.

שאסור לנשים להיבחר או לבחור. הרב קוק זצ"ל שהיה בין החתומים על האיסור קבע
"שאשה" המשתתפת בבחירות עוברת על "דת יהודית"... הרב פישמן, הרב אוסטרובסקי
והרב יצחק ניסנבוים שאלו: במו ידינו נוותר על חמישים אחוז מעם ישראל? מה זאת אומרת
שאשה לא תצביע, לא תבחר ולא תיבחר? אנחנו הצבור הדתי במסגרת המאבק של החיים
הדתיים שלנו מנטרלים במו ידינו חמשים אחוז של הצבור וגוזרים כליה על עצמנו... הרב
הראשי בן־ציון חי עוזיאל זצ"ל התיר בהיתר גמור לבחור ולהיבחר. אומר "הראשון לציון"
הסברה נותנת לומר דבכל כנסייה רצינית ושיחה מועילה אין בה משום פריצות. כל יום ויום
אנשים נפגשים עם נשים למו"מ מסחרי, ונושאים ונותנים ובכל זאת אין שום פרץ ושום
צווחה". (שו"ת "משפט עוזיאל" חו"מ ס'). אמנון שפירא, יחזקאל כהן — האשה בתמורות
הזמן — הקיבוץ הדתי — נאמני תורה ועבודה, תשמ"ד דף 12־13.

Index

Page numbers in *italic* indicate places in the text where Hebrew technical terms are defined.

217

BIBLICAL CITATIONS

Contributors

JOSEPH A. BRODIE
Instructor in Bible

GERSON D. COHEN
Chancellor Emeritus,
Jacob H. Schiff Distinguished Service
Professor in Jewish History

ISRAEL FRANCUS
Professor in Rabbinics

ROBERT GORDIS
Professor Emeritus in Philosophies of Religion
Professor Emeritus in Bible

SIMON GREENBERG
Professor of Homiletics and Education

ANNE LAPIDUS LERNER
Assistant Professor in Hebrew Literature

MAYER RABINOWITZ
Associate Professor in Talmud

JOEL ROTH
Associate Professor in Talmud

DAVID G. ROSKIES
Associate Professor in Jewish Literature

GORDON TUCKER
Assistant Professor in Jewish Philosophy